INTERNATIONAL DEVELOPMENT COOPERATION

Theory, Practice, and Evaluation

INTERNATIONAL DEVELOPMENT COOPERATION

Theory, Practice, and Evaluation

Jianzhi ZHAO

Fudan University, China

Translated by

Qin LIN

Shanghai Normal University, China

 **World Scientific**

NEW JERSEY · LONDON · SINGAPORE · BEIJING · SHANGHAI · HONG KONG · TAIPEI · CHENNAI · TOKYO

Published by

World Scientific Publishing Co. Pte. Ltd.

5 Toh Tuck Link, Singapore 596224

USA office: 27 Warren Street, Suite 401-402, Hackensack, NJ 07601

UK office: 57 Shelton Street, Covent Garden, London WC2H 9HE

Library of Congress Cataloging-in-Publication Data
Names: Zhao, Jianzhi, author.
Title: International development cooperation : theory, practice, and evaluation /
    Jianzhi Zhao, Fudan University, China ;
    translated by Qin LIN, Shanghai Normal University, China.
Description: Hackensack, NJ : World Scientific, [2023] | Originally published in Chinese by
    China Social Sciences Press. | Includes bibliographical references and index.
Identifiers: LCCN 2022021904 | ISBN 9789811258879 (hardcover) |
    ISBN 9789811258886 (ebook) | ISBN 9789811258893 (ebook other)
Subjects: LCSH: Economic assistance, Chinese. | China--Foreign economic relations. |
    Economic assistance. | International economic relations.
Classification: LCC HC60 .Z399 2023 | DDC 338.951--dc23/eng/20221025
LC record available at https://lccn.loc.gov/2022021904

British Library Cataloguing-in-Publication Data
A catalogue record for this book is available from the British Library.

国际发展合作: 理论、实践与评估
Originally published in Chinese by China Social Sciences Press
Copyright © China Social Sciences Press, 2018

For any available supplementary material, please visit
https://www.worldscientific.com/worldscibooks/10.1142/12906#t=suppl

Desk Editors: Jayanthi Muthuswamy/Pui Yee Lum

Typeset by Stallion Press
Email: enquiries@stallionpress.com

Printed in Singapore

About the Author

Jianzhi ZHAO is an Associate Professor of Economics and Public Policy at the School of International Relations and Public Affairs of Fudan University in Shanghai, China. His current research interests are international development, public policy, public economics, and development economics. He has worked at multiple international organizations, including the World Bank, Asian Development Bank, and Inter-American Development Bank. He was also a visiting researcher at the Bank of Finland. He has been invited to present his research at various government agencies, such as the Congressional Budget Office (CBO) and Bank of Finland. He has served as a referee for many international journals and published papers in many peer-reviewed journals. He was a Shorenstein Postdoctoral Fellow at Stanford University and received PhD in International Economic Policy from the University of Maryland, College Park.

About the Translator

 **Qin LIN**, PhD, is a lecturer at the School of Foreign Languages, Shanghai Normal University, China. Her research interests include Early Modern English literature and English poetry.

Contents

About the Author   v

About the Translator   vii

Part One   Theory of International Development Cooperation   1

Chapter 1   Definition of International Development Assistance   3
     Section 1. Introduction   3
     Section 2. Latest Developments in International Development
              Assistance   9

Chapter 2   Research on the Effectiveness of International
           Development Assistance   13
     Section 1. Literature Review of Aid Effectiveness   13
     Section 2. Aid Ownership and Global Governance   27

Chapter 3   International Development Cooperation Models
           and China's Experience   37
     Section 1. A Comparative Study of Aid Models: Japan vs.
              Europe and America   37
     Section 2. China's Experience: South–South Cooperation   81

**Part Two   Practice of International Development
            Cooperation**   **111**

Chapter 4   Introduction to the Management Systems of
            International Development Cooperation   113
  Section 1. The Concept of Aid Management System   113
  Section 2. Research on Aid Management System and
              Aid Effectiveness   118

Chapter 5   Participants in International Development
            Cooperation   127
  Section 1. Governments or International Development
              Agencies: Latest Developments   127
  Section 2. Non-Governmental International Development
              Organizations: A Perspective of Government
              Funding   131
  Section 3. Multilateral Development Banks: A Comparative
              Perspective   143
  Section 4. International Cooperative Governance: A Global
              Governance Perspective — Cooperation
              between G20 and DWG   171

Chapter 6   A Comparison of the Aid Management Systems
            of Traditional Donor Countries   193
  Section 1. The United States' Aid Management System   193
  Section 2. Japan's Aid Management System   195
  Section 3. The United Kingdom's Aid Management System   198
  Section 4. France's Aid Management System   200

Chapter 7   A Comparison of the Aid Management Systems
            of Emerging Donor Countries   205
  Section 1. Introduction to the Aid Management Systems
              of Emerging Donor Countries   205
  Section 2. India's Aid Management System   208
  Section 3. Brazil's Aid Management System   210
  Section 4. South Africa's Aid Management System   212
  Section 5. A Comparison of Aid Management Systems
              between China and Other Emerging
              Donor Countries   214
  Section 6. China's Aid Management System: A
              Path-Dependence Perspective   221

Part Three   Evaluation of International Development Projects   243

Chapter 8   Introduction to Evaluation of International
             Development Projects   245
     Section 1. Introduction   245
     Section 2. Basic Categories of Evaluation of International
                Development   251
     Section 3. Impact Evaluation and Its Importance   255

Chapter 9   Methods of Impact Evaluation for International
             Development   263
     Section 1. Non-Experimental Methods of Impact Evaluation   263
     Section 2. Randomized Controlled Trials (RCTs)   280

Index   291

Part One

Theory of International Development Cooperation

Chapter 1

Definition of International Development Assistance

Section 1. Introduction

As a new interdisciplinary research and teaching field, international development is becoming increasingly important; however, there are still many disputes about the precise definition of it in international academic and policy circles. Although international development is basically synonymous with "economic development" from a historical point of view, this definition is too simple to reflect the whole picture of the development of human society.[1] With the introduction of Human Development Indicators (HDIs) by the United Nations Development Programme (UNDP) and the World Bank, the definition of international development that most people can accept is a holistic one that includes economic development, social development, health development, and educational development. Although there is not enough consensus on its definition, the

---

[1] The discussion of development is generally believed to have first appeared in the inauguration of President Truman of the United States on 20 January 1949. In his inauguration speech, he said that "we must embark on a bold new program for making the benefits of our scientific advances and industrial progress available for the improvement and growth of underdeveloped areas. More than half the people of the world are living in conditions approaching misery. Their food is inadequate. They are victims of disease. Their economic life is primitive and stagnant. Their poverty is a handicap and a threat both to them and to more prosperous areas". URL: www.kekenet.com/Article/63275.shtml.

academic and policy circles, on the whole, agree that the core content of international development needs to focus on poverty eradication.

After a preliminary discussion of the definition of international development, now we can examine the concept of international development cooperation. Traditional research holds that international development, as a special domain of international political economy, mainly refers to the international assistance policies of developed countries to help low-income countries eliminate poverty and develop economy. Therefore, the resultant international development assistance is more of an aid relationship, a kind of grants or concessional loans from developed countries to underdeveloped countries, so this mode is also considered as a form of international development assistance. According to different sources of funds, it can be divided into official aid and private aid. The former is also Official Development Assistance (ODA) defined by the OECD-DAC (see Table 1.1).[2] This kind of international development assistance has

---

[2]The Organization for Economic Cooperation and Development-Development Assistance Committee (OECD-DAC) is one of the committees affiliated to the Organization for Economic Cooperation and Development. This committee is responsible for coordinating official development assistance to developing countries and is the core institution of international assistance that gives aid to developing countries. The DAC now has 29 members (28 OECD countries and the EU), with the World Bank, the International Monetary Fund (IMF), and the UNDP being permanent observers. Among the 25 committees affiliated to the OECD, the DAC is one of the three major committees. As of 2016, the assistance funds contributed by the DAC have comprised more than 90% of the total funds to the world. Generally speaking, it is more difficult to become a member of the DAC than that of the OECD. The former has only 29 members at present, while the latter has 35 members. It can be said that being the latter is a necessary but without sufficient condition to become the former, so the DAC is called the "Donor Country Club". After becoming a member of the OECD-DAC, this country should set up a special international development assistance organization according to the requirements, formulate international development assistance policies, and increase the scale of international development assistance to above 0.2% of its Gross National Income (GNI). As of 2016, only Denmark, Luxembourg, the Netherlands, Norway, and Sweden have met the United Nations' requirement that the proportion of their international development assistance constitutes 0.7% of their GNI. As of 2018, the OECD-DAC has 29 members (including 28 OECD members and the EU), namely, Australia, Austria, Belgium, Canada, Czech Republic, Denmark, Finland, France, Germany, Greece, Iceland, Ireland, Italy, Japan, Korea, Luxembourg, Netherlands, New Zealand, Norway, Poland, Portugal, Slovakia, Slovenia, Spain, Sweden, Switzerland, the UK, the US, and the EU.

Table 1.1: Classification of capital flows to developing countries.

Sources	Preferential	Non-preferential
Official	(1) Official development assistance, e.g. — grants or concessional loans for development (2) Other official aids, e.g. — export credit with preferential interest rates — official military assistance (3) South–South Cooperation mode	All kinds of official funds based on market interest rates, e.g. — export credit with market interest rates — official lending based on market interest rates
Private	Some NPOs, e.g. — the Bill & Melinda Gates Foundation	Funds targeting market interest rates or yields, e.g. — foreign direct investment — investment in stocks, bonds, etc.

obvious characteristics: first, the main source of funds must be local governments at all levels or their subsidiary executive bodies; second, the funds must be used to promote economic growth and improve the welfare of the recipient countries; third, no less than 25% of the aid funds must be grants or concessional loans.[3]

However, in recent years, the concept of ODA defined by the OECD-DAC has been disputed, and these issues have become more significant and urgent after the 2008 financial crisis. It is believed there are several defects in its definition.

Firstly, scholars and policy circles hold that this definition is too narrow to cover the development assistance of emerging economies; especially in recent years, the proportion of ODA flows to developing countries has declined significantly, and the growth rate is far lower than the total of foreign direct investment (FDI) (Zheng, 2017).

Secondly, the scale of international assistance needs to be improved. The international community has made great progress in the field of development, especially in the areas of poverty reduction, disease reduction, and literacy, since the United Nations Millennium Development Goals were set. However, according to the United Nations, the scale of the

[3]The official website of OECD: http://www.oecd.org/dac/stats/officialdevelopmentassistancedefinitionandcoverage.htm.

current international assistance is far from enough compared with the challenges faced by international development. In addition, as the economic and financial conditions of DAC member countries are still not optimistic in the short term, the original weak economic conditions of emerging economies also face challenges with the Fed's interest rate hike. All of these factors make the future trend of international development assistance funds uncertain.

Thirdly, the efficiency and the effectiveness of international assistance need to be improved. At present, there is considerable controversy over the efficiency of national development assistance in the academic world. For instance, Angus Deaton, the Nobel Prize winner in Economics, claims in his famous book *The Great Escape* that international development assistance for most of the time is ineffective or even counterproductive. With the improvement of empirical testing tools and data availability, more and more causality research tools are used to diagnose the poor effect of development assistance. Until now, many studies have found that international development assistance funds often fail to be used where they are needed most. There are two major reasons. First, the labor expenditure of executing international development assistance is too high. According to the estimates of the OECD, at present, the labor expenditure of DAC countries' own staff constitutes half of their project expenditure (Perroulaz *et al.*, 2008). A similar situation happens in multilateral organizations. According to the World Bank, at least one-third of its loan expenditure is spent on the salaries and business trips of its own employees and consultants. The real funds used for the aid projects themselves are far less than the statistical data. Second, among the recipient countries, some weak and corrupt governments have kept the development assistance funds without permission, or even brought about illegal outflow of the funds, which makes it difficult for the funds to be used to develop the economy and get rid of poverty.

Fourthly, international development cooperation among countries is insufficient. At present, the institutions of international development assistance are mainly divided into three categories: the development agencies and development financial institutions of DAC countries, the multilateral agencies represented by the World Bank, and the private international development agencies represented by the Bill & Melinda Gates Foundation. Regarding the first type of development agency, it is mainly for the governments of the donor countries to determine the recipient countries and the objectives and to implement the aid projects.

The operation of this type of development agency is often more consistent with the political and diplomatic interests of their own countries. For example, the donor countries are more inclined to choose those countries which are on good terms with them or their former colonies, and the selection process of projects is mixed with strict premise conditions and terms. The second type of development agency is more objective. When determining a recipient country and the aid project, what it mainly considers is whether the actual needs of the recipient country are consistent with its operation objectives. And the operation of the project mainly focuses on concessional loans. The third type of development agency is booming in recent years. Its typical characteristics are its clarity in aid fields and professionalism. For example, the aid projects of the Bill & Melinda Gates Foundation focus on healthcare and education. However, cooperation in the aid process is relatively inadequate due to the different functions and operations of various development agencies. For instance, according to the OECD, it is often the case that multiple aid agencies carry out the same aid project repeatedly in a certain country. This lack of effective international communication makes it difficult for national aid agencies to play their distinctive advantages, resulting in a waste of development funds.

Currently, the discussion about these controversies and problems in international development academic and policy circles is centered on two aspects. For those who are on the side of the DAC, they hold that the reform should be carried out from the established definition and framework, which has been approved by the DAC. For example, on 19 February 2016, at the initiative of the UK and other countries, the DAC finally agreed to reconsider the definition of ODA after 40-years' use. However, its main purpose is to emphasize the role of official development assistance in poverty reduction in solving conflicting, fragile, and volatile political situations. In addition, the importance of private investment and development is also reflected. The three most important updates are:

(a) It agrees that official assistance can be used for the military assistance of vulnerable countries, especially regarding issues related to promoting the development of those countries, such as the protection of human rights and the prevention of sexual conflicts, which also means that the DAC believes that international development assistance should promote stronger governance so as to prevent chaos and fight terrorism and crime. Although this proposition does play an important role in the stabilization of recipient countries, it is essentially consistent with the national strategic interests of Western countries (which are also the leading countries of the DAC), and the assistance is not free of charge.

(b) Tackling extremism has been officially incorporated into the field of international development. The DAC believes that more than 90% of extremists are located in countries or regions with weak governance and a poor human rights record.

(c) Donor countries should make more policies to encourage cooperation with private investment, and facilitate the entrance of private capital into the field of international development, especially into low-income countries to improve their economic development and welfare.

Although the above-mentioned policies of the OECD are a progress compared with the existing guidelines, it is undeniable that the main modifications are centered on the interests of Western countries. For example, the extremist organizations or countries that receive aid in the military field are defined by Western countries, and the definition of weak governance countries and governments is also based on Western standards. Comparatively speaking, only the third modification corresponds to the broader definition of "international development assistance" advocated by developing countries.

In this context, more and more scholars (especially those from emerging donor countries) begin to propose the introduction of other concepts so as to reflect the new trend of international development more comprehensively. A good example is the "South–South Cooperation model" that the emerging donor countries with BRICS (Brazil, Russia, India, China, and South Africa) as the main body have been advocating, which is gradually accepted by the international development academia. Since most developing countries are located in the southern hemisphere or in the southern part of the northern hemisphere, "South–South Cooperation" is generally used to refer to cooperation among developing countries. It is a cooperative mechanism spontaneously formed by many Asian, African, and Latin American developing countries after they got rid of colonial control at the end of World War II but had to face an unfavorable international political and economic order dominated by the strong traditional Western countries. South–South Cooperation is characterized by wide coverage and high flexibility, covering political, economic, social, cultural, environmental, and technological fields. It aims to promote the sharing of knowledge or experience among developing countries and to achieve development goals through bilateral or multilateral cooperation, regional cooperation, subregional cooperation and interregional cooperation.

Section 2. Latest Developments in International Development Assistance

The mode of international development calculated by the DAC is mainly Official Development Assistance (ODA). According to the OECD, the calculation method of official assistance is grants plus concessional loans minus the principal and interest repayment of the existing aid loans. Since World War II, governments and multilateral organizations' ODA to low-income countries has been growing steadily; especially since the United Nations Millennium Development Goals were set, the absolute poverty rate in the world has been reduced by half. However, with the change of the global economic map, the flow and the scale of international development aid funds calculated by the DAC have changed. The following two trends deserve special attention especially after the global financial crisis in 2008.

Firstly, the scale of international development assistance calculated by the DAC has reached a record high (see Figure 1.1). International development aid funds have been growing steadily, especially since the implementation of the United Nations Millennium Development Goals. According to the estimates of the DAC, the global international development assistance funds increased from US $108 billion in 2005 to US $150.8 billion in 2013, an increase of 30%. Nonetheless, we also find that the growth rate of international development assistance funds is not stable. It declined in consequence of the decline of the economic growth of developed countries, especially after the global financial crisis in 2008. Fortunately, its annual average growth rate of about 4% is still higher than the global economic growth rate, especially compared with the average economic growth rate of less than 2% of the developed countries. The current scholarship has established that the residents of developing countries, those of the lowest income countries in particular, are more vulnerable to the economic crisis than those of developed countries (Besley and Burgess, 2012), which also makes the international development

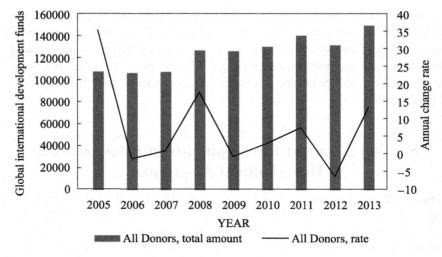

Figure 1.1:   Total amount and trend of international aid funds.
Source: The OECD.

assistance funds that are stable and even higher than the global economic growth rate more essential.

Secondly, the participants in international development have changed (see Figure 1.2). Compared with the steady growth of international development assistance funds, what deserves more attention is the change of its participants. As more and more developing countries become middle-income countries, some of them have also become "donors" from "recipients". According to the data of the DAC, the constitution of international development assistance funds underwent changes in nearly 16 years from 2000 to 2017. The proportion of the DAC countries, which are high-income economies in the traditional sense, was constantly decreasing, from 90% in 2001 to 80% in 2013. In the meantime, the proportion of non-DAC countries, which are mainly middle-income countries and emerging economies, increased from 2% to 10%, of which China's contribution is the largest (we will analyze separately next). In addition, development assistance from multilateral organizations also increased steadily, from 9% to 10%. Therefore, international development assistance in general has been optimized in terms of both the scale of funds and its constitution. In other words, as more and more countries graduate from the recipients of international development assistance funds and even

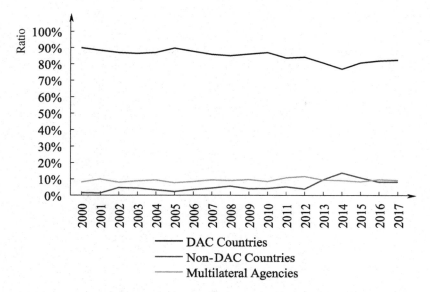

Figure 1.2:　Composition and trend of international assistance funds.
Source: The OECD.

become donors, the remaining recipients can get more development assistance funds. Besides, most emerging economies, such as BRICS, whose main international development cooperation mode is through South–South Cooperation, are not included in the DAC data. In Chapter 3, we will discuss South–South Cooperation in more detail.

References

Besley, Timothy and Robin Burgess. *Halving Global Poverty*. London School of Economics Working Paper, August 2012.

Perroulaz, Gérard, Claudie Fioroni and Gilles Carbonnier. "Trends and issues in international development cooperation". *International Development Policy\Revue Internationale de Politique Développement* [Online], 10 March 2010. URL: http://poldev.revues.org/142; DOI: 10.4000/poldev.142.

Zheng, Yu. "Aid effectiveness and conception of new development cooperation model". *World Economy and Politics*, No. 7, 2017.

Chapter 2

Research on the Effectiveness of International Development Assistance

Section 1. Literature Review of Aid Effectiveness

The effectiveness of international development assistance has always been an important research topic in the field of international development, especially since the setup of international development field changed from the dominance of traditional developed countries to their being on a par with emerging economies in recent years. This section divides the Western international development assistance into three stages, analyzes the evolution process of its theory and practice, and then describes its evolution path and the influencing factors behind it.

1. The First Stage: From the End of WWII to the Early 1960s

Although the research on international development assistance is interdisciplinary, it has a closer connection with the development of economic theory following World War II (Edwards, 2015).[1] With the shift of the

---

[1] The study of Western international development assistance has a long history, which can be traced back to Adam Smith's *The Wealth of Nations*. In the book, Smith discusses in detail why British colonies performed better than Spanish and Dutch colonies. His main point of view is that the British colonial system was superior to the latter two, or more conducive to the development of economy. This is an earlier theoretical research on how

territory of economics research from the UK to the US after World War II, quantitative research based on the use of a large number of mathematical tools gradually dominated the field. Consequently, economic theory also began to occupy a dominant position, one of whose important theoretical breakthroughs is the construction of the theory of economic growth. According to this theory, with the Harrod–Domar model being one of its pioneering models,[2] a country's long-term economic growth depends on its stock of capital, and its economic growth rate not only has no stable path but also rises with the increase of saving rates. Especially when there is an unlimited supply of labor in a country, the relative shortage of capital becomes more prominent.[3] However, when the developing countries themselves lack sufficient savings rate, the inflow of foreign capital, especially in the form of preferential or even free international aid, will enable them to solve the problems of lack of development funds and national savings. Therefore, such economists in the 1950s and 1960s as W. Arthur Lewis and Paul Rosenstein Rodan held that, the Western international development assistance can effectively help those developing countries which lack national savings and development funds to obtain the funds needed for investment in manufacturing industry, an industry that is crucial to the long-term economic growth of a country, meaning that the positive effect of international aid on economic and social development is obvious.

In practice, the US was also the main implementer of international development assistance after World War II. In 1948, after Truman launched the Marshall Plan as a whole, the US invested a large amount of aid funds into the less-developed countries and treated the aid as an

---

developed countries influence or help the development of underdeveloped areas. Since the formation and systematization of international development assistance mainly started after World War II, this section focuses on the situation after World War II.

[2] The Harrod–Domar model, namely the Harold–Domar economic growth model, is a kind of economic growth model which is mainly based on Keynesian economic theory. This model was respectively proposed by Roy Harold in his 1939 paper entitled "An Essay in Dynamic Theory" and by Evsey David Domar in 1946. This is the earliest mathematical model of modern development economics. Later, the neoclassical economists represented by Solow criticized this model and introduced the Solow model to replace it in 1950s.

[3] Representative views include W. Arthur Lewis' view of unlimited labor supply, which holds that developing countries, especially low-income countries, have unlimited labor supply in the primary stage of economic development.

important part of American foreign policy. However, despite the high enthusiasm of the US government for international aid, the US Congress took a dim view of it. In 1953, the US Congress clearly pointed out in the Mutual Security Act that the US' international aid to its allies would end in 2 years and military assistance in 3 years. Nonetheless, things changed when the Cold War began to escalate in the 1960s. In order to prevent low-income countries from becoming communist and to get more allies in view of the "One State, One Vote" voting system adopted by the UN, the US restarted its international development assistance as an important tool to expand its diplomatic space. At the same time, the US also led the establishment of the OECD–DAC with other developed countries to coordinate and guide the assistance of OECD member countries (mainly Western developed countries) to low-income countries.

Most countries adopted two parallel ways of international development assistance after World War II. The first way is bilateral aid mode, that is, it was the government departments of developed countries, usually ministerial aid agencies, that took charge of the management and implementation of aid to the target countries. The other way is multilateral aid mode, that is, donor countries handed their aid funds over to the World Bank and other multilateral development banks and entrusted them to implement the aid. There are differences in the proportion of these two kinds of aid among the Western countries. For example, the United States International Cooperation Administration received far more funding than multilateral development agencies, whereas the two kinds of aid adopted by the Nordic countries were basically at the same level. In addition, the traditional Western developed countries also resorted to the OECD-DAC to conduct the communication and coordination of aid among countries.

2. The Second Stage: From the Late 1960s to the Beginning of the 21st Century

Indeed, the traditional international development assistance led by Europe and the US, the Marshall Plan in particular, had played a significant role and made great achievements in the period from World War II to the 1960s;[4] however, the academic community from the 1970s began to

---

[4]Edwards (2015) holds that this stage covers from 1950 to 1982 and defines it as the stage of development assistance and planned economy.

reflect on the real effect of this way of assistance. In the past half century, Africa had received the largest share of development aid from the traditional developed countries in Europe and the US, but it failed to make obvious progress in terms of economic growth and poverty reduction. For example, according to Paldam (2005), international aid flows to low-income countries reached US $60 billion annually, accounting for an average of 7.5% of their GDP. In addition, the Solow model, which flourished in the 1960s and was praised as the "universal model" of the theory of economic growth, claims that human capital and projects have more weight in the contribution to economic growth and that human capital in particular makes more contribution to labor productivity growth than simple material investment. In the light of this theory, it became more important for developing countries to have absorption capacity and accordingly capacity building including training professionals should be prioritized so as to improve the quality and efficiency of aid projects. This voice continued for a long time and the definition of aid was further narrowed in the 1980s and early 1990s. International aid spent on capital intensive projects, especially large-scale infrastructure projects has become less. On the contrary, more international aid was invested in areas directly related to human capital, such as education, society, and health.

Meanwhile, with the introduction of econometrics into the Western academic community in the 1970s and its sustainable development as a new research method, scholars began to use transnational panel data to conduct quantitative research on the effectiveness of international aid at the national level, which lasted for more than 40 years.[5] Chenery and Strout (1966), who were among the earlier empirical research users, analyzed the short-term and long-term effects of aid by using economic growth model, Pakistan case study, and cross-border empirical research. Their research find that aid can promote economic growth in the short term, but in the long run its role in economic and social development will significantly decline if the recipient country continues to rely on international aid and fails to achieve self-sustainable growth. In the following decades, especially in the 1990s, a large number of articles on aid effectiveness began to emerge, but the research conclusions are quite different. In general, there are three different views.

---

[5]In the Western academic circles, even the US included, econometrics began to enter the academia as a new discipline until the 1970s. Moreover, there was little data available at that time (Doucouliagos *et al.*, 2008).

The first view highly praises the importance of international aid. It holds that international aid plays an important part in helping developing countries, especially low-income countries, either promote economic growth and improve long-term living standards or deal with poverty in a short time. Besides, this view believes that Western international aid can help developing countries break the vicious circle that "the poor become poorer", at least in the short term, because low-income countries do not have any domestic savings to make long-term fixed assets investment, not to mention long-term human capital investment such as education and healthcare. In fact, these scholars consider that the reason why low-income countries are still unable to achieve development is that international aid is not enough, since only a few countries have realized the Millennium Development Goal's commitment to spend 0.7% of their GDP on international development. Among the representatives who hold this view are Jeffrey Sachs, a famous economist in development economics, Paul Krugman and Joseph Stiglitz, two Nobel Prize winners in economics, and even Bill Gates.[6] Among them, Sachs can be said to be one of the staunchest supporters of international aid. He severely criticizes the Western developed countries for not offering enough international aid to low-income countries. In his book *The End of Poverty: Economic Possibilities of Our Time*, Sachs points out that Western development assistance is a lifeline for many low-income countries, and cutting off aid means cutting off their lifeline. Therefore, development assistance is crucial for low-income countries. He also acknowledges that the current top-down aid management model, which relies on bureaucracy, needs to be changed so as to improve the efficiency of aid distribution. He maintains that if the mode of distribution and management of international aid can be improved and effectively distributed to the people in need, then international aid can still play an effective role, especially in solving the problems of insufficient water supply and basic infrastructure in medical fields such as AIDS and malaria, even if the recipient country is politically inefficient or even corrupt. Such views are also reflected in the aid practice of the UN and the US. For example, in 2004, the US Congress passed

---

[6]Bill Gates believes that international aid, including the efforts to fight AIDS, is extremely important for low-income countries to help them improve their human capital, stabilize their societies and promote their economic development. URL: http://time.com/4704550/bill-gates-cutting-foreign-aid-makes-america-less-safe/.

a bill[7] that more than half of the Microenterprise funds of USAID should reach the poorest individuals of the recipient countries directly, rather than be entrusted to the governments or management departments of the recipient countries.[8] In addition, Sachs holds that international development assistance should follow the principle of "Big Five Development Intervention", that is, providing investment in agricultural production, basic medical facilities, education, facilities for power, transportation and communication, and safe drinking water. He even used this theory to transform some "Millennium Villages" in Africa and found that the effect of such intervention and investment was remarkable. However, such policies have also been criticized. For example, Rich (2007) thinks that Sachs's intervention and investment may be effective only in the short term, lacking long-term evidence. On the other hand, through the use of more effective causal identification measurement tools, Galiani *et al.* (2017) find that international aid has an obvious effect on economic growth and welfare of low-income countries.

The second view, on the contrary, holds that international development assistance is not helpful or even counterproductive to the economic and social development of recipient countries. Influential or representative articles of this view include those of Boone (1996), Rajan and Subramanian (2007, 2008, 2011), among others, which further test the effectiveness of international aid by using more detailed data and evaluation tools. Through the regression of the reduced model of 96 countries, Boone (1996) finds that international aid does not significantly increase investment or growth nor does it improve the living standards of the poor, but unexpectedly increases the size of government.[9] More interestingly, he finds that this impact remains the same whether recipient governments are democratic or highly repressive, and that the ineffectiveness of international aid is quite obvious. In addition, after a more comprehensive test and strict control of endogeneity, Rajan and Subramanian (2008) find that international aid by Europe and the US does not significantly improve the economy of recipient countries, especially those countries whose

---

[7]The bill is called Microenterprise Results and Accountability Act of 2004. URL: http://smith4nj.com/laws/108-484.pdf.

[8]For this purpose, USAID also commissioned IRIS Research Group to develop the "poverty assessment tool", which is based on the poverty line of different countries. URL: https://www.povertytools.org.

[9]The human development index is used here.

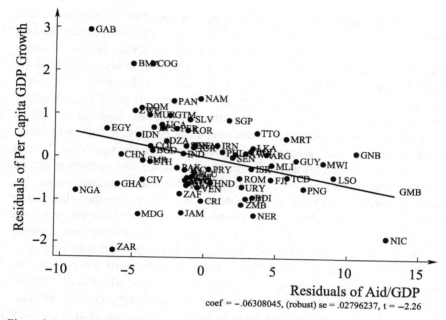

coef = –.06308045, (robust) se = .02796237, t = –2.26

Figure 2.1: Conditional correlation between growth and total aid, 1960–2000.

Note: The abscissa of the figure above shows the proportion of aid in GDP of a country, and the ordinate shows the economic growth rate of a country. Scattered points indicate the combination of abscissa and ordinate of the sample country. The negative fitting line indicates that there is a negative correlation between the proportion of aid in GDP and economic growth.

Source: Rajan and Subramanian (2008).

international aid accounts for a high proportion of their GDP (see Figure 2.1). Moreover, they also find that the underlying reason may be that international aid leads to an artificially high real exchange rate of recipient countries, which results in decrease in their export competitiveness and an illusory increase in imports. Of course, the most representative figures in this camp are William Easterly and Angus Deaton. In his masterpiece *The White Man's Burden*, Easterly points out that since international development assistance is basically dominated by top-down planners and bureaucrats, who lack adequate accountability, aid is meaningless to economic and social development and will end up helping increase rent-seeking space for these planners at most. Moreover, he is highly opposed to the US' linking international assistance with counterterrorism efforts, because international assistance will increase the possible birth of oppressive governments, thus increasing the number of extremists and terrorists. His ideas have influenced the US government's policymaking. For instance, the US Congress imposed a ban on giving aid to countries with human rights violations. The most influential study recently is by Angus Deaton, a Nobel Prize winner in 2014. In his book *The Great Escape: Health, Wealth, and the Origins of Inequality* (2014), Deaton points out that most of the current Western international development assistance is ineffective or even counterproductive; what is more, it will make those weak or corrupt government officials become more corrupt when there is a mismatch between local government governance and economic development, thus hindering their economic development. According to this book, the problem lies in that international aid can change the relationship between local governments and people. When there is no international aid, local government officials operate their governments and provide public goods and services through taxation. If the performance of a government or its officials cannot meet the expectations of the people, the people can protest by voting or refusing to pay taxes, which will result in *de facto* accountability of the government, thus forming a positive interaction between the government and the people. However, once a country gets international development assistance funds, this positive interaction may be broken because the operation of the government, especially a local one, no longer needs to depend on tax. Furthermore, owing to the disintegration of effective accountability system and supervision, the government may become corrupt in the process of using aid funds, and if it is originally corrupt or predatory, its corruption is more likely to be aggravated, which may affect the political stability, thus seriously doing harm to the development of the country. The more development assistance funds the government gets, the more destructive it becomes. This analysis that international aid reduces power, or that aid is used by corrupt political elites as rewards, which makes the originally benign political system become destructive or even increases the risk of civil war, thus resulting in negative effects on the economic and social development, is analogized as "resource curse" that brings about "international aid curse". Deaton further claims that there is another important problem in international development assistance, that is, the developed Western countries including the US often seek self-interests in the process of aid; in other words, Western countries often regard international aid as an extension of their national strategic interests and link it with their foreign policy. For example, according to Deaton, although the former President of Ethiopia

Meles Zenawi is a famous dictator in Africa, the US has constantly provided tremendous aid to Ethiopia for decades, not simply because Ethiopia is the poorest country, but mainly because Meles firmly opposes Islamic extremism, which is in line with the strategic goal of the US in Africa. Deaton goes a step further maintaining that although the world has made great progress in poverty reduction, this achievement has little to do with international aid and actually has a lot to do with China, whose goal of poverty reduction is chiefly achieved by its own economic development rather than foreign aid, which accounts for a very low proportion of its GDP. Of course, Deaton also agrees that some international development assistance is very important, such as assistance in the field of health, including the provision of vaccines and medical facilities.

The third view, which is also the most widely accepted in Western academic and policy circles, is relatively less extreme. People who hold this view believe that aid cannot be described as absolutely "effective" or "ineffective". Development is more closely related to the strength of a country's political and social system, which plays an important role in the interaction between the government and the people, which determines the development of a country and the effect of aid. In other words, aid effectiveness depends on certain conditions, which has a lot to do with the system, culture, and government governance of a country. If it is a good system, international aid can effectively promote its economic growth and achieve social development; by contrast, a predatory system will not only reduce aid effectiveness but also damage the long-term development of a country. Consequently, these people are also called conditionalism supporters. The article by Burnside and Dollar (2000) is influential in this regard. They believe that although international aid has a limited effect on the economic growth of recipient countries on average, it can bring about a relatively better effect in countries with good policies. In his famous work *The Bottom Billion* (2008), Collier points out that the argument that international aid is all or nothing is too extreme. According to him, international aid has in fact helped the economies of most African countries grow at an annual rate of about 1%, which is quite considerable, especially considering that the growth rate of some countries with the lowest income is zero and the economies and living standards of these countries will be actually in decline if the aid is removed, which will result in the deepening of poverty. Moreover, he thinks that although international aid is effective, its marginal efficiency will gradually decline; or to be more specific, when the aid volume doubles, its contribution to the economic growth will not continue to increase by 1%. Collier further divides the causes of falling into the poverty trap into four categories: conflict trap, natural resource trap, inland country trap, and poor governance trap. Through empirical data, he finds that international aid has little effect on getting rid of the first two traps, but significantly works on the latter two traps. Apart from emphasizing that marginal efficiency will gradually decline, Collier also stresses the importance of aid delivery methods, especially the quality of staff in the process of aid delivery and project implementation, which implies that technical assistance is crucial to the effectiveness of international assistance in practice. Daren Acemoglu is without question the most famous representative of this school in recent years. In the book *Why Nations Fail* written by him and James A. Robinson, they argue that institutional basis is not only a key factor in understanding economic development and growth but also a decisive factor in influencing the performance of recipient countries. They divide the economic and political systems of countries into being extractive and inclusive. They claim that the main reason why it is difficult for poor countries to develop lies in the fact that the extractiveness of their national economic and political systems will lead to the extraction of resources by the government or the upper society, hence international aid into these countries will only end up becoming resources to be extracted and cannot benefit the poor or promote their economic development. On the whole, the third view still belongs to institutional determinism of traditional Western economics or political science, and its definition of international aid is relatively narrow. It considers neither the aid that emerging donors receive nor the effect of international aid implemented by emerging donors.

3. The Third Stage: From the Beginning of the 21st Century to Now

This stage started at the beginning of this century, mainly due to the introduction of research tools, especially randomized controlled trials, into the field of development, and the issue of the effectiveness of international aid got reconsidered. Some scholars claim that, instead of discussing the effectiveness of Western international aid in a broad sense, it is better to focus on the heterogeneity of aid projects and evaluate and rank their effectiveness in detail so as to optimize the limited aid and avoid inefficiency and unnecessary waste. Esther Duflo and Abhijit V. Banerjee are representative pioneers of this view. In their book *Poor Economics: A Radical Rethinking of the Way to Fight Global Poverty*, they believe that the use of cross-border and macro-level data cannot help us understand the issue of aid effectiveness; on the contrary, aid project evaluation based on micro level is the most important. In the light of this, they introduced the approach of randomized controlled trials to evaluate the improvement of the recipient residents' welfare by different projects. In these experiments, the samples were randomly divided into the treatment group and the control group. The samples of the treatment group were involved in a specific aid project. After the completion of the project, they evaluated whether the implementation of the project had effects on the treatment group compared with the control group, and then demonstrated the effectiveness of the aid project. Scholars who support this view believe that poverty is caused not so much by geographical conditions, politics, or systems as by problems like imperfect distribution, incomplete information and market failure in the specific process of aid implementation. Therefore, how to distribute aid is the key to improving its effectiveness.[10] Although the evaluation of policy effect through randomized controlled trials can effectively overcome the problem of endogeneity, which enables a more accurate evaluation of causality rather than just correlation, its shortcomings have also been criticized. The most well-known criticism is from Deaton, who believes that the biggest problem with randomized controlled trials is external validity. To be more specific, if an aid project is proved to be effective in country A, it cannot be assumed that it can bring about the same effect in country B; likewise, some variables, which are removed from the experiment of country A due to difference and thus fail to be observed, may not be controlled in the aid practice of country B. Moreover, the results of randomized controlled trials are usually based on small-scale samples, so the applicability to larger populations is questionable, since in reality the scale of international aid is often much larger than that of experimental samples in terms of quantity and amount. For these reasons, although randomized controlled trials

---

[10]Since the introduction of randomized controlled trials by Duflo and Banerjee in their academic papers, institutions have been set up to apply this approach to international aid practice. Famous ones include the Poverty Action Lab at Massachusetts Institute of Technology (MIT), which was established by Duflo and Banerjee, and the Bureau for Research and Economic Analysis of Development at Yale University.

provide a new perspective and method for understanding the effectiveness of international aid, especially in solving endogeneity and identifying causality, the theory and practice of international aid should not solely rely on randomized experiments, which should develop in coordination with theories and concepts (Deaton and Cartwright, 2017).

Table 2.1 summarizes the development stages, viewpoints, theoretical basis, and representative works of the theories related to international aid. Generally speaking, although the above-mentioned four viewpoints are quite different or even diametrically opposed, they still share three similar characteristics. First, despite of different research methods, almost all Western literature defines aid based on the definition by the OECD-DAC, and there is no in-depth discussion on other alternative concepts of aid. Second, the theories of and debate on international development assistance have a lot to do with the evolution of economic methodology, especially that of development economics: from the original Harold–Domar economic growth model that claims that savings and capital stock determine economic development, to the neoclassical economic growth theory represented by the Solow growth model, which attaches great importance to human capital investment, then to the second and third viewpoints dominated by empirical research based on transnational macro data, and then to the introduction of randomized controlled trials which made development economics become a new research paradigm. The development of economics played a major role in this course, but other disciplines and perspectives, such as political science and the practice in the field of international development, were neglected. Third, the research target is solely the aid of Western countries, especially European countries and the US, which means that the research lacks not only Japan's aid which is different from the Western aid paradigm to a certain extent but also the aid of emerging donors represented by BRICS countries. Therefore, the traditional Western international aid theory lacks sufficient diversity and inclusiveness in research targets, research methods, and research materials.

As a result, Japan's aid model, which is different from that of Western countries, has been thoroughly studied. Since Japan's aid model focuses more on promoting economic growth through projects and infrastructure, it is also considered to have a better impact on recipient countries (Islam, 1993; Hansen and Tarp, 2001). In view of this, the Yokohama Declaration was issued by the Japanese government in 2008, with a core purpose to promote the transformation from ODA to international development cooperation and to establish a "Japanese model" in

Table 2.1:   The stages, main views, representative literature and policy practice of the literature of international aid effectiveness.

Stage	Major hypothesis	Theoretical or empirical basis	Theories or empirical findings	Representatives	Policy practice
The first stage: From the end of WWII to the early 1960s	Aid can make up for developing countries' shortage of savings, thus effectively promoting their economic growth and social development	The Harrod–Domar growth model	Based on Keynesianism, aid, as an inflow of capital, can make up for low-income countries' lack of savings and capital. In addition, low-income countries usually have an almost unlimited supply of labor, so increase in capital per capita can effectively improve their living standards	Roy Harrod, Evesey Domar, W. Arthur Lewis	Aid should be used for projects that increase capital stocks, especially the ones in capital intensive areas, including infrastructure
The second stage: From the late 1960s to the beginning of the 21st century	Aid can effectively promote economic growth, but endogenous growth chiefly depends on human capital	The Solow growth model	Economic growth will converge in the long run, and human capital accumulation is the core	Jeffrey Sachs, Joseph Stiglitz, Paul Krugman	Aid should be increased, especially in the fields of health, education, and so on
	Aid is counterproductive to economic growth and the improvement of living standards	Transnational macro empirical panel data	International development assistance does not help the economic and social development of recipient countries, or even has a counterproductive effect. The main reasons include that aid will damage the original accountability system of the government and push up the real exchange rate	William Easterly, Angus Deaton, Raghuram G. Rajan	Developing countries should reduce the inflow of aid and give priority to their own endogenous growth

(Continued)

Table 2.1: (Continued).

Stage	Major hypothesis	Theoretical or empirical basis	Theories or empirical findings	Representatives	Policy practice
	Aid effectiveness depends on certain conditions	Transnational macro empirical panel data	If the recipient country has a good system, international aid can effectively promote its economic growth and social development; on the contrary, a predatory system will not only reduce aid effectiveness, but also damage the long-term development potential of the country	David Dollar, Paul Collier	The amount of aid and where it goes should depend on the circumstances of the recipient country
The third stage: From the beginning of the 21st century to now	The effectiveness of aid should be measured based on the randomized controlled trials of the project	Randomized controlled trials based on micro projects	Limited aid should be optimized through detailed assessment and grading of the projects so as to avoid large-scale, inefficient and unnecessary waste	Esther Duflo, Abhijit V. Banerjee	Implement an aid project on a small scale and evaluate its effectiveness. Expand it on a large scale if the effect is good, such as the classic mosquito net case

Source: Zheng Yu.

the field of international development. Similarly, China's mode of international development cooperation has also been studied. For example, scholars have discussed the pros and cons of China's model from the angle of the effectiveness of "South–South Cooperation". Mwase and Yang (2012) consider China's international development cooperation model to be very effective, but of course it also has problems like having paid excessive attention to the economic returns of projects and insufficient attention to transparency, governance, debt sustainability, and so on. Similar view can also be found in Bräutigam (2010). Therefore, although there are disputes about the effectiveness of many different aid models in the international academic community, scholars all agree that there is room for improvement.

Section 2. Aid Ownership and Global Governance

In the last section, we mainly discussed the relevant theories of international aid, including where it can be distributed, whether it is worth distributing, and its amount. However, the effectiveness of aid implementation in practice is highly related to an important variable: ownership of aid implementation. This section will elaborate the importance of aid ownership and its importance to global governance from three aspects: the concept of aid ownership, empirical evidence, and the coordination in the international community.

1. The Background and Definition of Aid Ownership

Although the importance of country ownership to aid was officially highlighted in the *Paris Declaration* (2005) as a consensus of the conference, it has been discussed for a long time, at least dating back to the 1980s.

From 1950 to 1970, international aid mainly took the form of large-scale capital project investment. Generally speaking, the recipient country put forward a list of projects to the donor country, and then the donor country selected the projects according to their own preferences, which acted as a solution to the recipient country's shortage of savings or capital. But with the exception of food aid, most of the projects were managed by donor countries, and the aid was usually conducted in the form of a package deal, including mandatory purchase of capital goods or

technology from the recipient country, so the aid was bundled with investment and forced import.

In the 1980s, with the increasingly fierce debate on the effectiveness
of international aid, the behavior of some international organizations in
recipient countries got criticized. For instance, the extremely arrogant
and even "hegemonic" behavior of the IMF in providing aid to Tanzania
in the 1980s evoked strong objection from the then president Julius
Nyerere, who publicly criticized the IMF and expressed an unwilling-
ness to cooperate. This view got widely echoed in other developing
countries, which raised further objections to the international order and
global governance model at that time and demanded that developed
countries give the third world more voice, especially in the management
of domestic aid projects.[11] Finally, in the late 1980s, the World Bank,
another important institution of the Bretton Woods system, responded to
the developing countries' demands and proposed to give them more
ownership in aid projects and initiatives. The World Bank believes that
increasing the local ownership of the recipient country will improve the
legitimacy and credibility of the aid projects and reduce the local government and people's resistance and aversion to the projects, thus
improving the effectiveness and efficiency of the project implementation. Before long, some countries such as the Nordic countries began to
respond to the World Bank's call for giving more ownership to recipient
countries. In 1995, considering Tanzania's long-term criticism of
Western donors and thanks to an influential report by a Canadian economist Gerry Helleiner, Tanzania was listed as one of the first countries
with certain aid autonomy.[12] That report emphasizes that aid ownership
means that the recipient country has the final say on aid projects, and
believes that increasing ownership can help improve the coordination
and implementation rate of projects by the recipient country. This notion
has been rapidly extended to other African and developing countries
(Edwards, 2014).

---

[11] For more on Tanzania's aid ownership and its relationship with major donors, please see
Furukawa (2017).

[12] For detailed background information on the report and the Helleiner Commission associated with it, please see Edwards (2014).

2. Empirical Evidence of Aid Ownership

With the World Bank changing its position and endorsing the ownership of recipient countries, a large number of studies began to discuss the role and impact of aid ownership. In addition, the factors affecting aid effectiveness have been gradually identified. One of the commonly recognized factors is the process of aid delivery; especially whether the aid management system is coordinated will directly affect the effectiveness and efficiency of aid delivery. Accordingly some problems arise, such as how to improve the coordination of aid management system so as to improve the efficiency of aid delivery? Many scholars' answer is to improve the ownership of recipient countries for aid projects. For example, by using cross-border panel data, Burnside and Dollar (2000) find that aid can significantly improve the welfare of the people of the recipient countries when their governments are committed to reform, provide good policies, and use their "owning" international aid to finance the people. Of course, the earliest study about ownership and aid effectiveness was conducted by Johnson and Watsy (1993). It is also an influential internal evaluation study of the World Bank. Based on the analysis of more than 100 projects of the World Bank in 42 countries, the study examines project ownership from two dimensions: the independence of knowledge and technology and whether there are key politicians to promote the implementation of the projects. Based on these two dimensions, the study then divides the independence of the World Bank's projects into four specific aspects: (1) whether the project is ready for implementation when the loan is granted (which is used to judge whether the project is originally initiated by the recipient country); (2) the knowledge and technical support obtained from policy makers; (3) the political willingness to support the project; and (4) the efforts of politicians and governments to build consensus in support of aid. In addition, they evaluate the performance of the projects by four degrees: "highly satisfied", "satisfied", "dissatisfied", and "very dissatisfied" according to the rating of the independent assessment team within the World Bank. They find that, overall speaking, the higher the degree of project ownership the recipient country has, the higher the degree of satisfaction and rating of the project performance is. Moreover, aid ownership has also provided inspiration for case studies at the national level. For example, Kim and Kim (2014) hold that the important reason why Korea can grow from an aid dependent country in the 1950s to a donor country is that it not only has its own autonomy to make its own development blueprint and plan but also has a high degree of ownership when formulating and implementing the recipient projects and can highly match it with its national development strategic plan. Even though this approach is criticized by donor countries, Korea remains unmoved and continues to uphold its aid ownership.

Of course, there are often side-effects of or objections to improving aid ownership. For example, Alesina and Weder (2002) find that the more corrupt the government is, the more easily it gets official assistance. They also find that official aid does not effectively reduce corruption in recipient countries. At the same time, by comparing multilateral development institutions with private investment, they find that the situation of multilateral development banks is slightly better, but not significantly different from bilateral official assistance, whereas private investment performs better, since the more corrupt a country is, the less likely it is to get private investment. Moreover, the definition of national ownership — whether it is only for the ownership of the project itself or for the national development strategy behind the project — still remains controversial. Sometimes the ambiguous concept of "ownership" is even used as an excuse by both aid countries and recipient countries. One the one hand, donor countries will give aid projects to the recipient country in the name of "ownership" so as to reduce their own burden. On the other hand, recipient countries or aid implementing agencies often use "ownership" as a bargaining tool when formulating and implementing policies, even if they themselves are corrupt or lack sufficient capacity to implement these projects.[13]

3. Aid Ownership and Global Governance Change

Judging from the emergence of the concept of aid ownership and its subsequent disputes and evolution, we can see that developing countries' demand for aid ownership is consistent with their struggle for a greater say in global governance. The reform of global governance requires developing countries to have more aid ownership, which is also an inevitable trend. Behind this, we should pay special attention to the efforts made by multilateral organizations to demand a greater say in global governance.

---

[13]For more on aid ownership, please see Booth (2012).

Apart from participating in some multilateral organizations with other Western countries, Japan was among the earlier developed countries to endorse the aid ownership of developing countries. As early as 1991, at the Tokyo International Conference on African Development, all countries reached an agreement on helping African countries develop through "ownership" and "partnership". In the subsequent Tokyo Action Plan of 1998, it clearly put forward that "ownership" and "partnership" were the fundamental principles for the action plan. Then, at the 10th anniversary of the Tokyo International Conference on African Development in 2003, the participants further stressed that "the 'ownership' of African countries in their own development process and the 'partnership' of the international community in support of such ownership are of great importance to the development of Africa", and called upon international organizations like the UN and the World Bank to be active in cooperating with African multilateral institutions (Li, 2008; Zhao and Zhou, 2013). It is undeniable that, although the Tokyo International Conference on African Development is a multilateral framework, the actual leader behind it is Japan. Therefore, the change mainly reflects Japan's ideas about foreign aid, however, it still carried little weight in Western developed countries.[14]

In Western countries, people and governments were dithering over whether to increase foreign aid in view of the rising doubts about aid effectiveness in the 1990s. Then in March 2002, organized by the UN, the OECD-DAC member countries and major international organizations met in Monterey, Mexico to have the United Nations International Conference on Financing for Development and signed the Monterey Consensus, which requires developed countries to make earnest efforts to achieve the goal of allocating 0.7% of their GNP to international development assistance.

As a follow-up to the Monterey Conference, developed countries signed the *Paris Declaration* in 2005, which clearly proposed shifting their focus to the quality and effect of aid oriented by practice and action, especially focusing on the ownership of aid projects of recipient countries, which was listed as the first principle to clarify the leadership and decision-making power of recipient countries for projects. The second principle is that donor countries and recipient countries should be aligned,

---

[14]In the third chapter, this book will focus on the differences between Japan's international aid and that of Europe and America.

and the local systems of recipient countries should be used to jointly achieve the aid goals.[15] In order to strengthen the concept and implementation of the *Paris Declaration*, developing countries and donor countries signed the *Accra Agenda for Action* (AAA) at the 12th United Nations Conference on Trade and Development held in Accra International Conference Center, Ghana in 2008. Apart from continuing to regard aid ownership as the primary principle, further elaborating the definition of ownership, and requiring recipient countries to participate in the formulation of aid projects and use their own systems to implement aid, the AAA also introduced the principle of inclusive partnerships to call on more subjects to participate in aid projects. As a result, aid ownership of developing countries has been continuously strengthened.

4. Summary

Through the analysis of the concept, background, and empirical research of aid ownership and its relationship with global governance, we can see that there is a clear correlation between aid ownership and developing countries' struggle for a greater say in international affairs: Tanzania's fierce criticism of donor countries in the early stage enabled its early acquisition of aid ownership, the African Union as a whole negotiated with developed countries for greater ownership, and then the *Paris Declaration* and the *AAA* explicitly required the recipient countries to have greater ownership. Objectively speaking, developing countries have gained a significant voice in foreign aid. However, the factors behind this change are worth further discussion. First of all, global economy over the past decades has changed. Emerging economies appeared and the economic map has changed from being dominated by developed countries to their being on a par with emerging economies. Second, with the rise of more developing countries, including emerging

---

[15]The other three principles of the *Paris Declaration* are harmony, which requires donor countries to coordinate and simplify aid processes and share information with recipient countries to avoid duplication, results, which means that both developing countries and donors should shift their focus to results and make them assessable, and mutual accountability, which means that donors and recipients should be jointly responsible for aid results.

economies, the dependence of the developing world on aid is greatly in decline, which has improved the negotiating power of developing countries to a certain extent. Third, with the rise of emerging donors, more aid or cooperation models have been introduced. From equal bilateral dialogue rights in South–South Cooperation to emerging multilateral development institutions such as the Asian Infrastructure Investment Bank, developing countries that need external development funds have more choices. Finally, the changes in this process are mainly dominated by developed countries, which have been patronizing the developing countries by giving them aid, aid ownership this time, whereas developing countries have always been in a relatively weaker position. Therefore, on the whole, although it seems that developing countries do have a greater say than before, it is in essence a concession made by the developed countries, especially the OECD-DAC countries, in view of the changes in the global economic map and governance. They have not really regarded the recipient countries as equal partners and they have failed to cooperate with them or to help them develop in a mutually beneficial and win–win manner.

References

Alesina, Alberto and Beatrice Weder. "Do corrupt governments receive less foreign aid?" *American Economic Review*, Vol. 92, No. 4, 2002, pp. 1126–1137.

Boone, Peter. "Politics and the effectiveness of foreign aid". *European Economic Review*, Vol. 40, No. 2, 1996, pp. 289–329.

Booth, David. "Aid effectiveness: Bringing country ownership (and politics) back in". *Conflict, Security & Development*, Vol. 12, No. 5, 2012, pp. 537–558.

Bräutigam, Deborah. "China, Africa and the international aid architecture". *African Development Bank*, 2010.

Burnside, Craig and David Dollar. "Aid, policies, and growth". *American Economic Review*, Vol. 90, No. 4, 2000, pp. 847–868.

Chenery, Hollis B. and Alan M. Strout. "Foreign assistance and economic development". *The American Economic Review*, Vol. 56, No. 4, 1966, pp. 679–733.

Collier, Paul. *The Bottom Billion: Why the Poorest Countries are Failing and What Can Be Done About It*. Oxford: Oxford University Press, 2008.

Deaton, Angus and Nancy Cartwright. "Understanding and misunderstanding randomized controlled trials". *Social Science & Medicine*, Vol. 210, 2017, pp. 2–21.

Doucouliagos, Hristos and Martin Paldam. "Aid effectiveness on growth: A meta study". *European Journal of Political Economy*, Vol. 24, No. 1, 2008, pp. 1–24.

Edwards, Sebastian. *Economic Collapse and Recovery in Tanzania*. Oxford: Oxford University Press, 2014.

Edwards, Sebastian. "Economic development and the effectiveness of foreign aid: A historical perspective". *Kyklos*, Vol. 68, No. 3, 2015, pp. 277–316.

Furukawa, Mitsuaki. "Management of the international development aid system: The case of Tanzania". *Development Policy Review*, February 2017.

Galiani, Sebastian *et al.* "The effect of aid on growth: Evidence from a quasi-experiment". *Journal of Economic Growth*, Vol. 22, No. 1, 2017, pp. 1–33.

Hansen, Henrik and Finn Tarp. "Aid and growth regressions". *Journal of Development Economics*, Vol. 64, No. 2, 2001, pp. 547–570.

Islam, Shafiqul. "Foreign aid and burdensharing: Is Japan free riding to a coprosperity sphere in Pacific Asia?" *Regionalism and Rivalry: Japan and the United States in Pacific Asia*. Chicago: The University of Chicago Press, 1993, pp. 321–390.

Johnson, John H. and Sulaiman S. Wasty. "Borrower ownership of adjustment programs and the political economy of reform". World Bank Working Paper, 1993.

Kim, Eun Mee and Phi Ho Kim. "From development to development cooperation". In E. Kim (Ed.), *The South Korean Development Experience: Beyond Aid*. Berlin: Springer, 2014.

Li, Anshan. "Tokyo International Conference on African Development and Japan's Aid Policy to Africa". *West Africa Asia*, No. 5, 2008.

Mwase, Nkunde and Yongzheng Yang. "BRICs' philosophies for development financing and their implications for LICs". IMF Working Paper, 2012.

Paldam, M. "A look at the raw data for aid and growth". Working Paper, 2005.

Rajan, Raghuram and Arvind Subramanian. "Does aid affect governance?" *American Economic Review*, Vol. 97, No. 2, 2007, pp. 322–327.

Rajan, Raghuram G. and Arvind Subramanian. "Aid and growth: What does the cross-country evidence really show?" *The Review of Economics and Statistics*, Vol. 90, No. 4, 2008, pp. 643–665.

Rajan, Raghuram G. and Arvind Subramanian. "Aid, Dutch disease, and manufacturing growth". *Journal of Development Economics*, Vol. 94, No. 1, 2011, pp. 106–118.

Rich, Sam. "Africa's Village of dreams". *The Wilson Quarterly (1976)*, Vol. 31, No. 2, 2007, pp. 14–23.

Zhao, Yue and Zhou Shengkun. "Intervention or subsidy? A review of the research on the ownership of development assistance of recipient countries". *Policy Making and Information*, No. 1, 2013.

Zheng, Yu. "Aid effectiveness and conception of new development cooperation model". *World Economy and Politics*, No. 7, 2017.

Chapter 3

International Development Cooperation Models and China's Experience

Section 1. A Comparative Study of Aid Models: Japan vs. Europe and America[1]

The comparison and evolution of international development aid models have always been an important research topic in the field of international political economics; equally important are the strategic considerations behind the selection of different paths. With the rapid increase of China's foreign aid, how to learn from other countries' experience and lessons and optimize China's foreign aid is becoming increasingly important, for which Japan provides a valuable reference system. Japan's foreign aid has always been an important topic of concern to the international academic and policy circles. This is not only because it has provided an enormous amount of long-term international development assistance but also because it, despite belonging to the Western camp in terms of ideology and geopolitics, has adopted relatively independent international development assistance policies that differ from those of European and American countries. Based on Japan's international development assistance data of the past 60 years, this section, by employing a comparative analysis framework, tries to conduct a detailed data analysis of the dynamic evolution of Japan's foreign aid after World War II and to analyze the

---

[1] This part is based on the author's article published in the *Journal of Contemporary Asia-Pacific Studies*. For details see Zhao Jianzhi and Ouyang Zhe (2018).

strategic considerations behind its continuous evolution. It finds that Japan's foreign aid data reveal three distinct stages, which are highly consistent with the period of exploratory development, the period of seeking political power, and the period of forming its unique style since joining the "Colombo Plan" in 1954. The findings of this section can not only help to understand the dynamic path evolution of Japan's post-war international development assistance and the underlying internal logic of the relevant international circumstances and its domestic development but also provide an important research foundation for optimizing China's foreign aid practice.

1. Introduction

Shortly after World War II, Japan initiated its foreign aid. As a country prohibited from resorting to military means, foreign aid has become an important diplomatic weapon for Japan. As the first Asian economy to enter the OECD and the DAC, Japan had remained a crucial power in foreign aid till 2018. In an international aid agency mainly comprising European and American countries, Japan has played a pivotal role in that it overtook its European and American counterparts to become the one providing most ODA among DAC member countries in 1989 and had maintained the status for nearly a decade. How many stages can Japan's foreign aid, which started after World War II and has lasted more than 60 years, be divided into? What are the features of each stage in the distribution of aiding regions and fields? What are the differences between Japan's foreign aid and that of European and American countries? What are the international and domestic factors that have prompted Japan to move from one stage of foreign aid to the next? What constitute the benefits consideration, foreign aid concepts, and constraints reflected, and what are the diplomatic styles and policies shown in the context of Japan's foreign aid? An in-depth discussion of these questions would help to reveal the strategic thinking behind the evolution of foreign assistance and clarify the internal logic behind the relationship between the strategic evolution and the changes in international situations and domestic development in Japan.

As China's economy develops and its connections with other countries and regions deepen, foreign aid has become an important diplomatic exchange medium between China and the recipient countries and regions and has gained more importance in its national strategy. As a developing country, China has been providing foreign assistance to other countries and regions within the "South–South Cooperation" framework. In terms of foreign assistance concepts, it adheres to the principles of "not imposing any political conditions, not interfering in the internal affairs of the recipient countries, and fully respecting their right of independently choosing their own paths and models of development".[2] Its foreign assistance has received both friendly praise and sharp criticism, which strikingly resembles the development course of Japan's foreign aid history. Therefore, we intend to present an in-depth analysis of the development course of Japan's foreign assistance and summarize its experience and lessons, which would be of great importance to optimize the international development assistance of China.

Foreign academic circles have studied more extensively on Japan's foreign aid, whereas scholars in China have conducted relatively fewer studies in this respect. Generally speaking, the shortcomings of relevant research are shown as follows. First, the diachronic analysis of Japan's foreign aid strategies is not detailed enough. Second, there is a lack of full application and systemic display of the existing detailed foreign aid data when using evidence to discuss Japan's foreign aid. This section examines two programmatic ODA documents — the "Official Development Assistance Charter" and the "Development Cooperation Charter" issued by Japan in 1992 and 2015, respectively — and sorts out the strategic characteristics of Japan's foreign aid at each stage. Accordingly, the development of Japan's post-WWII foreign aid is divided into three periods: the period of exploratory development, the period of seeking political power, and the period of forming its unique style. Through the systematic display and comparison of the foreign aid data between Japan and the US and Western European countries since 1960, this section also presents the characteristics of Japan's foreign aid at each stage.

The innovation and contribution of this section lie in that, based on solid data, it systematically synthesizes and analyzes the development of Japan's post-WWII foreign aid, and summarizes its prominent features by means of comparison with those of European and American countries. The main conclusions of this section are as follows. The development of

---

[2]The State Council Information Office of The People's Republic of China. *China's Foreign Aid (2014) White Article*. See: http://www.scio.gov.cn/zfbps/ndhf/2014/document/1375013/1375013_4.htm.

Japan's foreign aid can be divided into three distinct stages — the period of exploratory development, the period of seeking political power, and the period of forming its unique style — each of which has its own highly compatible themes of foreign aid strategy. Despite being an important donor country in the OECD-DAC system, Japan's foreign aid in practice is not completely consistent with the DAC concepts dominated by European and American countries, that is, Japan has had its own concepts and characteristics based on its own foreign aid strategy. In the dynamic evolution of Japan's foreign aid, there are also three distinct features from beginning to end: taking Southeast Asia as its stronghold in geography, never giving up economic interests when setting objectives, and serving its ideal of becoming a political power in diplomacy. This section is of great significance in further understanding Japan's foreign aid and providing new perspectives, new evidence, and new methods for studying foreign aid. It is also of important reference value for grasping Japan's strategic intentions of using foreign aid and for predicting the development trend of Japan's foreign aid in the future.

This section is mainly divided into six parts. The first part, i.e. the introduction, briefly narrates the basic research framework of this section. The second part summarizes the findings and shortcomings of previous research on Japan's foreign aid by worldwide scholars. The third to fifth parts systematically synthesize the three stages of the dynamic evolution of Japan's foreign aid in comparison with Europe and America based on historical analysis and data presentation. Finally, there is a brief evaluation of Japan's foreign aid policy and a summary of the whole section.

2. Literature Review

In 1954, Japan joined the "Colombo Plan" to become a donor country. Since then, along with Japan's post-war reconstruction and economic take-off, its foreign aid has also begun to develop rapidly. In 1989, it became the world's largest foreign aid donor country and had maintained this status for nearly a decade. As a non-European-and-American OECD-DAC donor country with long-term foreign aid to China, Japan's foreign aid practice has attracted extensive attention worldwide. At present, except for a few comprehensive monographs with general introduction to Japan's foreign aid (Zhang, 1996; Jin, 2000; Rix, 1980; White, 1964), most discussions on Japan's foreign aid focus on the following aspects.

2.1 *Perspective of national interests*

From the perspective of international relations, national interests have always been the core element in reviewing foreign aid. As the realist master Hans Morgenthau points out, despite of various forms of a country's foreign aid, all forms of aid are ultimately political in nature and are essentially planned to maintain and promote the donor country's national interests.[3] When considering Japan's foreign aid, national interests are also unavoidably an important perspective.

Lin Xiaoguang (2005) believes that foreign aid is the Japanese government's "strategic choice to exploit its strengths and avoid weaknesses". As a defeated country, Japan is disqualified to use military means as a diplomatic weapon owing to the peaceful constitution. Therefore, economic diplomacy has become an inevitable choice for Japan to maintain and expand its national interests. Zhu Fenglan (2003) points out that foreign aid is not only a special economic means that Japan has to use to fulfill its national strategy after World War II as it could not use military means but also an important tool for Japan to obtain national interests. Japan's large expenditure on foreign aid is because the "output" of foreign aid is much higher than the "input". After combing through the history of Japan's foreign aid, Yasutomo (1989) points out that in the 1980s, foreign aid stood out from Japan government's multiple policies and became the core of its foreign policy to safeguard its national interests. As a diplomatic tool subject to Japan's independent control, foreign aid would not provoke frictions or conflicts with other countries (especially the US) like military or trade issues, thereby effectively achieving Japan's diplomatic goals in practice. It has won broad international and domestic support, elevated Japan's international status, and presented Japan with an ideal and feasible path to becoming a non-military yet active and promising international power. These factors that perfectly suit Japan's national interests jointly motivated Japan to become a major donor country in a self-reinforcing way.

Economic benefits have always been an important goal of Japan's foreign aid, which was particularly obvious in its early stage. Through foreign aid, Japan has gained access to the markets of recipient countries,

---

[3]Hans Morgenthau divided foreign aid into six categories: Humanitarian aid, subsistence aid, military aid, prestige aid, bribery aid, and economic development aid (see Morgenthau (1962).

promoted their infrastructure construction, and fostered the development of its foreign investment and trade, thereby advancing the development of its own economy. The academic circles have reached a consensus that economic benefits are an important driving force for Japan's foreign aid. Matsui (1983) believes that foreign aid to developing countries can boost the economic benefits of developed countries; in the early studies on Japan's foreign aid, White (1964) even maintains that basically there is no non-economic motivation in foreign aid.

Political and security interests are another major goal of Japan's foreign aid. Brooks and Orr (1985) point out that Japan cannot resort to military power but suffers the threat of world military turmoil to its politics and security; hence, it is of great importance for it to use foreign aid ingeniously to protect the peace and stability of countries and regions with political and security significance to it. Samurai Igarashi (1990) believes that Japan's foreign aid has gradually turned to its political and ideological interests, reflecting its intention to maintain the international order dominated by Western countries. Yasutomo (1986) points out that from the late 1970s to the early 1980s, Japan's foreign aid has become politicized in practice and is no longer limited to economic and commercial interests. This politicization has also spread to the security field, as reflected in Japan's "comprehensive security" claim, whereby foreign aid is instrumental in ensuring Japan's economic and military security in an all-round manner.

2.2 *Perspective of aid philosophy*

Aid philosophy refers to the guidelines for a country to practice foreign aid, which reflects the perspective and logic of its foreign aid. The discussions on national interests by academic circles consist of an important perspective for understanding Japan's foreign aid. However, national interests have different facets, and the focus of national interests is constantly evolving along with historical advancement; all are closely related to international situations and domestic development. Therefore, the investigation of national interests is inseparable from the analysis of historical circumstances. Nonetheless, most of the existing research treats historical circumstances merely as a brief background introduction, lacking sufficient analysis of the international situations and domestic development in a specific historical context as well as of how the mechanism could affect Japan's consideration of the national interests behind its foreign aid.

Mawdsley (2012) distinguishes the aid philosophy of traditional Western developed countries represented by DAC members and that of emerging countries. Traditional Western developed countries emphasize the charitable nature and moral obligations of foreign aid, believing that developed countries should provide unilateral transfer payments without asking for returns to help underdeveloped countries. By contrast, the emerging donor countries emphasize the establishment of an equal partnership via foreign aid with recipient countries that are also Third World countries and seek for win–win cooperation. Hattori (2003) holds that developed countries' assistance to developing countries through unilateral resource output that seems to require no return is not in itself gratuitous. This kind of free aid from developed countries actually gives them moral superiority over developing countries, and somehow obliges the recipient developing countries to align their ideological and political stance with the donor countries as a reward. By citing Hattori's view on the moral nature of foreign aid, Japanese scholars Fukuda-Parr and Shiga analyze the impact of the aid-generated interactions between the donor and recipient countries on foreign aid. After studying the development process of Japan's own foreign aid, they point out that though it belongs to the European and American camps and is an important member of DAC, Japan does not completely agree with the DAC norms while striving to comply with these norms. As for aid philosophy, Japan emphasizes the autonomy of the recipient countries and its economic cooperation and common development with them, which is closer to the foreign aid philosophy of emerging countries (Fukuda-Parr and Shiga, 2016). The accounts of some native Japanese scholars also reflect Japan's aid philosophy as such. Kubota (1992) believes that Japan's foreign aid is not only out of humanitarian concern but also gains economic returns and enhances its own international image. Nishikawa (1993) points out from another angle that Japan's prosperity depends on international prosperity and stability; therefore, its foreign aid to developing countries is also a help to Japan itself. Some European and American scholars express similar views from other perspectives. European and American countries have always criticized Japan's foreign aid for paying too much attention to geo-economic benefits and their poor quality of aid. This reached a peak after Japan became the world's largest donor country in 1989. Under various considerations, Japan vowed to improve the quality of aid and attach more emphasis to caring for people, which was clearly stated in the "Official Development Assistance Charter" first promulgated in 1992.

After respectively examining the general situations of Japan's aid to all countries and a rural life improvement plan in the Philippines in particular, Hook and Zhang and Scheyvens maintain that, though the Japanese government has vowed to continuously improve the quality of foreign aid, it has not done much in practice; in fact, economic considerations still account for a considerable proportion of Japan's foreign aid (Hook and Zhang, 1998; Scheyvens, 2005). This shows that, despite following the DAC norms in expressing its aid philosophy, Japan still emphasizes the mutual economic benefits of foreign aid.

As the publicity of the principles, standards, means, and methods of foreign aid, aid philosophy should comply with the internal logic of the country's foreign aid strategy at home and strive for international support and legitimacy for the practice of foreign aid abroad. Most of the existing studies on Japan's foreign aid philosophy have focused on the quality of Japan's foreign aid and the relative weight of economic benefits and moral assistance. However, the existing studies have failed to realize that aid philosophy reflects a country's foreign aid strategy to some degree, and rarely analyzed how Japan, a member of the Western allies, managed the complex interaction between advocating its aid philosophy under the Western discourse system on the one hand and independently voicing its aid strategy on the other hand from the perspective of its aid philosophy.

2.3 *Perspective of aid characteristics*

Japan's foreign aid has many characteristics of its own, and many scholars have analyzed it based on these characteristics.

First, Japan's foreign aid is closely linked to its economic development. Japan's foreign aid, trade, and investment go hand in hand, which has jointly promoted the development of the Japanese economy. This model is called the "trinity approach", which is officially recognized by the Japanese government and widely discussed in academia (Araki, 2007; Fukuda-Parr and Shiga, 2016).

Second, the domestic mechanism of Japan's foreign aid has also received some attention. Hook and Zhang point out that, the fact that Japan's two goals of improving the quality of aid and pursuing the economic benefits of aid are at odds with each other reflects the gaming between different domestic institutions. The Ministry of Foreign Affairs of Japan hopes to improve Japan's international status and therefore insists on improving the quality of aid; nonetheless, the Ministry of

International Trade and Industry of Japan mainly represents the interests of the Japanese business community and therefore emphasizes the economic goals of foreign aid. Katada (2002) inherits this view and believes that the wishes of the domestic people and the pressure of the international community have rendered the gaming more complicated. Hirata (1998) also takes into consideration the influences of the Ministry of Finance of Japan, Japan International Cooperation Agency, the Japan Overseas Economic Cooperation Fund, and non-governmental organizations (NGOs) on Japan's foreign aid.

Third, Japan has made outstanding achievements on some international aid issues, which has also aroused some scholars' thinking. Since Japan successfully hosted the first Tokyo International Conference on African Development (TICAD) in 1993, it has been playing an important role in African development issues since. Watanabe (2008) analyzes the fourth TICAD and points out that the success of the conference shows that Japan's foreign aid agenda has become more and more autonomous and flexible than following the international practice in the past. Japan's vigorous assistance to Africa is conducive to strengthening Japan's ties with African countries, winning political support from them on the international arena, and expanding business cooperation opportunities with them. Some Japanese scholars including Ishikawa (2005) believe that Japan's own experience of transforming from a developing country to a developed country is of great significance for the majority of African countries which are mostly poor and underdeveloped. Japan is also an important leader in global environmental issues. Moni (2009) points out that global environmental issues have always been an important topic of international concern and an important issue of the UN, but previously no country in the international community had taken the initiative to assume the leading responsibility. As one of the biggest donor countries in the world, Japan has been providing great assistance to environmental undertakings for a long time and has made outstanding achievements in tackling domestic environmental problems. These factors helped Japan gain large-scale international support and praise when it stood up for the world's environmental problems and became a leading country on this issue.

The characteristics of foreign aid are the external manifestations of aid strategy. For example, the Japanese model of "trinity approach" embodies the weight of economic interests in Japan's foreign aid. The disagreements between the Ministry of Foreign Affairs and the Ministry of International Trade and Industry on Japan's foreign aid represent the difference between the economic interests and political interests in Japan's foreign aid in different periods. Japan's outstanding performance in global climate change reflects its posture on pursuing its status as an international power. This section combines the characteristics and the strategy of Japan's foreign aid, regards the aid characteristics as the external manifestations of Japan's realization of its aid strategy at each level, and integrates them into an overall framework.

2.4 *The analytical framework of Japan's foreign aid strategy*

In summary, though the existing research on Japan's foreign aid has made certain achievements, there are still aspects in need of improvement.

First, historical circumstances need to be further analyzed when discussing Japan's foreign aid strategy. In its foreign aid practice for more than 60 years, Japan's aid strategy has also undergone a major evolution. Many existing studies have mentioned this evolutionary process, but they often use specific events at specific time points as simple evidence in their discussions or arguments, falling short of a systematic analysis framework. The evolution of Japan's foreign aid strategy is a historical process. In this process, the international political and economic situation and Japan's domestic development have played a major restraining and shaping role in its evolution, which is subsequently manifested in Japan's definition of national interests, expression of aid philosophy and aid characteristics. In the process of analyzing the evolution of Japan's foreign aid strategy, existing research lacks systematic review of the historical contexts and continuous investigation of two key influencing variables: the international situations and Japan's domestic development.

Second, in the use of evidence, existing research failed to make full use of current detailed data. A direct reflection of the evolution of Japan's foreign aid strategy consists of changes in aid data and indicators. Since Japan joined the DAC, Japan's foreign aid has left detailed records and data, which faithfully reflects changes in its distribution, focus, and quality, which reveals the evolutionary process of Japan's foreign aid strategy. However, there is no coherent and systematic display and analysis of such data in existing research. Therefore, this section proposes an analytical framework for the evolution of Japan's foreign aid strategy so as to integrate the systematic processes that affect the evolution (see Figure 3.1).

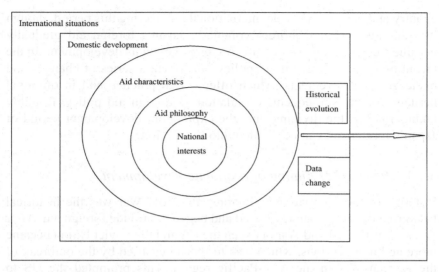

Figure 3.1:   The analytical framework for the evolution of Japan's foreign aid strategy.

Based on the above framework, taking two programmatic policy documents on Japan's official development assistance — the "Official
Development Assistance Charter" in 1992and the "Development
Cooperation Charter" in 2015 — promulgated by the Japanese government
as the dividing lines, this section divides the complex history of Japan's
foreign aid after World War II into three stages: the first stage is the period
of exploratory development (1954–1991), the second stage is the period of
seeking political power (1992–2014), and the third stage is the period
of forming its unique style (2015–).

3. The Exploratory Development Period of Japan's Foreign Aid (1954–1991)

3.1 *Analysis of the historical background and aid strategy of the exploratory development period*

The first stage is the exploratory development period of Japan's foreign
aid. Soon after World War II, Japan joined the foreign aid system of the
European and American camp both as a recipient country and a donor

country and began to provide international aid. During this period, though its initiation was not entirely voluntary, Japan's foreign aid gradually became a core element of Japan's foreign policy in its development. In the meantime, Japan's foreign aid policy underwent a series of changes and made great achievements, which offered rich practice and institutional heritage for the subsequent formulation of foreign aid policy. Roughly taking 1973 as the dividing line, the exploratory development period of Japan's foreign aid can be divided into two periods.

3.1.1   *1954–1972: Aiming at economic development*

In terms of the international situation, the Cold War was the historical background when Japan recovered and began to provide foreign aid. After World War II, the Cold War between the US and the Soviet Union became more and more serious, which was further intensified by the outbreak of the Korean War in the Asia-Pacific region. This prompted the US to change its Asia-Pacific strategy and subsequently change its previous policy of weakening Japan that meant to prevent it from staging a come-back. The US quickly began negotiations with Japan and signed the "San Francisco Agreement" with Japan in 1951, effectively ending its occupa-tion of Japan; at the same time, the two sides signed the "Japan–US Security Treaty" and became allies, making Japan an important part of the US's global strategy. The US also placed high hopes on Japan, hoping it to become a bridgehead for the US to contain the Soviet Union's sphere of influence to expand to Southeast Asia. "The San Francisco Agreement" stipulates that Japan must pay compensation to the Southeast Asian coun-tries and regions that it invaded and occupied during World War II. In 1954, Japan joined the "Colombo Project" led by the UK to aid the devel-opment of South Asia and Southeast Asia, marking its official entry into the international aid system of the European and American camp. In the same year, Japan and Myanmar signed the "Japan–Myanmar Peace Treaty" and the "Japan–Myanmar Compensation and Economic Cooperation Agreement", which kicked off Japan's foreign aid practice. The historical heritage of the Japanese occupation period and the histori-cal background of the Cold War between the US and the Soviet Union determined the beginning of Japan's foreign aid, and also determined that the beginning period of Japan's foreign aid was mainly concentrated in Southeast Asian regions.

In terms of the domestic development situation in Japan after World War II, the destructed economy was awaiting revival and the economic situation was grim. The policy of weakening Japan during American occupation made Japan's domestic development situation even worse. Before World War II, as an industrial power with a shortage of resources, Japan's economy was inextricably linked with Southeast Asia. On the one hand, Southeast Asia was the most important source of raw materials for Japan; on the other hand, the region was also an important export market for Japanese commodities. The invasion of Southeast Asia by Japan during World War II had severed post-war diplomatic relations and political and economic exchanges between Japan and Southeast Asian countries. As a result, Japan fell into a dilemma of declining domestic industries on the one hand and the loss of foreign raw materials and commodity markets on the other hand.

Confronted with such domestic and foreign situations, Japan established a development strategy that prioritizes economic development to restore its vitality and power. On the one hand, Japan's "Pacifist Constitution" and the signing of the "San Francisco Agreement" and the "Japan–US Security Treaty" determined that Japan could no longer embark on the path of military expansion. At the same time, Japan was also relieved of security concerns and gave up the idea of expanding and developing military strength. On the other hand, Japan's domestic economy was in urgent need of revival and development. When Japan turned into the US's friend, the US provided a series of aids to Japan's economic development, including orders from the Korean War, whereby Japan's economic recovery got a historical opportunity. The unanimous strategic choice of all post-war Japanese governments is to abandon the strategy of becoming a militarized country and to integrate the current bargaining chips and constraints at home and abroad to vigorously develop its economy.

Under such circumstances, Japan's foreign aid, initiated by the "San Francisco Agreement" not on an entirely voluntary basis, proved to be effective in promoting the recovery and development of the Japanese economy and fully conformed to Japan's national interests and strategies with priorities for economic development during this period; therefore, it has gradually been placed at a more central position by the Japanese government. During this period, Japan referred to this kind of aid as "economic cooperation" rather than "international assistance" in its official expressions. On the one hand, the expression of this kind of aid philosophy certainly entails "compensation" liabilities of the aid; on the other hand, it also implies that the Japanese government recognizes the role of such aid in promoting economic development.

The boosting effects of Japan's foreign aid on its economic development in this period are mainly embodied in the following aspects. First, by providing foreign aid to such Southeast Asian countries as Myanmar, Japan had re-established ties with Southeast Asian countries and opened the door to their markets of raw materials and commodities. Second, Japan's foreign aid usually attached a series of special conditions that are conducive to Japan's economic development, which is also a distinctive feature of its foreign aid during this period. On the one hand, it is stipulated in Article 14 of the "San Francisco Agreement" that Japan's payment of "compensation" shall be made by providing services such as "production" rather than directly providing currency, and the Allies should consider providing Japan with raw materials for production.[4] This arrangement actually helped Japan retain foreign exchange, encouraged the development of Japan's domestic industrial production, promoted Japan's export trade, strengthened the international competitiveness of Japanese companies, and opened up the international market. On the other hand, the great majority of Japan's foreign aid during this period was administered in the form of loans rather than grants. Meanwhile, there were additional conditions attached to these loans, that is, these loans could only be used to purchase Japanese goods and services. This is tantamount to "eating the cake and having it", which had greatly promoted Japan's foreign trade and investment. In fact, promoting foreign trade and investment was exactly the focus of Japan's strategy for economic revival. Japan's foreign aid during this period had greatly promoted its foreign trade, foreign investment, and economic growth, and the Japanese government even generalized this model as the "Japan ODA Model".[5] In this model, Japan first signed a compensation or economic cooperation agreement with the recipient country and promised to build roads, power plants,

[4]United Nations. "Treaty of Peace with Japan", in United Nations — Treaty Series, 1952. URL: https://treaties.un.org/doc/Publication/UNTS/Volume%20136/volume-136-I-1832-English.pdf.

[5]Ministry of Economy, Trade and Industry of The Government of Japan, "White Article on International Economy and Trade". 2007, p. 377. URL: http://www.meti.go.jp/english/report/downloadfiles/2007WhiteArticle/Section4-3.pdf.

ports, and other infrastructure for the recipient country (mostly in the form of loans in Japanese yen); the recipient country also had great motivation to build up and maintain a better investment environment for Japanese companies. At the same time, with improved hardware and software infrastructure, the private sector in Japan became more motivated to carry out investment in these countries through cooperation with ODA or independent access, which had in turn further promoted the development of Japan's trade and economy. Having accumulated a large trade surplus, Japan got more inclined to further increase its foreign aid and raw material imports, thus forming a virtuous circle of "aid loans–investment–trade". It is precisely in the exploration and development of this "Japanese model" in aid strategy that the crucial role of foreign aid in Japan's economic development has gradually emerged. Therefore, foreign aid has become a common tool more and more frequently used in Japan's foreign policy as well as an important weapon for the realization of its national strategy.

3.1.2 *1973–1991: Diversification of aid objectives*

In 1973 and afterwards, some new situations and new realities contributed to the transformation of Japan's foreign aid strategy. Although the objective of economic development remained the focal point of Japan's foreign aid, other objectives such as economic security and the improvement of international political status also began to surface in Japan's foreign aid.

With the continuous development of Japan's economy and trade, the economic and trade exchanges and connections between Japan and other countries and regions in the world had increased and become closer. In terms of international circumstances, Japan experienced several major crises from 1973 to 1974, which prompted it to begin to reflect on its previous aid policies.

The "oil crisis" of 1973 had a huge negative impact on the Japanese economy. In October 1973, the Fourth Middle East War broke out, and the Organization of Petroleum Exporting Countries (OPEC) imposed an oil embargo on Western countries such as the US and Japan that supported Israel. As a country extremely dependent on imported natural resources such as oil, the "oil crisis" caused huge fluctuations in Japan's economy and society. Japan began to realize that its economic prosperity and economic security were heavily dependent on energy, whereas the US could not guarantee its oil security. As a result, it began to consider how to establish good relations with oil-producing countries, and the "energy diplomacy" began to come to the stage. A large volume of Japan's foreign aid began to flow to the Middle East and to some Third World countries and regions such as Africa and Latin America, which means Japan began to globalize its foreign aid. In 1974, Japanese Prime Minister Kakuei Tanaka visited Thailand and Indonesia, but was greeted by huge demonstrations in Bangkok and Jakarta. As Japan's foreign aid had long focused on Southeast Asia, it assumed that trust and friendly relations should have been established between it and Southeast Asian countries long ago. However, the two demonstrations dealt a heavy blow to Japan's belief in the effectiveness of its foreign aid. Its explicit goal of pursuing its own economic interests in its foreign aid and the loan policy with various conditions attached had not won trust from the people of Southeast Asian recipient countries; on the contrary, the foreign aid had aroused the people's deeper dissatisfaction with it. Japan began to relax conditions for its subsequent aid to Southeast Asia. In addition to its economic objective, it also began to emphasize the diplomatic and political significance of foreign aid, focusing on improving its relationship with recipient countries as well as its international image. In the mid-1970s, Japan accumulated a large trade surplus due to the rapid growth of its trade with Africa. In 1975 alone, its trade surplus with Africa reached US $1.02 billion,[6] which led to dissatisfaction and trade frictions in many African countries, with some countries adopting sanction policies against it. Japan alleviated the trade frictions by providing Japanese yen loans as aid, thus opening the door to foreign aid in Africa. This also provided new ideas and practical experience for Japan to resolve international conflicts and achieve political and economic goals through foreign aid.

Judging from the international situations in a broader context, the US–Soviet Cold War situation underwent major changes in the 1970s, forming a state of "the Soviet Union on the offensive and the US on the defensive", consequently the US began to face tremendous strategic pressure from the Soviet Union. Under such circumstances, the US began to require Japan to cooperate with its global Cold War strategy and assume the responsibility of "strategic cooperation", mainly by providing foreign aid to countries and regions of great strategic significance to the

---

[6]Calculated by the author based on the data retrieved from IMF Direction of Trade Statistics (DOTS) database. URL: http://data.imf.org/?sk=9D6028D4-F14A-464C-A2F2-59B2CD424B85.

US–Soviet Union Cold War (such as Turkey, Pakistan, and Egypt). On the other hand, as Japan had accumulated a large trade surplus in foreign trade, it was easy to have trade frictions with many countries, especially the US. Major Western aid donor countries led by the US imposed pressure on Japan and demanded that Japan increase its foreign aid in a bid to return the trade surplus to developing countries. While maintaining its ally with the US, Japan began to have differences of interests with the US, so Japan–US relations faced reexamination in Japan.

In terms of Japan's development, the Japanese economy had taken off after the long-term development of about 20 years after World War II. In the 1980s, it further prospered and became a pivotal economic power in the world. In view of the status of having become an economic power, Japan's ambition started to grow at home and its desire to become a major political power gradually surfaced up.

Against this background, while it still emphasized the goal of economic development, Japan also began to pay more attention to its status in the international society on the other hand. The importance of diplomatic and political interests in Japan's national strategy became more prominent.

In view of this situation, Japan began to reflect on its previous foreign aid policies and started to construct new aid philosophy and strategic choices such as "comprehensive security safeguard" or "comprehensive economic cooperation". Although these aid notions were still under discussion in Japan at that time, the consensus behind them was consistent: as a non-armed country, it was impossible for Japan to resolve international conflicts and frictions with threats of military force; moreover, as a country with little resources, Japan's economic development depended on trading raw materials and energy with other countries. Due to the "Japan–US Security Treaty", Japan did not have to worry too much about direct military threats to its homeland; however, resources were crucial to its economic security, which was dependent on orderly and safe international surroundings and diplomatic relations; therefore, resolving international disputes or even preventing them through foreign aid had become the only choice to ensure Japan's economic security. At the same time, with the growth of its economic power and its desire to become a political power, Japan began to seek to establish a better international image. Among the many non-military means, foreign aid had become the best choice for Japan to seek a higher international status, thus being gradually and widely recognized as the core of Japan's diplomatic tools.

In practice, Japan's foreign aid during this period mainly has the following characteristics. First, Japan's foreign aid began to internationalize, whereby more and more aid began to flow to the Middle East and Africa. While this practice embodied Japan's "energy diplomacy" and showed that Japan intended to seek support from developing countries including African countries to improve its international status, it was also because Japan actively cooperated with the US in "strategic cooperation" with the expectation of improving its status among the Western allies of the US as well as its own image as a major power on the international stage. Second, Japan's foreign aid had increased substantially. The rapid growth of Japan's economy prompted the international community, especially Western countries, to demand it to assume more international responsibilities and provide more foreign aid. On the one hand, Japan had a large foreign trade surplus and was pressured by the US and other Western donor countries to provide more foreign aid so as to return the trade surplus to developing countries; on the other hand, it itself was willing to assume more international responsibilities in order to establish a good international image. In fact, Japan had successfully formulated five ODA medium-term target clauses since 1978 to continuously promote the growth of its foreign aid. Third, Japan's previous foreign aid, mainly in the form of Japanese yen loans with many additional conditions, had focused more on economic objectives and was largely invested in economic production sectors and economic infrastructure sectors, which resulted in much criticism from the international community and the recipient countries for the poor quality of its aid. During this period, Japan began to focus on improving the quality of aid, gradually increasing the proportion of aid to medical care, education, and other social infrastructure sectors and the proportion of grants in the total volume of aid.

3.2 *Aid evolution in the exploratory development period and its comparison with Europe and the US*

Judging from the data of Japan's aid, trade and investment, Japan's foreign aid underwent rapid development from 1960 to 1991, especially after the 1985 "Plaza Accord" with a sharp rise of the exchange rate of Japanese yen.[7] Although Japan's net exports and foreign exchange

---

[7]The budget and expenditure of Japan's ODA are calculated in yen, but the ODA statistics are calculated in US dollar. After signing the "Plaza Accord" in 1985, Japanese yen

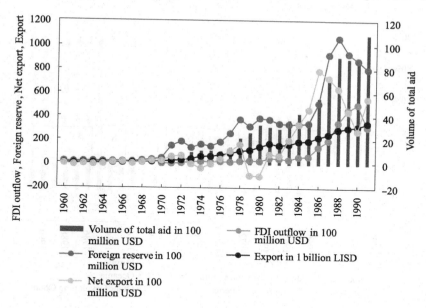

Figure 3.2: Survey of Japan's foreign aid, foreign trade, and foreign investment (1960–1991).

Source: Data from the World Bank WDI database and the International Monetary Fund International Financial Statistics database. URLs: http://databank.worldbank.org/data/reports.aspx?source=world-development-indicators, http://data.imf.org/?sk=4C514D48-B6BA-49ED-8AB9-52B0C1A0179B.

reserves declined during the two oil crises and the bursting of its economic bubble in 1990, they had generally maintained a relatively high upward momentum; meanwhile, the export volume reflecting its export competitiveness had also maintained long-term stable and rapid development. In addition, Japan's foreign direct investment (FDI outflow) also experienced rapid development (see Figure 3.2). As can be seen, Japan's foreign aid, foreign trade, and foreign investment all developed rapidly at this stage, and the growth of foreign aid was not contradictory with its strategy of promoting trade and foreign investment that centered on economic development.

Judging from its regional distribution of aid, Japan's foreign aid in general was mainly concentrated in Southeast Asia; especially before

---

appreciated robustly against US dollar. Objectively speaking, this had resulted in the rapid growth of Japan's ODA priced in US dollars.

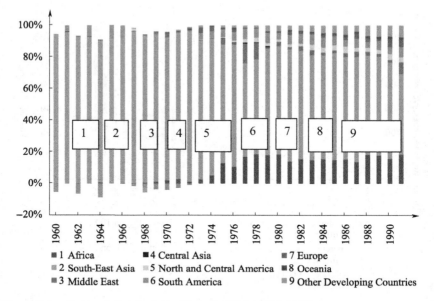

Figure 3.3:   Regional distribution of Japan's ODA (1960–1991).
Source: Data from OECD-DAC database. URL: http://stats.oecd.org/qwids/.

1972, its aid was almost entirely concentrated in that region. Since 1973, its aid to the Middle East region has increased substantially. In fact, throughout the 1960s, Japan's ODA to the Middle East was less than US $500,000 per year; whereas by 1977, the aid amount had jumped to US $110 million, accounting for 12.4% of Japan's ODA that year. This vividly illustrates Japan's "energy diplomacy" at that time.[8] In addition, since 1973, the developing countries in Africa, South America, and other continents began to receive relatively stable aid from Japan's ODA, especially the aid to African countries having maintained a relatively high proportion of 15% and above since the mid-1970s (see Figure 3.3).

Comparatively speaking, the US's foreign aid during this period served its containment strategy, with Asia being its focus but also distributed in other parts of the world (see Figure 3.4). Before 1974, the US's foreign aid in Asia was also mainly distributed in Southeast Asia. Since

---

[8]Calculated by the author based on the data retrieved from OECD-DAC database. URL: http://stats.oecd.org/qwids/.

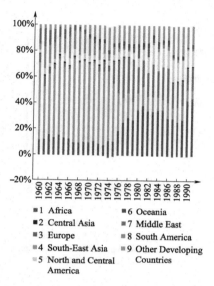

Figure 3.4:   Regional distribution of the US ODA (1960–1991).

Source: Data from OECD-DAC database. URL: http://stats.oecd.org/qwids/.

then, with the Cold War having changed, the US's aid to Southeast Asia and South America has greatly decreased, but its aid to the Middle East, Africa, and other developing countries has greatly increased. In general, though the US's foreign aid was widely distributed, it still had many similarities to Japan in terms of structure, which reflects to some degree the characteristics of Japan's foreign aid that it was greatly influenced by the US during this period and assumed the assistance obligation of "strategic cooperation" to the US.

The foreign aid of Western European countries[9] also scattered all over the world during this period. Nonetheless, with Asia only being its secondary focus, the focus of Western European aid was the African countries that have historical sovereign-colonial connections and closer geographical relationship with them and become independent since 1960 (see Figure 3.5). Generally speaking, the assistance structure of Western Europe in various

---

[9]This refers to 18 Western European countries among OECD member states, including Austria, Belgium, Denmark, Finland, France, Germany, Greece, Iceland, Ireland, Italy, Luxembourg, Netherlands, Norway, Portugal, Spain, Sweden, Switzerland, and the United Kingdom.

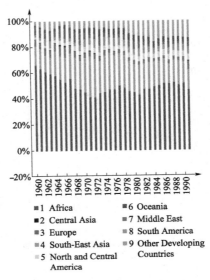

- 1 Africa
- 2 Central Asia
- 3 Europe
- 4 South-East Asia
- 5 North and Central America
- 6 Oceania
- 7 Middle East
- 8 South America
- 9 Other Developing Countries

Figure 3.5: Regional distribution of Western European countries' ODA in OECD (1960–1991).

Source: Data from OECD-DAC database. URL: http://stats.oecd.org/qwids/.

regions of the world during this period was relatively stable, with relatively few changes.

Judging from the regional distribution of aid, compared with Europe and the US, Japan's aid during this period showed a clear Asia-centered and then gradually globalized feature.

Judging from the distribution of sectors, Japan's aid during this period showed an obvious characteristic of focusing on economic construction aid (see Figure 3.6). The vast majority of sectoral assistance had entered the economic infrastructure and service sectors (such as roads, energy supply, etc.) and the production sectors (such as agriculture, forestry, fishery, and industrial production); moreover, there was generally more economic assistance to economic infrastructure and services than to the production sectors. However, there was relatively little aid to social infrastructure and service sectors (such as education, medical care, health, etc.) that can reflect the so-called quality of aid. In fact, it was not until the 1970s that Japan began to provide substantial and stable assistance to social infrastructure and service sectors, and it was not until 1978 that the social infrastructure and service sectors received a relatively stable aid, maintaining a level of 10% or above of all Sector Allocable ODA.

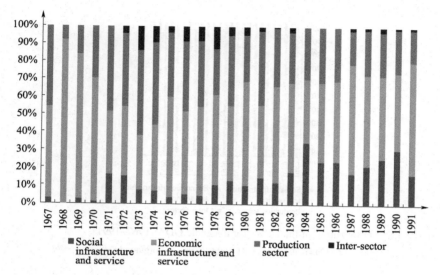

Figure 3.6: Distribution of Japan's sector allocable ODA (1967–1991).

Source: Data from OECD-DAC database. URL: http://stats.oecd.org/qwids/.

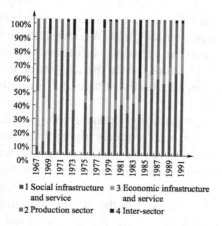

Figure 3.7: Distribution of the US sector allocable ODA (1967–1991).

Source: Data from OECD-DAC database. URL: http://stats.oecd.org/qwids/.

By contrast, the US's aid mainly concentrated in the economic sector and much less in the social sector before 1970. However, the US provided less economic assistance to economic infrastructure and service sectors but more to the production sectors (see Figures 3.7 and 3.8). After 1970, the assistance to social infrastructure and service

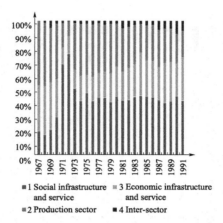

Figure 3.8:   Distribution of the US sector allocable ODA (1967–1991).

Source: Data from OECD-DAC database. URL: http://stats.oecd.org/qwids/.

sectors grew rapidly, and eventually maintained a relatively high level of more than 50%. The foreign aid of Western European countries was similar to that of the US: the aid to social infrastructure and services began to increase greatly after 1970. Western Europe provided roughly equivalent assistance to the economic infrastructure and service sectors and to the production sectors, while the assistance to social infrastructure and service sectors eventually remained at a relatively high level of about 40%.

Judging from the proportion of loans in foreign aid, the proportion of loans in Japan's foreign aid is much higher than that of the US and Western Europe, which served as another evidence for Japan's Western allies to criticize the poor quality of Japan's aid (see Figure 3.9). Judging from Japan's own evolution, the loan ratio in the 1970s was significantly higher than that in the 1980s, with the latter remaining below 50% for a long time, which reflected its efforts to improve its aid quality in order to meet Western aid standards.

There is another indicator — the level of humanitarian aid — that can reflect the characteristics of Japan's aid structure during this period (see Figure 3.10). European and American countries generally emphasized the significance of humanitarian aid. This not only has something to do with the ideological factors of the Cold War at that time but also reflects the

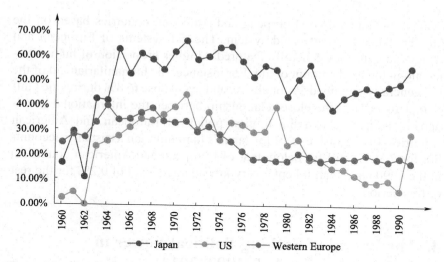

Figure 3.9: The proportion of loans in the foreign aid of Japan, the US and Europe (1967–1991).

Source: Data from OECD-DAC database. URL: http://stats.oecd.org/qwids/.

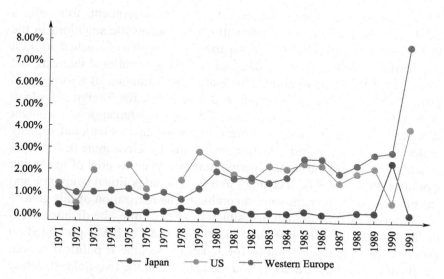

Figure 3.10: The proportion of humanitarian aid of Japan, the US, and Europe (1967–1991).

Source: Data from OECD-DAC database. URL: http://stats.oecd.org/qwids/.

evaluation standards of European and American countries based on the OECD standard-oriented aid system. The aid systems of European and American countries generally featured a higher proportion of humanitarian aid in the total amount of aid. For instance, the humanitarian aid of the US generally remained 2% or above, and even close to 8% during the Gulf War. This reflects the close relationship between the international development assistance and the foreign policy of European and American countries. In contrast, except for Japan's humanitarian assistance accounting for 2.39% (still far below that of European and American countries) in the 1990 Gulf War, it kept a very low average level of 0.2% for the rest of this period.

4. The Period of Seeking Political Power in Japan's Foreign Aid (1992–2014)

4.1 *Analysis of historical background and aid strategy in the period of seeking political power*

After more than 30 years of exploration and development, following a series of events affecting the international and domestic situations in the late 1980s and early 1990s, the Japanese government launched its first "Official Development Assistance Charter" with its national interests and strategies at that time in mind. This marks the formation of a formal and institutionalized concept, program, and framework for foreign aid which is the core of Japan's diplomatic tools. In 2003, the Japanese government revised the Charter to make it more fitting with Japan's national strategy under the changed world situation and domestic environment. In short, Japan's foreign aid during this period mainly served its goal of becoming a political power, and both changes in international political landscape and Japan's own development were favorable to the realization of this goal.

In terms of the international situation at that time, the disintegration of the Soviet Union in 1991 and the end of the Cold War presented an excellent historical opportunity for Japan to become a political power. Firstly, the end of the Cold War and the collapse of the two-polar structure generated a huge power vacuum in international political power, thus making it possible for Japan and other Western allies of the US to play a greater strategic role. Secondly, the end of the Cold War meant the relaxation of many constraints of traditional two-polar confrontation that Japan was subject to, such as temporarily ending its obligation of "strategic cooperation" with the US and the disappearance of the huge strategic and security pressure from the Soviet Union. Consequently, Japan had gained more independent strategic space and was expected to obtain an independent political status commensurate with its economic strength in the international arena.

On the other hand, it must be mentioned that, because of the long-term expansion of its economic power and the domestic and international predications of its future development, Japan was considered to be another major power that continued to catch up with the US, with the probability of forming a "tripolar" structure of the US, Japan, and Europe. This became more apparent when the Cold War ended. However, due to Japan's pursuit of power and increasing self-expectations, the contradictions that emerged between it and the US in the late Cold War period further intensified after the Cold War, so Japan began to face continuous strategic suppression from the US. This situation had changed owing to the long-term economic downturn after the bursting of the Japanese economic bubble and the rise of China and other emerging developing countries, when the threat to the US posed by Japan was gradually reduced and that posed by China and other emerging countries increased. Hence, the tension between Japan and the US was eased. Therefore, compared with the previous period, Japan had generally gained more space for strategic autonomy after the Cold War, while the international situation also provided greater space and possibilities for Japan to become a political power.

In terms of Japan's domestic development, though the desire to become a political power emerged in the 1980s, it was not until the end of the Cold War that formal and clear strategic goals were formed, which was partly attributed to its long-term rapid economic development. After World War II, Japan became the second largest economy in the world (as of 2009) following a long period of rapid economic growth. In 1985, a long-term trade surplus made Japan the world's largest creditor nation. In 1987, its GNP per capita surpassed that of the US. In 1988, its foreign reserves became the world's largest. In 1989, Japan surpassed the US and became the world's largest donor country.[10] At this time, regardless of its political status, Japan had become the "leader" of the international community economically, especially in terms of international aid. The

---

[10]Calculated by the author based on the data retrieved from OECD-DAC database. URL: http://stats.oecd.org/qwids/.

long-term economic growth and outstanding achievements made its domestic desire of becoming a great power continue to expand. Under such circumstances, competing with the US in various fields and trying to become a political power had earned a common voice in the Japanese society, while pursuing a more important political role on the international stage gradually came to be the core of Japan's national strategic agenda. Therefore, seeking the status of being a political power became one of Japan's strategic themes and core national interests during this period. At the 48th UN General Assembly in 1993, Japan officially expressed its desire to become a permanent member of the UN Security Council, thereby starting its long-term diplomatic efforts to become a political power. How could it make good use of foreign aid, its core tool of foreign policy, to exert its influence as the world's largest donor country and serve its national strategic goals? This constituted an important strategic choice for Japan's foreign aid during this period.

In 1992, Japan issued the first "ODA Charter". In this programmatic guideline document for Japan's foreign aid, the Japanese government systematically expounded its foreign aid concepts, principles, priorities, and standards. In the 1992 ODA Charter, it put forward the "four principles" for foreign aid: (1) coordinate environmental protection and development; (2) prevent any use of ODA for military purposes or aggravating international conflicts; (3) pay close attention to the recipient country's military expenditure, weapons of mass destruction and missiles, and weapon imports and exports; and (4) pay close attention to the recipient country's promotion of democratization, economic marketization, and protection of human rights, and freedom.[11] It can be seen that the Japanese government had stepped out of the ODA era of merely focusing on economic interests, and had placed more weight on the political, security, and ideological factors in foreign aid. Compared with the 1992 Charter, the 2003 revised ODA Charter[12] stated in more details the importance of world peace (as a non-armed country) and trade (as a small country in resources) for Japan's security and prosperity, and established the concepts that Japan, as a peaceful country, would use ODA to promote world

---

[11]Ministry of Foreign Affairs of Japan. *Official Development Assistance Charter (Old ODA Charter)*, 1992. URL: http://www.mofa.go.jp/mofaj/gaiko/oda/seisaku/taikou/sei_1_1.html.

[12]Ministry of Foreign Affairs of Japan. *Official Development Assistance (ODA) Charter*, 2003. URL: http://www.mofa.go.jp/mofaj/gaiko/oda/seisaku/taikou.html.

peace and the development of developing countries. Moreover, the new ODA Charter also mentioned several times the important role of ODA in improving Japan's international status. What is particularly noticeable is that it put humanitarianism and the protection of personal safety and rights in an especially important position.

As Japan put forward the goal of becoming a political power and recognized the crucial role of ODA in achieving this goal, Japan's use of ODA had gradually formed its own aid philosophy under new international situation and domestic environment despite the great influence of the US; in particular, Japan had formulated its unique aid feature as for how to play a leading role, enhance its political influence, and improve its international political status in the field of international aid.

The first was to maintain the aid structure that focused on Southeast Asia while taking into account countries in need of assistance from other parts of the world. In the ODA Charter issued in 1992 and revised in 2003, Japan recognized the importance of Southeast Asian countries, especially ASEAN countries, to its stability and prosperity, and clearly stated that Southeast Asia would be the focus of its foreign aid. Meanwhile, it claimed that it would pay attention to other parts of the world with emphasis.

Second, the emphasis of aid was on "structural adjustment" rather than "quantitative increase". On the one hand, as Japan had become the largest donor country, it did not make much sense for it to focus on expanding its aid volume. Moreover, there were successive international criticisms of the poor quality of Japan's aid, which became more prominent after it became the largest donor country. On the other hand, in fact, when the Japanese economic bubble began to burst in 1990, Japan's economic development was on the decline with sharply mounting fiscal pressure, therefore, it was unrealistic for it to maintain high growth in foreign aid. Against this backdrop, it was no longer appropriate to improve Japan's international status through continuous expansion of foreign aid. Therefore, Japan withdrew its economic goals in foreign aid to some degree, added more political and moral elements, and improved the structure and quality of aid to demonstrate its international image and moral style. These adjustments were of greater significance to enhance its international status.

The third was to play a leading role in a series of world issues. In some global issues without clear leadership, Japan had proactively played a leading role, which effectively enhanced its international influence and status. The most typical example of this kind was in the field of environmental protection. In the 1992 ODA Charter, Japan placed environmental protection on the top of the "Four Principles", which showed its concern about environmental issues in foreign policy. The "Kyoto Protocol" signed in Japan in 1997 was a major international achievement for Japan. So far, it is still a leader in the field of environmental issues such as global warming and climate change. The African issue was another key field where Japan's foreign aid played a leading role. In 1993, Japan successfully organized the first Tokyo International Conference on African Development, and the conference has been successfully held for six times to this day. Through these conferences and corresponding actions, Japan has strengthened its partnership with African countries and elevated its international status. In addition, it also made attempts and efforts on public health and medical care, gender discrimination, and other world issues.

The fourth was to focus on UN diplomacy. As Japan clearly expressed its desire to become a permanent member of the Security Council, UN diplomacy had also become the top priority in its foreign aid. In this regard, Japan had spared no effort in either proactively airing its voice in the UN or vigorously assisting the UN peacekeeping forces. Its vigorous assistance to developing countries also consisted of an important guarantee for it to get extensive support within the UN system. With its successful election as a non-permanent member of the UN Security Council from 2016 to 2017 at the end of 2015, Japan had been elected for 11 times, setting a record high in the number of times a country has been elected within the UN, which evidently showed the significance Japan attached to UN diplomacy and the achievements of its foreign policy of seeking more international support.

4.2   *Aid evolution in the period of seeking political power and its comparison with Europe and the US*

Judging from Japan's aid and economic data from 1992 to 2014, its volume of foreign aid generally maintained at a relatively stable scale, matching the changes in its fiscal revenue. This reflects that, with the slowdown of Japan's economic growth and the increasing pressure on its fiscal revenue, its foreign aid reform changed from "quantitative increase" to "structural adjustment". Specifically, before 2003, the volume of Japan's foreign aid began to decline after the last increase due to the medium-term target clause (1993–1997) regarding the expansion of foreign aid volume, while its foreign trade and foreign investment also remained at a relatively stable level. After 2003, the volume of Japan's foreign aid began to increase, and its foreign trade and foreign investment also began to grow except for 2009 after the financial crisis (see Figure 3.11).

In terms of the regional distribution of Japan's foreign aid, it was roughly divided by 2004 shortly after the Japanese ODA Charter was issued. Before 2004, Japan's ODA remained concentrated in Southeast Asia. After 2004, its foreign aid to the Middle East and Africa began to increase. In some years, the aid to Africa or the Middle East even surpassed that to Southeast Asia. As can be seen, Japan's foreign aid since 2004 has become more scattered in regions (see Figure 3.12).

By comparison, the focus of US's foreign aid during this period was still in Africa and the Middle East, while a considerable part of aid flew to other developing countries (see Figure 3.13).

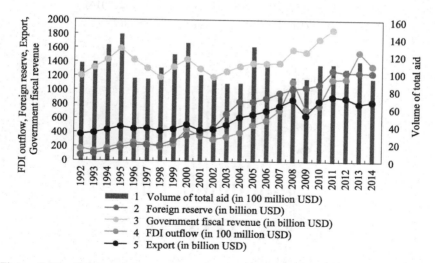

Figure 3.11: Survey of Japan's foreign aid, foreign trade, and foreign investment (1992–2014).

Source: Data from the World Bank WDI database and the International Monetary Fund International Financial Statistics database. URLs: http://databank.worldbank.org/data/reports.aspx?source=world-development-indicators, http://data.imf.org/?sk=4C514D48-B6BA-49ED-8AB9-52B0C1A0179B.

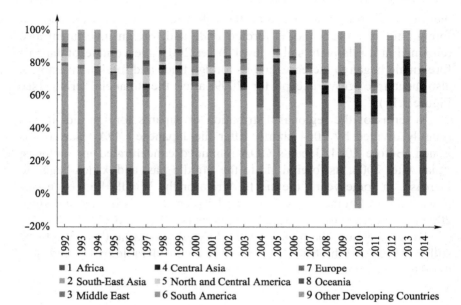

Figure 3.12:   Distribution of Japan's sector allocable ODA (1992–2014).

Source: Data from OECD-DAC database. URL: http://stats.oecd.org/qwids/.

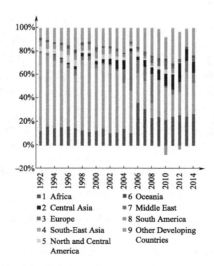

Figure 3.13:   Regional distribution of the US' ODA (1992–2014).

Source: Data from OECD-DAC database. URL: http://stats.oecd.org/qwids/.

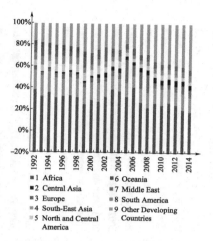

Figure 3.14: Regional distribution of the OECD Western European countries' ODA (1992–2014).

Source: Data from OECD-DAC database. URL: http://stats.oecd.org/qwids/.

From the perspective of the regional distribution of aid, though it still saw Southeast Asia as the focus of foreign aid, Japan began to place Africa in an increasingly important position like what Europe and the US did. Western European foreign aid still concentrated in Africa, while the aid to other developing countries gradually increased and the aid to Southeast Asia roughly maintained at around 10–15% (see Figure 3.14).

In terms of the distribution of aid by sectors, Japan still retained a high proportion of aid expenditure for economic infrastructure and services during this period, consistent with its 2003 revised ODA Charter which explicitly emphasized the concept of "self-help" in developing countries' development as well as the aid logic and characteristics of supporting economic infrastructure construction. However, compared with the previous period, Japan's aid to the production sector underwent substantial decrease and that to the social infrastructure and services sector increase. This reflected its efforts in lessening the economic purpose of foreign aid, emphasizing the protection of human rights and improving the quality of aid (see Figure 3.15).

By comparison, the lion's share of European and American aid expenditure went to social infrastructure and services sector, with the US spending an average of more than 60% and Western Europe maintaining an average of about 50%. This reflected the emphasis on human rights

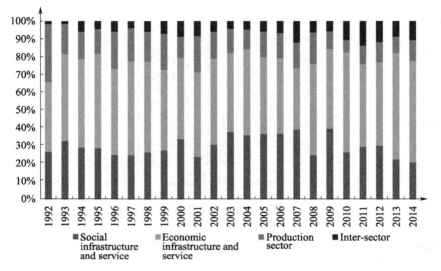

Figure 3.15:   Distribution of Japan's sector allocable ODA (1992–2014).

Source: Data from OECD-DAC database. URL: http://stats.oecd.org/qwids/.

protection and the interpretation of high aid quality under the European and American value systems and ideologies. As can be seen, Japan's aid structure during this period reflected that on the one hand, it adhered to its own aid philosophy, and that on the other hand, it was also moving closer to the European and American aid philosophy so as to improve the aid quality and present a good international image (see Figures 3.16 and 3.17).

In terms of the proportion of loans in foreign aid, though still relatively high since 1992, the proportion of loans in Japan's foreign aid generally revealed a downward trend and did not rise until after 2006 (see Figure 3.18). This reflected Japan's efforts to improve the quality of aid from another aspect. By contrast, the aid of Europe and the US during this period still mainly took the form of large-scale grants rather than loans; therefore, the quality of Japan's foreign aid was still being questioned measured by DAC standards.

Based on the comparison of the level of humanitarian assistance, Europe and the US still maintained a relatively higher proportion of humanitarian assistance, especially the US. During the 1999 Kosovo War, the proportion of humanitarian assistance provided by the US reached a historical high of 25.83% and had been on the rise since 2000 until 2014. The proportion of humanitarian assistance provided by Western Europe

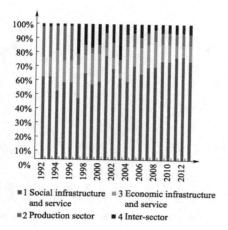

Figure 3.16:   Distribution of the US's sector allocable ODA (1992–2014).
Source: Data from OECD-DAC database. URL: http://stats.oecd.org/qwids/.

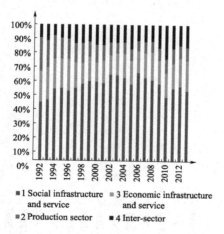

Figure 3.17:   Distribution of the OECD Western European countries' sector allocable ODA (1992–2014).
Source: Data from OECD-DAC database. URL: http://stats.oecd.org/qwids/.

was relatively stable, maintaining at around 6%. That by Japan also increased significantly. Since it issued the ODA Charter in 1992, despite the concerns about human rights stated in the "Four Principles", Japan's humanitarian assistance in reality remained at a very low level except during the Kosovo War in 1999; only after 2003 when it revised the ODA

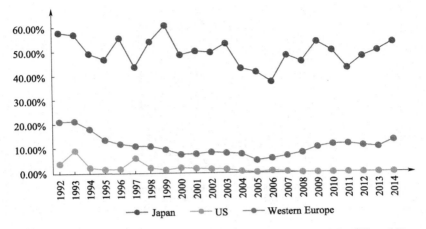

Figure 3.18: The proportion of loans in the foreign aid of Japan, the US and Europe (1992–2014).

Source: Data from OECD-DAC database. URL: http://stats.oecd.org/qwids/.

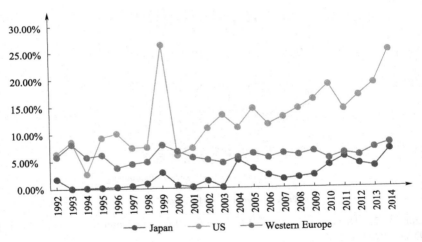

Figure 3.19: The proportion of humanitarian aid of Japan, the US and Europe (1992–2014).

Source: Data from OECD-DAC database. URL: http://stats.oecd.org/qwids/.

Charter which more explicitly put forward the protection of human rights did Japan begin to increase its expenditure on humanitarian assistance, gradually bringing its level close to that of Western Europe (see Figure 3.19).

5. The Period of Forming a Unique Style in Japan's Foreign Aid (2015–)

The year 2015 marked the 60th anniversary since Japan first provided foreign aid in 1955. Upon reviewing and reflecting on its ODA history, the Japanese government proposed a new ODA Charter in 2015 with the title "Development Cooperation Charter". Compared with the name of the previous version "Official Development Assistance Charter", the 2015 version crossed the word "official" and changed "assistance" into "cooperation", from which we can predict Japan's foreign aid philosophy in the new era. In short, compared with the previous two major periods, the biggest feature of Japan's foreign aid in this period was that it clearly put forward its unique concept of foreign aid different from European and American values, thereby showing a series of new characteristics.

Viewing from the international situations, Japan has experienced a long period of peace after World War II and the setup of the world has undergone major changes. Firstly, there were major changes in international power balance. The rise of emerging countries, especially China, has further diversified the leadership system of global governance. Secondly, the constant development of globalization driven by technological progress and global economic and trade exchanges has made the interdependence between countries closer and closer, and also made many non-state entities, such as private capital and NGOs, play an increasingly important role in global affairs. Thirdly, non-traditional security issues have increasingly become major factors threatening international peace and stability. Environmental issues and climate change, infectious diseases, international terrorism and transnational crime, cyber security, and refugee issues from the collapse of fragile countries have generated new challenges for the international community; moreover, owing to the strengthened interdependence between countries, the political instability or economic collapse in some emerging countries would affect other countries, thereby leading to world economic turbulence. As a result, Japan linked the stability and development of other countries and regions in the world with its own security and prosperity more closely.

Viewing from Japan's own development, despite the constant impacts from emerging countries such as China, Japan has become a pivotal country in the world after a long-term stable and peaceful development, and is at the forefront of the whole world, especially in coordinating human capital accumulation, science and technology, industrial development, and development and environmental protection, as well as in dealing with problems such as crossing the middle-income trap and aging population. Although Japan's goal of becoming a permanent member of the Security Council has not yet been achieved, it has played an increasingly important role as a political leader on issues such as global climate change and the Asian Development Bank. Japan still strives to play a more important role in the international community and regards it as part of important national interests. In the long-term development course, Japan has become more and more confident in its own development experience and path, and believes that its development path can be used as a source of reference for other countries and regions and thus deserves a more important position in the international society.

In 2013, the Japanese government issued the "National Security Strategy", which systematically elaborated its response to the new international environment. Japan believed that the essence of safeguarding its national security lies in creating a stable and predictable international environment and preventing dangers before they occur. Therefore, its strategy should be, based on the principle of international cooperation, playing a proactive role to promote peace, stability, and prosperity of the international community, with a view to creating an international order and security environment beneficial to Japan.[13] Japan positioned itself as a "Proactive Contributor to Peace". Driven by such self-expectations, it believed that it should play a more active leadership role in the international community.

In 2015, in compliance with the "National Security Strategy", the Japanese government issued the "Development Cooperation Charter". As the guidelines of Japan's foreign aid in the new era, the new ODA Charter displays the following brand-new features when using foreign aid tools in its choice of aid strategy.

First, Japan has built up confidence in its own foreign aid capabilities and concepts and intended to promote its concepts and play a leading role. In the new ODA Charter, the Japanese government pointed out shortly after the opening that "Japan's years of solid efforts (in foreign aid for world peace and prosperity) have won respect and confidence from the international community, which also expects Japan to play a more proactive role commensurate with its national power to promote international

---

[13]The Government of Japan, "National Security Strategy", 2013. URL: http://www.cas.go.jp/jp/siryou/131217anzenhoshou/nss-e.pdf.

peace, stability, and prosperity".[14] In addition, it emphasized that Japan would assume the duties and obligations of a "responsible power". It can be said that based on the Japanese government's own recognition and explanation, Japan has basically fulfilled the goal of the previous period and grown into an influential political power (although it has not yet entered the UN Security Council). In fact, Japan not only has enough confidence in its own political status but also has greater confidence in its "soft power". It believes that its own experience of growing into a developed country and its unique values and culture have been widely recognized by the international community, and so considers adding its "soft culture", including Japanese language, to its foreign aid endeavors. In addition, Japan also proposed to promote "the integration of Japan's own policies into the concept of international foreign aid and future development trends",[15] and even further "play a leading role in international organizations and the entire international community and shape international norms".[16]

Second, Japan has clearly affirmed the role of foreign aid in its national interests and planned foreign aid from the perspective of national interests. The Shinzo Abe administration clearly pointed out in the 2013 "National Security Strategy" that Japan's foreign aid is an important tool for it to realize its national security strategy.[17] In the 2015 "Development Cooperation Charter", Japan more explicitly stated that its foreign aid is an important part in protecting its national interests.[18] Although national interests have always been an important criterion for the Japanese government to consider its foreign aid policy, this is the first time that it clearly stated this viewpoint in official documents, especially in its programmatic documents on foreign aid. It even put forward the argument that ODA is "an investment for the future".[19]

Third, Japan has broken away from the traditional conventions of foreign aid and attempted new practices. First, just as indicated by

---

[14]Ministry of Foreign Affairs of Japan. *Development Cooperation Charter*, 2015. URL: http://www.mofa.go.jp/mofaj/gaiko/oda/seisaku/taikou_201502.html.
[15]*Ibid.*
[16]*Ibid.*
[17]National Security Council of Japan. *National Security Strategy*, 2013. URL: http://www.kantei.go.jp/jp/kakugikettei/2013/__icsFiles/afieldfile/2013/12/17/20131217-1_1.pdf.
[18]Ministry of Foreign Affairs of Japan. *Development Cooperation Charter*.
[19]*Ibid.*

removing the word "official" from the ODA Charter, Japan now only regards government foreign aid as part of its foreign aid system. The Japanese government would use governmental ODA as a lever to fully mobilize the local government, private sector, and NGOs of the recipient country at all levels and various sectors to jointly serve the development goals. Second, though Southeast Asia is still the focus, Japan has played down its emphasis on this region in wording and highlighted the global vision of its foreign aid. Third, Japan has stepped out of the international convention of providing aid to a recipient country until that country becomes a "middle-income country", emphasized the "middle-income trap", and pointed out that it would continue to provide assistance to those middle-income countries according to the specific circumstances. Then, Japan emphasizes its focus on regional development while stepping out of the perspective of only providing aid to specific countries, and proposes that its foreign aid would focus on affairs that are transnational or related to the whole region. Last but not least, although Japan still claims that ODA only serves non-military purposes, the new ODA Charter specifies that if the recipient country's army serves non-military purposes, the Japanese government may also provide assistance to the army upon careful consideration. These attempts at new practice not only suggest the future direction of Japan's foreign aid but also demonstrate its sufficient self-confidence in its own concept of aid; therefore, it has the ability to independently deviate from international conventional practice based on European and American standards.

Fourth, Japan has started to re-emphasize the important role of the traditional "Japanese model". As was implied by changing the word "aid" into "cooperation" in the ODA Charter, Japan has transformed itself from a one-way aid provider to a participant benefiting from the win–win situation in aid. In fact, it also put forward the concept of "joint development" with recipient countries in the new ODA Charter. Moreover, it once again proposed the "Japanese model" that integrates "aid-investment-trade", that is, by improving the local investment environment through investment in hardware and software infrastructure and through cooperation between government and social capital, it can vigorously promote the development of the private sector and materialize the economic development led by the private sector, which can boost the expansion of investment and trade and simultaneously fuel the economic development of both Japan and the recipient countries. In the initial period of Japan's foreign aid, when the "Japanese model" greatly boosted its economic development, it was also widely criticized by the international community for having low quality. When trying to enhance its political influence, Japan gradually downplayed the economic goals of foreign aid and began to place more emphasis on high-quality foreign aid. Under the current circumstances, especially when facing the long-term downturn of its economy and the arduous challenges like aging, Japan began to re-emphasize the economic goals of foreign aid, thus bringing about a revival of the "Japanese model".

6. Conclusions and Inspiration for China

Through detailed data display, historical combing, and comparative analysis of Japan's foreign aid with Europe and the US, we can see that its development has experienced three stages. Behind this dynamic evolution lies a series of strategic considerations in response to the evolution of the domestic and foreign political and economic setup. We can summarize three characteristics that run through Japan's foreign aid, especially through comparison with Europe and the US.

First, it takes Southeast Asia as its stronghold. The US as a global superpower often changes its focus of foreign aid based on the varied international situations and its interest needs, from Southeast Asia to the Middle East and Africa. The focus of Western European countries' foreign aid has been relatively stable, consistently being in Africa, which echoes with the fact that the former suzerain states try to maintain their influence in Africa. As for Japan, despite substantial increase in aid to Africa since 2003, Southeast Asia has always been the base and stronghold of its foreign aid, as it is very important to Japan's own economy and security. Japan has also always been an extremely important economic partner of Southeast Asian countries and has been playing an important role in promoting the course of regional integration in Southeast Asia.

Second, it never gives up economic interests in its goal. The foreign aid of European and American countries always takes social infrastructure and services such as health and education as the focus, while in Japan's aid structure, the biggest focal point has always been economic infrastructure and services. The so-called "Japanese model" initiated in the early days of its foreign aid has served as a powerful boost to its economic development. When it tried to seek more political influence, it focused on improving the diversification of foreign aid, but its aid to the economic sectors did not decrease substantially. Its total ODA aid to the production sectors and the economic infrastructure and service sectors still accounted for nearly 70% for a long term. After the release of Japan's new ODA Charter in 2015, the economic goals of foreign aid and the "Japanese model" were further emphasized in the institutionalized document, with unprecedented attention to economic benefits. Facing domestic and international challenges such as the depressing international economic environment, long-term downturn of the Japanese economy, and the prominent aging problem, the Japanese government must take boosting economic development as its major task. In the foreseeable future, how to seamlessly combine foreign aid with domestic economic interests will become a significant goal in Japan's foreign aid for a long term.

Third, it serves the ideal of becoming a political power in diplomacy. As a defeated country in World War II, the most prominent feature of Japan is the mismatch between its political status and its economic strength compared with European and American countries, which gets particularly obvious when compared with the leadership status of another defeated country, Germany, in the EU. After World War II, as a member of the allies of Western countries, Japan has gradually restored diplomatic relations and political ties with other countries. In the 1980s, after it expressed its desire to enhance its international influence in view of its continuous economic development, its foreign aid and its political rise were closely connected. The "Development Cooperation Charter" of 2015 reveals Japan's confidence in improving its political status. Its desire to apply its soft power and shape international rules as expressed in the new Charter further demonstrates its political ambitions. Though having not become a permanent member of the Security Council, Japan has never stopped this effort. The ideal of becoming a political power will be an important factor in understanding Japan's foreign aid for a long time.

Despite the great difference in national situations between China and Japan, China's foreign aid model that focuses on infrastructure construction resembles Japan's model most, thus Japan's foreign aid experience can provide a valuable reference system for China. Based on the findings of this section, we make the following policy-making recommendations for China's foreign aid.

First, China should establish a more systematic assistance framework and objectives. This section finds that, despite the dynamic evolution of Japan's foreign aid goals, what remains unchanged is the existence of a mature assistance framework and clear objectives from beginning to end, and the foreign aid at all stages has been implemented around this framework and the objectives. With rapid growth in the amount of China's foreign aid, its effects were undermined by over-concentration to certain countries or fields, lacking an overall and coordinated framework, as well as by relatively vague goals in some cases. This not only leads to compromised efficiency of foreign aid but also raises the risk of aid fund using and even the repayment of some funds. Therefore, it is recommended that China strengthen the top-level design of foreign aid and unify all aid departments under a consistent aid framework and goals by strengthening coordination and management so as to improve the systematicness and effectiveness of its foreign aid.

Second, China's foreign aid should adhere to the principle of conforming to its national conditions and comparative advantages. Although Japan belongs to the Western camp in terms of ideology and geopolitics, its methods of aid were often criticized by European and American governments and social organizations; nevertheless, it has managed to adhere to a relatively independent international aid policy for a long time. In recent years, China's foreign aid has similarly been criticized by European and American countries, which claim that China's aid pays too much attention to short-term economic benefits, tied aid, and infrastructure rather than the social fields. Although there are some problems about China's foreign aid in certain aspects and projects, such as failing to pay enough attention to the macroeconomic and fiscal debt of the recipient countries, China should still clearly understand and consolidate its national conditions and comparative advantages, follow the guidelines of foreign aid benefiting both the donor and recipient countries without being shaken by Western criticism, and insist on taking a path of foreign aid that conforms to China's national conditions and comparative advantages.

Third, China's foreign aid should closely serve its foreign policy and national interests. Although our data indicate that some countries, such as the Nordic countries, regard foreign aid as an international welfare for low-income countries, these countries are mainly small or neutral countries. As a matter of fact, our research data also show that the foreign aid policies of the US and Western Europe are largely the manifestations of their foreign policies, which is especially true of Japan. Behind the dynamic evolution of Japan's foreign aid lies a series of considerations for its national strategies and interests. Therefore, as the largest developing country, China, with numerous diplomatic goals and huge national interests, should not shy away from emphasizing the fact that its foreign aid is an extension of its foreign policy and national interests. Especially when considering the increasing importance of economic diplomacy in the entire Chinese diplomatic work, how to most effectively use this "leverage" to serve China's foreign policy and maximize its national interests has become an important issue.

Finally, in this new era, China should also be prepared to compete with Japan in the field of foreign aid. In the 2015 ODA Charter, Japan emphasized the international vision of its foreign aid, whereas China's foreign aid is also increasingly going global, which will become more evident in its present implementation of the Belt and Road Initiative. Since 2015, the Japanese government under Prime Minister Shinzo Abe has greatly increased its assistance in Southeast Asia and Central Asia.[20] These two regions are also key areas around China as well as the important regions and bridgeheads on China's "Belt and Road" blueprint. Consequently, China should be fully prepared for the competition with Japan's foreign aid. China has two major advantages to meet this challenge. The first is China's vast market. Compared with Japan, China has a broader market and greater demand, which is extremely attractive to Southeast Asian and Central Asian countries that are accepting industrial transfer and expanding industrial construction. The second is China's strong capabilities of infrastructure construction. Southeast Asian and Central Asian countries still have huge demand for infrastructure construction, then China's strong construction capabilities and cost advantages in this regard are of great significance to its foreign aid and investment. On the other hand, there is also much room for its foreign aid to improve. The first is to improve its tailor-made ability when providing aid to recipient countries. As China started late in its country-specific assistance projects, there is still much to be done in formulating special aid projects based on the characteristics of specific countries and regions,

---

[20] According to a report by Caijing.com on 22 June 2015, Japanese Prime Minister Shinzo Abe announced in May 2015 a plan called "High-quality Infrastructure Partnership: Investing in the Future of Asia", which will invest US $110 billion in Asian infrastructure construction in the next five years, just exceeding the US $100 billion of capital fund of the China-sponsored Asian Infrastructure Investment Bank. See http://yuanchuang.caijing.com.cn/2015/0622/3909969.shtml. In October 2015, Prime Minister of Japan visited five Central Asian countries for the first time in 9 years and signed an agreement on huge amount of aid. URL: https://thediplomat.com/2015/10/what-did-abe-accomplish-in-central-asia/.

strengthening mutual trust and understanding with the recipient countries, and improving the specificity and efficiency of assistance. The second is to increase aid projects in the fields of social services and people's livelihood. Although China has a comparative advantage in infrastructure construction assistance, assistance in the fields of social services and people's livelihood can be more conducive to improving its international image and gaining local people's trust and support. The third is to realize the mutual promotion of politics and economy, that is, to establish a more profound strategic relationship based on the Belt and Road Initiative and the growth of aid. China should capitalize on multiple policy tools and exert the leverage role of foreign assistance on many issues such as economy, education, military, and counter-terrorism so as to enhance its regional influence.

Section 2. China's Experience: South–South Cooperation

1. Introduction

"South–South Cooperation" came into being after the end of World War II, which is the first and the most profound development initiative put forward by developing countries. As an important concept of international development, it has gone through dynamic development following constant changes in international political and economic situations. Nowadays, as the emerging economies are occupying an increasingly important position in global economy, the discourse of South–South Cooperation resurfaces as a central topic for discussions on development. Based on the relevant studies by the academic circles worldwide and development-oriented international organizations, this section tries to sort out the historical development of the concept of "South–South Cooperation", analyze the practice models of various agencies under its framework, and point out its dilemma in the present situations.

This section is divided into six parts. By integrating historical events, the first part describes the three historical stages of South–South Cooperation, analyzes the structural factors for the emergence of "New South–South Cooperation", and gives the definition of South–South Cooperation. The second part elaborates the interactive relationship between South–South Cooperation initiated by developing countries and the international economic order dominated by developed countries. The third part expounds the development programs provided by South–South Cooperation in different periods by taking developing countries as the research objects. The fourth part discusses the core principles and differentiated methods of South–South Cooperation based on the practices of various countries. The fifth part discusses the pros and cons of the existing international coordination mechanisms in the South–South Cooperation agenda. The sixth part analyzes the realistic dilemma South–South Cooperation faces.

2. History and Stages of South–South Cooperation

Foreign scholars have generally divided South–South Cooperation into three stages, though they differ in the specific cut-off points.

Morvaridi *et al.* characterize the three stages with landmark events: the 1960s was the embryonic stage, when the establishment of G77 and United Nations Conference on Trade and Development (UNCTAD) gave rise to the dependency theory of economic development and the South–South Cooperation idea that advocated changes in the international economic order; the 1970s was the hidden stage, when the structural adjustment of neoliberalism was embraced by the mainstream academic circle and development practice; and in the 21st century, with the OECD's "Triangular Cooperation" initiative, South–South Cooperation has returned to the mainstream development research along with the aid effectiveness agenda and become a technical agenda (Morvaridi and Hughes, 2018).

Silva (2015) gives a more clear-cut chronological division: 1949–1979 being the first stage, with the signing of the "Buenos Aires Plan of Action" by the G77 as the cut-off point; 1980–1998 being the second stage, with the World Bank starting to establish the Global Partnership Network as the cut-off point; and 1999 to present being the third stage.

Despite the difference in the specifics of division, the above division of phases aims to distinguish the first phase of South–South Cooperation from the third phase. Some research literature terms the third stage of South–South Cooperation as "New South–South Cooperation" (New SSC) (Gosovic, 2016), a term preserved by the present study. The following will detail the evolution of South–South Cooperation in the three stages.

2.1 The first stage: From the Non-Aligned Movement to the alliance of developing countries

The idea of South–South Cooperation can be traced back to the Bandung Conference in 1955 and the Non-Aligned Movement thereafter. Huang and Tang (2003) points out that the principle of South–South Cooperation is consistent with the spirit of the Bandung Conference. In the initial stage, the Non-Aligned Movement embraced South–South Cooperation in political issues. After the beginning of the Cold War, the small and medium countries, especially some emerging independent countries, were forced to form alliances in the bipolar structure of the US and the Soviet Union and to give up some sovereignty, such as the power to formulate macroeconomic policies, to attach themselves to the two superpowers. In order to protect their national sovereignty and their place in the international system, the small and medium countries had to unite with each other.

In the early days of the Non-Aligned Movement, the keynote of South–South Cooperation was opposing power politics and hegemonism. Meanwhile, at the first UNCTAD, two camps, the North and the South, once again emerged during discussions on global economic issues. The developing countries issued the "77-State Declaration" and established the "Group of 77" (G77), with the purpose of negotiating economic issues in the UN system on behalf of the developing countries. Subsequently, the focus of the Non-Aligned Movement shifted to the economic field, and it cooperated with the G77 to propose building a "New Economic International Order". Following the discussions on trade inequality and the advancement of the dependence theory, the South–South Cooperation of developing countries centered on the aim of "collective self-reliance", which emphasized mutual help among developing countries so as to enhance each other's economic growth (Zhou *et al.*, 1983). Due to the limited resources available to the developing countries, technical cooperation as an important content of cooperation became an important part of the agenda. In 1978, the UN Conference on Technical Cooperation among Developing Countries was held in Buenos Aires, where 138 countries passed the "Buenos Aires Plan of Action" and formally established the guideline of "Horizontal Cooperation" for South–South Cooperation.

South–South Cooperation in this stage exhibited a distinctive political color against the backdrop of the Cold War, since it was a political choice for the developing countries to "huddle together for warmth" and fight against hegemony. The rhetoric of "solidarity" symbolized South–South Cooperation in the 1970s. In the economic field, South–South Cooperation directly pointed to the goal of achieving development, emphasized the inequality of North–South development and tried to resolve the developmental inequality through political actions with the slogan of a "New International Economic Order". However, limited by the resources available, the practice of South–South Cooperation was confined to the field of "technical cooperation". In addition, owing to the difference in the economic systems, economic development concepts, and macroeconomic policies among the southern countries, they can only treat each other without interference rather than export development experience.

2.2 The second stage: The impact of neoliberalism and the attempts of South–South Cooperation

South–South Cooperation was immensely impacted by global capital in the 1980s. The financial institutions for international development represented by the World Bank and the IMF, together with transnational capital, had forged the structural adjustment plans for developing countries. The reform slogan of "New International Economic Order" was not realized, what is more, the elites of many southern countries even helped global capital to initiate neoliberal reforms in the developing countries.

In this round of neoliberal reforms, the development-oriented financial institutions such as the World Bank gradually transformed from a funder to an intellectual authority on economic development, thus distorting the development agenda into a depoliticized technical agenda (Morvaridi and Hughes, 2018). The World Bank began to disseminate the so-called "best practice" of the developed countries' market economy to promote liberalization reforms.

The wave of liberalization reforms witnessed the states' declining intervention ability and policy autonomy. The sense of solidarity and the resistance to inequality in South–South Cooperation had been continuously dissolved by the "global market". Global South–South

Cooperation gradually disappeared, while regionally differentiated South–South Cooperation began to emerge. Both the OPEC and the Bolivarian Alliance for the People of Our America represented the attempts made during that period.

2.3 The third stage: The economic power of emerging market countries and the revival of South–South Cooperation

At the end of the 20th century, the economy of East Asian countries developed rapidly. All the fast-growing economies in East Asia adopted the means of state intervention more or less. The emerging manufacturing powers such as China and India demonstrated the necessity of appropriate state intervention with their own development, which broke the monopoly of the neoliberal interpretation of economic development. The extent to which the developing countries accepted the Washington Consensus varied (Esteves and Assunção, 2014). In addition, the practice of the structural adjustment programs in Latin America and Africa in the 1980s did not achieve similar progress to that in East Asia. Traditional development assistance was criticized as being inefficient. Meanwhile, the southern countries that had achieved economic development (such as emerging market countries) were eager to expand their national influence and seek common progress with development partners. Therefore, they began to provide developing countries with development assistance that is different from traditional ODA (such as China's cooperation package in Angola).

Due to the difficult situations posed by the traditional model as well as the different options offered by developing countries, the agenda of aid effectiveness has become a major issue of international development in the 21st century.

The OECD-DAC, as the coordinator of traditional ODA of developed countries, established the High-Level Forum (HLF) on aid effectiveness to promote discussions on the effectiveness of development assistance. Since the ownership of recipient countries was introduced in *Paris Declaration*, HLF has continuously advanced the discourse power of developing countries in development assistance. In 2008, the *Accra Agenda for Action* recognized that South–South Cooperation is an important complement to North–South Cooperation (Esteves and Assunção, 2014). At the HLF-4 Busan meeting, South–South Cooperation was officially included in the partnership document, which summarized various development cooperation models such as South–South Cooperation, triangular cooperation, and traditional ODA as the "global partnership" (Renzio and Seifert, 2014).

Under the frameworks of OECD and HLF, South–South Cooperation refers to all cooperation between developing countries in order to promote development, which downplays the "political solidarity" part of its previous concept. As a path choice for development cooperation, South–South Cooperation is in the interests of all parties. Developed countries and traditional donor countries could continue to maintain the existing institutional framework by compromising with other effective development cooperation models when the original model was met with obstacles. Emerging economies (i.e. developing countries with faster development) were included as shareholders of international development financing and became important participants. The southern countries, no longer subject to conditional ODA, could use the opportunity of South–South Cooperation as a bargaining chip to facilitate fair negotiations between donor countries and recipient countries.

Some scholars believe that the OECD's definition has depoliticized South–South Cooperation, which better adapts to the logic of capital flow (Morvaridi and Hughes, 2018), and is more conducive for the traditional donor countries to maintain their existing power. Meanwhile, some other scholars hold that the recognition of South–South Cooperation by the OECD proves that the development experience of some southern countries has also gained recognition, thus diversifying the knowledge on international development (Renzio and Seifert, 2014). However, not all developing countries have depoliticized South–South Cooperation, as the political rhetoric such as "solidarity" still prevails in the propaganda of South–South Cooperation. Therefore, there is not a fixed model shaped for the revitalized New South–South Cooperation.

Based on its historical stages, South–South Cooperation has exhibited the following characteristics.

(a) The definition of "South" determines that the purpose of South–South Cooperation is to get rid of inequality. "South" is defined not only by social geography, but also by historical memory. From a socio-geographic perspective, the South is the oppressed end of an unequal international system. In the early period of the Cold War, the inequality mainly manifested itself in political power. Therefore, the political power of former colonial countries that had gained independence became an important issue of South–South Cooperation at that time (Muhr, 2016). After the 1970s, the inequality in economic development received more attention, whereby the category of southern countries basically overlapped that of developing countries. At the same time, the range of participants in South–South Cooperation became broader, since all the countries with a history of being exploited and excluded had developed a cross-border political identification with each other and participated in South–South Cooperation. Even if some of them had achieved considerable development, they were still linked by the previous political identification.[21] Therefore, South–South Cooperation essentially serves to put an end to the unequal status.

(b) The trend of South–South Cooperation is to become a sub-item of the development agenda. Nearly all the demands of the developing countries for the international system were condensed in South–South Cooperation during the 1970s. As a political rhetoric, the voice of South–South Cooperation for reforming the global order reached its peak in the 1970s. Nonetheless, South–South Cooperation failed to substantially promote the reform of the global order, and its political voice gradually quieted down after the 1990s, with more emphasis on "solidarity". On the other hand, in terms of economic development, South–South Cooperation took technical cooperation as the starting point and produced practical results in sharing development experience and economic and trade cooperation. Various southern countries have also developed their own preferences and cooperation models of South–South Cooperation in the economic field (Mwase and Yang, 2012). Under the development agenda, South–South Cooperation will have more room for development as an alternative to traditional development assistance and as a technological agenda. It is more likely to strengthen national power through economic development so as to promote the transformation of global order based on the agenda of political reform.

---

[21] For instance, Singapore remains a member of G77; and despite having leaped to be an OECD country, Korea is often viewed as a participant of South–South Cooperation in the aid field.

3.   South–South Cooperation and the World Economic Order

Judging from the historical stages of South–South Cooperation, both South–South Cooperation and New South–South Cooperation once became important topics. Compared with South–South Cooperation that was formed spontaneously and featured interactions within the South, New South–South Cooperation became the subject of discussion chiefly because of the promotion by actors outside the South and reached a consensus that the South and the North should interact with each other. There are multiple explanations for this phenomenon in the academic circle.

By analyzing the changes in the international economic order, some scholars are optimistic that New South–South Cooperation signifies that the southern countries represented by emerging market countries are reconstructing the international economic order. Just like the G20 that replaced the G7, South–South Cooperation has been recognized by the OECD, which indicates that the practical experience derived from the economic strength of the developing countries is being recognized by the world.

By analyzing from the perspective of actor motivation, some scholars believe that the reason why the OECD integrated South–South Cooperation into the HLF agenda and spared no effort to persuade important developing countries (China, India, Brazil, etc.) to sign the "Global Partnership" document at the Busan Conference is that it wanted to continue its control of the development aid agenda. Similarly, by launching GPEDC along with the "Global Partnership", the OECD aimed to obtain comprehensive information on South–South Cooperation in the first place.[22] The inclusion of South–South Cooperation in the agenda of traditional donor countries is still to incorporate the South into the existing order dominated by the North.

Other scholars believe that the New South–South Cooperation may even advance the expansion of the liberal economic order. From a historical point of view, the southern countries in the 1970s differed in economic system. However, with the advancement of globalization, even emerging economies that conduct state intervention have generally adopted export-oriented economic development models and integrated

---

[22]Not all the developing countries that have signed the Global Partnership participated in GPEDC, where China, India, and Brazil are not included.

into the global market. Regardless of the speed difference in development, the development experience of the southern countries is invariably based on the market economy. Therefore, global capital will surely play an important role in the New South–South Cooperation. Even if the southern countries can share the successful experience of state intervention, the capital is still needed to be introduced to stimulate development. Besides limited official capital, the flowing global private capital will benefit from the practice and development of the New South–South Cooperation. Therefore, new inequality may result from dependence on the mature capital markets of developed countries.

Based on the above viewpoints, it can be found that the southern countries have the motivation to get rid of their economic backwardness, but they still lack the ability to change the world economic order. Even if some of the rapidly developing southern countries have successful experience of development and share with their development partners, it remains difficult for them to jump out of the liberal economic order framework.

That the New South–South Cooperation has been accepted by other actors in the field of international development shows that the practice of development cooperation by southern countries has formulated a new model different from the traditional development assistance. However, their acceptance of South–South Cooperation as an alternative is extremely limited. The OECD-DAC has not abandoned "good governance" and other inherent notions of development cooperation, nor has it fully accepted the concepts of "non-interference" and "abolition of the donor-recipient country dichotomy" proposed by the southern countries (Abdenur and Fonseca, 2013).

The New South–South Cooperation and the traditional ODA are two paths of development cooperation that coexist with each other under the liberal economic order, between which a new path of triangular cooperation has also emerged. Under this framework, the New South–South Cooperation does not have the ability to reform the world economic order but more resembles a depoliticized and devalued technological agenda.

4. South–South Cooperation and the Notion of National Development

An important component of South–South Cooperation is experience sharing. Since the signing of the "Buenos Aires Plan of Action" in 1978,

South–South Cooperation has launched a full range of experience sharing, with technology sharing as the starting point. The ministerial declaration issued by the G77 and China in 2009 claimed that "South–South Cooperation supports the promotion of best practices in developing countries so as to promote the broad development goals of these countries".[23]

After the waves of neoliberalism and globalization in the 1980s, the development speed among the southern countries varies.

The southern countries whose development relies on petroleum resources have established the OPEC. Relying on coordination and cooperation, they have realized economic growth through the export of oil, which provides a model of achieving development through the formation of primary product cartels for southern countries that extensively export primary products. In East Asia, China and India have used a variety of policy tools on the basis of a market economy to moderately intervene in the market, supported industries with comparative advantages, formed an export-oriented economy, promoted the development of manufacturing, and achieved economic growth. In Africa, there are cases like South Africa that rely on the boom in commodities to achieve rapid economic growth, and there are also countries like Ethiopia that try to replicate China's development trajectory.

Although the southern countries have all quickly adapted to the market economy in the process of globalization, their comparative advantages and development concepts are not completely the same, thus making it hard to reach a consensus. As a result, it would be difficult to practically summarize the best practice within the southern countries or to verify by data the value of South–South Cooperation on such basis, especially the sharing of development experience (Muhr, 2016).

This also reflects that the best practice in South–South Cooperation is more for reference to development partners than for forced transplantation.

---

[23] South–South Cooperation encourages the exchange of best practices and support among the developing countries in order to jointly achieve their broad development goals (including all aspects of international relations, not just in traditional economic and technological fields), quoted from G77 Statement: After the adoption of the resolution at the UN High-level Conference on South–South Cooperation, the Ambassador, Permanent Representative of the Republic of the Sudan to the United Nations and Chairman of the Group of 77, His Excellency Mr. Abdul Mahmoud Abdul Khalem Ohamad, New York, 6 October 2009. URL: http://www.g77.org/statement/getstatement.php?id=091006b, accessed on 20 June 2018.

Development partners shall respect each other's sovereignty rather than interfere in the choice of other countries' development path, which is quite different from the idea of propagating neoliberal reforms in the structural adjustment program.

Although South–South Cooperation does not entail forced export of the concept of development, the trade activities of the faster-developing countries exporting manufactured products to and importing primary products from the least developed countries have actually formed a trade structure similar to that of the colonial times. In this regard, some scholars maintain that such trade interdependence cannot be interpreted as neocolonial dependency, since the essence of the dependency relationship is to make one party lose its autonomy. When the least developed countries cannot manage to be fully self-reliant, the complementary trade transactions carried out by the developing countries, based on the principle of non-interference in internal affairs and sovereign equality, actually serve to materialize the collective self-reliance of the developing countries (Muhr, 2016).

5. The Practice and Characteristics of South–South Cooperation

When the G77 was established, it endowed South–South Cooperation with three principles: solidarity, complementarity, and cooperation (Muhr, 2016). The "Nairobi Outcome Document" adopted by the UN through the high-level meeting on South–South Cooperation has established five normative principles of South–South Cooperation: national sovereignty and autonomy, equality, no strings attached, non-interference, and mutual benefit. It also identified four operational principles: mutual accountability and transparency, coordination, results-based planning, and multi-stakeholder approach (UNDP and MOFCOM, 2016).

In practice, the development cooperation carried out by all countries based on the concept of South–South Cooperation has displayed differentiated characteristics. The fifth annual high-level meeting of the Development Cooperation Forum under the UN Economic and Social Council summarizes this phenomenon like this: the long-term conceptual framework of South–South Cooperation is non-normative and built upon common principles. With this approach, South–South Cooperation can coordinate various priorities among the stakeholders and ensure shared autonomy and progress (ECOSOC, 2017). It can be found that South–South Cooperation has reached a political consensus that is almost the same as that of the Non-Aligned Movement due to the political interactions of developing countries in history. However, due to the varied economic development experiences and development models of those countries, there is no standard practice model for South–South Cooperation, thus being described as being non-normative.

The normalized political consensus of South–South Cooperation has formed a "development partnership" for such cooperation. The developing countries, especially those providing development cooperation, differ in their ways of practicing "development partnership". The choice of these ways is determined by differences in their capabilities, comparative advantages, economic and trade preferences, international relations as well as concepts of development.

5.1 *The principle of political consensus*

The principles of national sovereignty and autonomy, which are virtually identical with the autonomy principle on the agenda of aid effectiveness, emphasizes that developing countries have the right to determine their own national development policies. Before putting forward the aid effectiveness agenda, the traditional donor countries, when providing development aid, required that the developing countries should meet various requirements in the aspects such as government expenditures, debt levels, and democratic levels in order to ensure that aid is implemented under the norms of "good governance". This model had severely restricted the autonomy of the developing countries, giving rise to disadvantages such as the emergence of indolent governments that relied on aid and the unavailability of aid resources to the least developed countries. By contrast, South–South Cooperation maintains that national sovereignty is related to autonomy, making it clear that the right of development is part of national sovereignty.

In history, the developing countries had suffered from political and economic oppression, but no such oppression occurred among them and they even must unite to resist the oppression. Therefore, the developing countries respect each other's national sovereignty, resulting in the principles of equality and non-interference. The concrete manifestation of the principle of non-interference in South–South Cooperation is to have no political strings attached for development cooperation, but to truly support each other (i.e. be complementary) and obtain mutual benefit in development.

According to the research by the IMF, with South–South Cooperation as a foreign aid program, China often adopts a cooperation package when providing development cooperation for development partners. In this way, the turn-key projects can be completed through the circulation of Chinese funds among Chinese construction teams, which cannot only avoid local corruption risks, but also avoid setting any attached strings (Mwase and Yang, 2012). Some studies also point out that, unlike the West's approach of setting attached strings on governance and political systems, the purpose of South–South Cooperation investment in economic infrastructure is to provide material conditions for the improvement of governance capabilities and institutional changes of the development partners (Amanor, 2013).

5.2 *Non-normative features in practice*

Although South–South Cooperation emphasizes "mutual benefit" in principle, different actors resort to various channels and methods for South–South Cooperation in different periods.

In the 1970s, the developing countries generally lacked resources, so they carried out development cooperation based on technical cooperation and sharing. Take India as an example. India launched the Indian Technical and Economic Cooperation Programme (ITEC) in 1964, which continues to this day. According to the Agrawal statistics and in terms of foreign development assistance projects, 60% of the activities were composed of building capacity and training civil servants, engineers and public sector managers in other developing countries; 30% of the activities were composed of providing preferential export credits for project assistance, which enabled foreign governments to purchase Indian equipment and services; and 10% of the activities were auxiliary activities that supported the first two activities, such as feasibility studies and the deployment of technical experts from India (Agrawal, 2007). Technical cooperation and the derivative people-to-people exchanges happened to circumvent the problem of lacking funds in developing countries, which allowed every country to contribute to collective self-reliance and enhanced internal unity.

Since the revival of New South–South Cooperation, actors at different stages of development have emerged within the group of developing countries. Each actor has launched different forms of development cooperation based on their own development experience, national strategies and capabilities. As a group, the BRICS countries have shown remarkable characteristics in practice. Take China, Brazil, and India as examples.[24]

Based on its own development experience, China has attached great importance to economic infrastructure investment and usually employs preferential loan tools or bundled aid. But at the same time, various forms of free aid, grants and interest-free loans are used in social infrastructure cooperation and humanitarian assistance, such as education, health and other fields. In terms of the targets of assistance, China's targets are relatively scattered, as it has carried out various types of cooperation with any development partner who has no political conflicts with it.[25] In addition to development cooperation, China's development assistance is often linked with foreign investment, thus resulting in development partnerships such as the Angolan model.

Brazil pays more attention to technical assistance in education, health, and agriculture, and uses debt relief to encourage Brazilian companies to perform local business in its development partners' places. In terms of the targets of assistance, Brazil is keen on assisting countries in the Portuguese-speaking cultural circle as well as Latin American and African countries that have similar colonial experiences (Mwase and Yang, 2012).

Since World War II, India has provided extensive development cooperation and technological assistance on capacity building. At the same time, after the establishment of the Export-Import Bank of India in the 1980s, it has been keen to use credit facilities to carry out its foreign development cooperation. Its preferential loan exchange rate meets the requirement of the OECD-DAC on ODA, but it also stipulates that more than 75% of the preferential loans should be used to purchase Indian equipment and products, which has in practice boosted its own exports (BGP, 2017). In terms of cooperation projects, India prefers to invest in economic infrastructure. However, in its development cooperation with its neighboring countries, India will also resort to various methods in line

---

[24]As a member of OECD-DAC, Russia's assistance model differs from that of South–South Cooperation; South Africa's foreign development cooperation is very small in volume.

[25]China does not engage in development cooperation with countries that violate the "one China" principle.

with South–South Cooperation, such as budget assistance and free gifts, etc.

Besides the BRICS countries with outstanding development achievements, other countries are also using their own methods to carry out development cooperation. South–South Cooperation in Latin America and the Caribbean is dominated by Cuba and Venezuela, which emphasizes comprehensive alliance among countries. Based on the initiative of the two countries, the Peoples of Our America — Peoples' Trade Agreement and PetroCaribe, an oil cartel in Latin America, were established. These two organizations, together with the Caribbean Community, have formed the sub-regional common market for South–South Cooperation in Latin America (Santander and Alonso, 2017).

In addition, some documents point out that the developing countries such as Indonesia, Turkey, and Mexico have actively participated in the governance activities advocated by the OECD. They coordinate South–South Cooperation with triangular cooperation initiatives under the GPEDC framework, and coordinate the developing countries that act independently and the developed countries that wish to coordinate with South–South Cooperation.

As a member of the G20, Indonesia actively participates in South–South Cooperation, mainly in the form of technical assistance. As early as 1981, Indonesia launched the Indonesian Technical Cooperation Programs for developing countries in response to the "Buenos Aires Plan of Action". In 2010, in order to enhance its influence in South–South Cooperation and strengthen its inter-projects coordination capacity, Indonesia established the National Coordination Team to coordinate the South–South Cooperation projects provided by different Indonesian departments. In terms of development initiatives, Indonesia is one of the initiators of the New African-Asian Partnership. Meanwhile, it responded to the GPEDC of OECD, being one of the co-chairs.

In 1992, Turkey established the Turkish International Cooperation Agency under the Ministry of Foreign Affairs, which takes charge of foreign development cooperation and has established offices in 33 countries. Turkey specifically provides development cooperation to its "sister countries" based on common culture, which largely focuses on education, capacity building, humanitarian assistance and infrastructure construction. As a member of the OECD and an observer of the DAC, Turkey's development cooperation meets the OECD standards on ODA, so it is often included in the statistics on ODA. Turkey defines its development cooperation as South–South Cooperation, yet spontaneously recognizes the OECD standards, thereby playing the role of coordinating South–South cooperation and North–South cooperation.

As an observer of the DAC, Mexico's development cooperation resembles that of Turkey, as it also acts as a coordinator of South–South cooperation and North–South cooperation. Mexico is also one of the few developing countries equipped with a coordinated aid data system. The difference is that its development partners are mainly located in Latin America, and its development cooperation is mostly in the form of technical cooperation.

After half-a-century's development, the principle of political consensus still guides the practice of South–South Cooperation. Compared with ODA by the OECD-DAC, South–South Cooperation is distinctly different in terms of its respect for sovereign equality, non-interference in internal affairs, and emphasis on mutual benefit. The practice of South–South Cooperation displays different models in accordance with the characteristics of each country; nevertheless, all the developing countries with successful development experience are keen to participate in South–South Cooperation and engage in development cooperation with partners in the South. The practices of South–South Cooperation are indeed diversified. Although diversified practices help to break the monopoly of traditional ODA in development cooperation, it is also featured by fragmentation in development cooperation, which reflects the insufficiency of coordination in South–South Cooperation.

6. Coordination of South–South Cooperation

Since the group of the southern countries is maintained by the political identity derived from the experience of oppression, there is no absolute leader. They implement the principle of non-interference in internal affairs, and the sovereign countries absolutely have the dominant right to select development partners, design South–South Cooperation strategies, and manage the results of South–South Cooperation. Therefore, South–South Cooperation has shown distinct differences, lacked uniform standards, and also been questioned on issues such as transparency.

Establishing an entity that can coordinate South–South Cooperation can help summarize the experience, construct a knowledge system, promote the development agenda for South–South Cooperation, and achieve the goal of reforming the world economic order.

Currently, there are three entities that are more active in attempting to coordinate or lead South–South Cooperation: the GPEDC platform guided by the OECD, the DCF platform initiated by the G77 within the UN system, and the development financing agencies represented by the New Development Bank (NDB) established by the BRICS countries.

6.1 *Analysis of the pros and cons of GPEDC as a coordination platform for South–South Cooperation*

GPEDC is the outcome and continuation of the agenda on aid effectiveness. At the Fourth High-Level Forum on Aid Effectiveness in 2011 initiated by the OECD, the meeting proposed the Global Partnership for Effective Development Cooperation, which transformed the agenda on aid effectiveness into the agenda on development cooperation effectiveness. A total of 161 countries and 56 organizations have joined this Partnership, which has also accordingly developed into a discussion platform for complex stakeholders.

According to the Busan Partnership Agreement, GPEDC put forward four principles: guaranteeing the ownership of the developing countries, attaching importance to the fruits of cooperation, adopting an inclusive development partnership, and implementing transparency and accountability. The platform is promoted by three high-level government officials who concurrently serve as co-chairs, with a steering committee meeting held every two years where the stakeholders are invited to discuss how to advance the partnership.

Although it is an open platform, GPEDC inherits the development concept that has evolved from the aid effectiveness agenda formulated by the OECD. As for the path of development cooperation, it advocates boosting triangular cooperation by incorporating South–South Cooperation into the partnership framework (Esteves and Assunção, 2014).

As one of the options for South–South Cooperation coordination platform, GPEDC has the following advantages.

(a) GPEDC includes all the stakeholders in the development field, and has built a platform that integrates the voices of actors in all development fields.
(b) The "Busan Partnership Agreement" is the consensus basis for GPEDC when coordinating the actions of relevant stakeholders in the

field of development cooperation. Regarding North–South cooperation, South–South cooperation, and triangular cooperation as equally important development cooperation paths, this agreement has broken the power difference between the donors and the recipients and laid the foundation for the dialogue between developing and developed countries on an equal basis. In addition, the agreement contains the mature concepts in the agenda on aid effectiveness (such as the developing countries' ownership of development policies), which reflects the basic consensus in the community of development knowledge.

Meanwhile, it has the following disadvantages.

First, GPEDC is a continuation of the agenda on aid effectiveness advocated by the OECD, whereas the degree of participation by the southern countries varies. The pursuit of transparency and accountability conflicts with the principle of non-interference in South–South Cooperation; hence the southern countries are concerned whether, under the advocacy of the OECD, this mechanism can be more tolerant of the South–South Cooperation practice.

Second, GPEDC has the function of collecting information on South–South Cooperation yet with a questionable stance on analysis and evaluation, which is highly likely to be affected by the OECD's concepts and may become the basis for developed countries to criticize South–South Cooperation.

Third, the main activity of GPEDC is a biennial forum, which has difficulty in coordinating South–South Cooperation, summarizing its experience, and conducting regular activities.

Fourth, the results of GPEDC are not politically binding, nor does it have the capacity of arbitration. Therefore, all the stakeholders can only express their views on the platform, which can barely solve practical problems.

In summary, as a platform advocated by the OECD, GPEDC is affected by the OECD in terms of both partnership promotion and daily management. The enthusiasm for participation on the part of the southern countries is not high. Studies have shown that the role of GPEDC lies more in building a communication channel between the North and the South in development cooperation. The developing countries that are active within GPEDC often lack the ability to take the lead in development cooperation. Nonetheless, such countries as Mexico, Indonesia, etc. hope to carry out development cooperation on an equal footing with the developed countries in order to boost their own development (Renzio and Seifert, 2014).

6.2 *Analysis of the pros and cons of UN-DCF as a coordination platform for South–South Cooperation*

Developing countries, especially the G77, support the establishment of a coordination platform for South–South Cooperation within the UN system. At present, within the UN system, the UNDP under the UN General Assembly has established the UN South–South Cooperation Office; under the UN Economic and Social Council, the Development Cooperation Forum (DCF) is devoted to high-level political dialogues on international development cooperation among member states in a two-year cycle. During the meeting period, the UN Department of Economic and Social Affairs (UN DESA) oversees the routine research activities.

As a coordination platform for South–South Cooperation, the UN-DCF as a dialogue platform has the following advantages.

First, as a forum under the UN, DCF has a more solid legitimacy foundation than other forums. Many concepts emphasized by the developing countries, such as sovereign equality and peaceful development, have long become the consensual principles of the UN. In terms of discussions and negotiations, the developing countries have stronger incentives to participate with fewer concerns. Under the dialogue rules of the UN Economic and Social Council, the southern countries can effectively express their views through the speaking channels of country groups such as the G77. The consensus reached at the meeting will be written into the resolution of the UN General Assembly, which in turn will exert profound political influence.

Second, as a UN-affiliated forum, DCF is more powerful in mobilizing resources; UN DESA, as a department implementing the results of the forum on a routine basis, can produce knowledge on development cooperation through its research capabilities and investigative activities to further advance South–South Cooperation.

Third, as a UN-affiliated forum, discussions under the DCF framework are more conducive to achieving the global development goals including the sustainable development goals, integrating South–South Cooperation into the system for achieving the sustainable development goals, and solving the problems such as the fragmentation of development cooperation and the legitimacy of South–South Cooperation.

On the other hand, the UN-DCF also has the following disadvantages.

First, the UN system is highly bureaucratic, with low efficiency in proceedings and actions. As part of the High-Level Political Forum, DCF is only one part of many agendas; and of the overall DCF agenda, South–South Cooperation is only one of the areas that DCF focuses on, therefore the resources available are limited. Besides, the developing countries in the G77 are not completely consistent in their demands for development, which means it is hard or even impossible for the Southern countries to reach a consensus. In addition, South–South Cooperation is not the exclusive task to UN DESA, as this function partially overlaps with those of other South–South Cooperation offices under UNDP, which may result in inconsistent coordination.

In summary, with the legitimacy advantage of coordinating South–South Cooperation within the UN system, the consensus reached can be more widely recognized by the developed and the developing countries. However, owing to its low operational efficiency, the UN system cannot mobilize enough resources to coordinate South–South Cooperation among all these countries. The coordination of South–South Cooperation within the UN is more to strive for the legitimacy of development cooperation for the developing countries, to conduct phased assessments in a timely manner, and to promote the realization of global development goals.

6.3 *Analysis of pros and cons of multilateral development banks initiated by developing countries as a platform for South–South Cooperation*

In 2012, the BRICS countries initiated the establishment of a new type of multilateral development bank; and during the Durban Summit in 2013, the leaders of the five countries agreed to establish the NDB. At the end of 2013, President Xi Jinping announced China's initiative to establish the Asian Infrastructure Investment Bank (AIIB) during a foreign visit. In 2016, the NDB went into operation in Shanghai. In the same year, the AIIB was put into operation. As a new type of multilateral development bank initiated by the developing countries, it has varied degree of innovation in terms of development concepts and development cooperation models, which echoes the voices of the developing countries in the field of development cooperation.

The advantages of taking the new type of multilateral development banks as the coordination platform for South–South Cooperation are as follows.

First, in the new multilateral development banks, the developing countries have advantages in equity and voting rights, which helps to promote the concept of South–South Cooperation. For example, the NDB adopts the host country system in project implementation to help the developing countries to increase their development policy ownership. For another example, the AIIB and the NDB both emphasize the development and cooperation partnerships, which can help to weaken the "donor-recipient country" dichotomy.

Second, as holders of funds and implementers of development cooperation, the new multilateral development banks are more conducive to implementing the concept of South–South Cooperation and further enriching the practical knowledge on it.

Third, the new multilateral development banks still maintain high standards of accountability and transparency and evaluate their own behaviors. This will attract the developed countries to participate (such as AIIB), thereby constructing the legitimacy of the concept of South–South Cooperation and further promoting the recognition of South–South Cooperation in the area of international development financing.

However, the new multilateral development banks still have limitations as a coordination platform.

First, the new multilateral development banks are limited to the development of a certain region or the participation of a few countries, and are less involved in South–South Cooperation with some other regions like Arab countries and Latin America. Therefore, the replicability of the knowledge of South–South Cooperation produced thereby remains to be verified.

Second, the new multilateral development banks have advantages in knowledge construction; however, as a coordination platform, they cannot produce political consensus.

Third, the new multilateral development banks are not yet mature in practice, as they have not completed the project cycle, nor completed the comprehensive evaluation, which awaits further observation.

To sum up, the new multilateral development banks, as autonomous actors in the field of international development financing, have advantages in turning the concept of South–South Cooperation into development financing actions and in constructing the practical knowledge about

South–South Cooperation projects. However, as the new multilateral development banks are limited by tasks, they cannot coordinate the development cooperation policies of all countries nor produce political consensus.

In general, the OECD, the UN, and the new multilateral development banks all have their advantages and disadvantages in coordinating global South–South Cooperation. However, in terms of the two indicators — political influence and action power, none of the three platforms can be regarded as the optimal choice for coordinating South–South Cooperation, which is difficult to be defined and standardized like ODA due to its non-normative characteristics.[26] Nonetheless, there is no doubt that South–South Cooperation still needs to be coordinated politically and in action in order to ensure its effectiveness and continuous progress in practice.

7. Challenges and Dilemmas of South–South Cooperation

As a concept, South–South Cooperation forms a political identity among developing countries through shared social memory and is rooted in development cooperation among developing countries. With the expansion of globalization and free markets, the antagonistic relationship between developing and developed countries has transformed into a cooperative one formed by the connection of transnational capital, and the political nature of South–South Cooperation has been gradually weakened. In the new century, developing countries have increasingly expanded their influence on the world economy and their willingness to participate in global governance has increased. Developed countries have begun to recognize South–South Cooperation, which has been credited as an important channel for international development cooperation.

However, South–South Cooperation still faces risks in three aspects.

7.1 *South–South Cooperation lacks global monitoring and coordination*

South–South Cooperation is characterized by being non-normative due to differences in the developing countries' capacity, development concept,

---

[26]DCF Resolution.

and development cooperation system. On the positive side, non-normative features can encourage innovation in South–South Cooperation and stimulate various attempts at development cooperation. However, non-normative features also make South–South Cooperation remain on the conceptual level of promoting the developing countries' participation in development cooperation, thus not being able to produce more profound impact on international development cooperation.

Therefore, South–South Cooperation needs a global monitoring and coordination mechanism to help it get rid of the fragmented practice and conceptual discussions.

On the one hand, the monitoring mechanism needs to possess research capabilities to conduct research and evaluation on various actors in South–South Cooperation and construct a relevant knowledge system. This can be achieved by conducting in-depth research on many key topics such as how to enhance the autonomy of developing countries, how to ensure aid effectiveness without interfering in internal affairs, and how to coordinate the relationship between micro-development cooperation projects and macro-national development ones, so as to form a consensus among the developing countries and break the knowledge monopoly of the traditional donors of the North. This can also be achieved by summarizing the excellent experience from the diversified cases of South–South Cooperation, identifying the existing problems, and providing references to follow-up practice. The construction of this knowledge system will contribute to South–South Cooperation by advancing its self-renewal and helping it gain broader international recognition.

On the other hand, the coordination mechanism needs to have political influence to promote the consensus on South–South Cooperation among developing countries and even in the international community. The developing countries are the main actors of implementing the consensus on South–South Cooperation. Their development cooperation and the knowledge on South–South Cooperation interact with each other to generate the influence of South–South Cooperation. Therefore, the coordination mechanism needs to convene the developing countries to participate in the promotion of the agenda and in continuous optimizing South–South Cooperation.

The existing South–South Cooperation coordination platform is insufficient in its power for action and influence, and the risks of its fragmentation and conceptualization remain serious and need to be addressed urgently.

7.2 *New South–South Cooperation may create new inequalities*

South–South Cooperation is gradually becoming a technical agenda on development after the wave of globalization and facing the risk of depoliticization. After market-oriented reforms, the political opposition between the developing and the developed countries has been gradually weakened. In discourse, South–South Cooperation is more associated with economic development, and the principle of "solidarity" seems to be giving way to "mutual benefit".[27]

On the one hand, the facilitative role of cross-border capital flow and investment on development is encouraging South–South Cooperation to embrace capital and encourage private capital to participate in development financing. Nonetheless, this model may create new inequalities, as it may deepen the dependence of developing countries (especially the least developed countries) on capital, thus resulting in political compromise. Different from the traditional donors' accusations that South–South Cooperation may cause excessive debt burden on developing countries, the dependence of South–South Cooperation on capital is not on any development partner, but on the capital market itself. As South–South Cooperation and North–South Cooperation have the same preference for capital, it makes the developing countries in need of development have to rely on the global capital market, thus being unable to make independent development decisions.

On the other hand, the party providing development cooperation among the development partners is more inclined to gain economic interests in project implementation while ignoring political cooperation. For example, China and India are currently exporting manufactured products and importing primary products in their trade with Africa, which may lead to difficulties in the development of Africa's manufacturing industries due to their disadvantage of productivity competitiveness. It is thought that the export buyer's credit facility may cause protectionist unequal competition. Hiring domestic labor force rather than that of the project host country is also considered to be the failure on the part of the development partners to achieve institutional trust.

Meanwhile, some studies point out that even if the existing South–South Cooperation projects pursue mutual benefit, they are not carried out in total pursuit of interests, but have formed a balance of benefits between

---

[27]In Nairobi Document, solidarity was replaced by equality.

development partnership and development cooperation. However, this balance is shifting its focus on economic interests with the cooperation between New South–South Cooperation and the capital market. Under this trend, the New South–South Cooperation still needs to emphasize the internal solidarity of developing countries, rather than interpreting South–South Cooperation as a technical agenda for development.

7.3 *New South–South Cooperation may cause macroeconomic risks to development partners*

The developing countries represented by China and India emphasize infrastructure investment in their development cooperation model. Take China as an example. China believes that more productive infrastructure will bring about economic growth, promote the development partners' development level, and thus fundamentally reduce their debt pressure (Mwase and Yang, 2012), which conveys the idea of "broadening income sources". Traditional donor countries pay more attention to the macro-debt level of the recipient countries, emphasize the reduction of government expenditures and give play to market capacities, which conveys the idea of "decreasing expenditures". At the same time, the developing countries represented by China regard the effectiveness of the project as their own responsibility and believe in the principle of non-interference by handing over the overall development at a macro level to the development partners themselves.

Since the developing countries lack an open and transparent evaluation system for their own cooperation, the South–South Cooperation model that emphasizes infrastructure investment may harbor the following risks.

On the one hand, it is difficult to ensure a high rate of return from infrastructure construction projects, because infrastructure investment loans entail a long repayment cycle and period (usually more than 15 years), and the cost of monitoring project benefits is relatively high. Meanwhile, the benefits of productive infrastructure are determined by its spillover effects. The lack of independent cost-benefit calculations may give rise to the possibility of false report of benefits.

On the other hand, the rate of return issue may even cause debt pressure on the least developed countries. Since the degree of correlation between infrastructure investment and economic growth has not been verified by research, and the economic backwardness of the least developed countries cannot only be attributed to the lack of infrastructure, the acceptance of infrastructure investment may cause their debt pressure, thus affecting the fiscal sustainability of the government and causing tremendous pressure on their macro economy.

8. Conclusion

To sum up, as the economy of the developing countries continues to grow, the influence of South–South Cooperation on international development is getting stronger and stronger. South–South Cooperation has increased the development cooperation options for developing countries and has injected new vitality into their development. International development cooperation is also shifting from traditional North–South cooperation to a development contract based on such factors as national experience, mutually beneficial relations, reciprocity, broad participation, and local control of resources (UNDP and MOFCOM, 2016). However, we also need to see that the non-normativeness and fragmentation of South–South Cooperation practice render political identification to be the knowledge ceiling of South–South Cooperation. How to build a system for monitoring and coordinating South–South Cooperation, whereby the limited resources can play a greater role and achieve effective development, remains a problem to be solved in South–South Cooperation.

References

Abdenur, Adriana Erthal and João Moura Estevão Marques Da Fonseca. "The north's growing role in South–South cooperation: Keeping the foothold". *Third World Quarterly*, Vol. 34, No. 8, 2013, p. 1486.

Agrawal, Subhash. "Emerging donors in international development assistance: The India case". Ottawa: Partnership and Business Development Division, *International Development Research Centre*, December 2007, p. 7.

Amanor, Kojo Sebastian. "South–South Cooperation in Africa: Historical, geopolitical and political economy dimensions of international development". *IDS Bulletin*, Vol. 44, No. 4, 2013, pp. 25–27.

Araki, Mitsya. "Japan's Official Development Assistance: The Japan ODA model that began life in Southeast Asia". *Asia-Pacific Review*, Vol. 14, No. 2, 2007, pp. 17–29.

BGP (Board Guidelines and Procedures). Export Lines of Credit: A safe and convenient export financing option, *Export-Import Bank of India*, 2017, p. 8.

Brooks, William L. and Robert M. Orr. "Japan's foreign economic assistance". *Asian Survey*, Vol. 25, No. 3, 1985, pp. 322–340.

ECOSOC. The High-level Political Forum on Sustainable Development presided by the Economic and Social Council, *Abstracts of the Fifth Biannual High-level Conference of the Development Cooperation Forum*, United Nations Economic and Social Council, E/2017/76, 28 June 2017.

Esteves, Paulo and Manaíra Assunção. "South–South cooperation and the international development battlefield: Between the OECD and the UN". *Third World Quarterly*, Vol. 35, No. 10, 2014, pp. 1780–1785.

Fukuda-Parr, Sakiko and Hiroaki Shiga. "Normative framing of development cooperation: Japanese bilateral aid between the DAC and southern donors". JICA Research Institute Working Article No. 130, JICA, Research Institute, 2016. URL: https://www.jica.go.jp/jica-ri/publication/working article/jrft3q0000006elo-att/JICA-RI_WP_No.130.pdf.

Gosovic, Branislav. "The resurgence of South–South cooperation". *Third World Quarterly*, Vol. 37, No. 4, 2016, pp. 733–743.

Hattori, Tomohisa. "The moral politics of foreign aid". *Review of International Studies*, 2003, Vol. 29, No. 2, pp. 229–247.

Hirata, Keiko. "New challenges to Japan's aid: An analysis of aid policy-making". *Pacific Affairs*, Vol. 71, No. 3, 1998, pp. 311–334.

Hook, Steven W. and Guang Zhang. "Japan's aid policy since the Cold War: Rhetoric and reality". *Asian Survey*, Vol. 38, No. 11, 1998, pp. 1051–1066.

Huang, Meibo and Tang Luping. "South–South cooperation and China's foreign aid". *International Economic Cooperation*, No. 5, 2003, p. 66.

Ishikawa, Shigeru. "Supporting growth and poverty reduction: Toward mutual learning from the British model in Africa and the Japanese model in East Asia". JBIC Institute, Japan Bank for International Cooperation, 2005. URL: https://www.jica.go.jp/jica-ri/IFIC_and_JBICI-Studies/jica-ri/publication/archives/jbic/report/discussion/pdf/dp08_e.pdf.

Jin, Xide. *Official Development Assistance*. Beijing: Social Sciences Academic Press (China), 2000.

Katada, Saori N. "Japan's two-track aid approach: The forces behind competing triads". *Asian Survey*, Vol. 42, No. 2, 2002, pp. 320–342.

Kubota, Isao. *ODA Introduction: Structure and Function*. The Society for Public Administration Printing Office, 1992.

Lin, Xiaoguang. "Japan's post-war economic diplomacy and official development assistance". *Asia & Africa Review*, No. 1, 2005, pp. 64–70.

Matsui, A. *Economic Cooperation*. Yuhikaku Publishing CO. Ltd., 1983, pp. 134–136.

Mawdsley, Emma. *From Recipients to Donors: Emerging Powers and the Changing Development Landscape*. London: Zed Books, 2012.

Moni, Monir Hossain. "Why Japan's development aid matters most for dealing with global environmental problems". *Asia Pacific Review*, Vol. 16, No. 1, 2009, pp. 8–36.

Morgenthau, Hans. "A political theory of foreign aid". *American Political Science Review*, Vol. 56, No. 02, 1962, pp. 301–309.

Morvaridi, Behrooz and Caroline Hughes. "South–South Cooperation and neo-liberal hegemony in a post-aid world". *Development and Change*, Vol. 49, No. 3, 2018, pp. 888–892.

Muhr, Thomas. "Beyond 'BRICS': Ten theses on South–South cooperation in the twenty-first century". *Third World Quarterly*, Vol. 37, No. 4, 2016, pp. 631–632.

Mwase, Nkunde and Yang Yongzheng. "BRICs' philosophies for development financing and their implications for LICs". IMF Working Article WP/12/74, 2012, pp. 4–13.

Nishikawa, Yoshimitsu. *The International Politics and Japan's National Strategy after the Cold War*. Koyo Shobo, 1993, p. 6.

Renzio, Paolo De and Jurek Seifert. "South–South cooperation and the future of development assistance: Mapping actors and options". *Third World Quarterly*, Vol. 35, No. 10, 2014, pp. 1863–1869.

Rix, Alan. *Japan's Economic Aid: Policy-making and Politics*. London: Croom Helm, 1980.

Samurai Igarashi, T. *Japan's ODA and the International Order*. The Japan Institute of International Affairs, 1990, p. 83.

Santander, Guillermo and José Antonio Alonso. "Perceptions, identities and interests in South–South cooperation: The cases of Chile, Venezuela and Brazil". *Third World Quarterly*. URL: https://doi.org/10.1080/01436597.2017.1396533, pp. 7–12.

Scheyvens, Henry. "Reform of Japan's Official Development Assistance a complete overhaul or merely a fresh coat of paint?". *Progress in Development Studies*, Vol. 5, No. 2, 2005, pp. 89–98.

Silva, Michelle Morais de Sá e. "South–South cooperation: Past and present. Conceptualization and practice" from Thomas Muhr, "South–South cooperation in education and development: The !Yo, SíPuedo! literacy method". *International Journal of Educational Development*, Vol. 43, July 2015, p. 127.

UNDP. Chinese Academy of International Trade and Economic Cooperation, *Inclusiveness and Adjustments? The Way Countries Carry Out Development Cooperation and Their Value of Reference for China*. China Commerce and Trade Press, 2006, pp. 6–8.

Watanabe, Matsuo. "Japan's foreign aid policy in transition: An interpretation of TICAD IV". *Japan Aktuell — Journal of Current Japanese Affairs*, Vol. 16, No. 3, 2008, pp. 7–26.

White, John Alexander. *Japanese Aid*. London: Overseas Development Institute, 1964.

Yasutomo, Dennis T. *The Manner of Giving: Strategic Aid and Japanese Foreign Policy*. Lexington, Mass.: Lexington Book, 1986.

Yasutomo, Dennis T. "Why aid? Japan as an 'aid great power'". *Pacific Affairs*, Vol. 62, No. 4, 1989, pp. 490–503.

Zhang, Guang. *Research on Japan's Foreign Aid Policies*. Tianjin: Tianjin People's Publishing House, 1996.

Zhao Jianzhi and Ouyang Zhe. "The dynamic evolution of Japan's foreign aid after World War II and analysis of its aid strategy: A comparative perspective of Europe and America". *Journal of Contemporary Asia-Pacific Studies*, No. 2, 2018.

Zhou, Jirong and Wang Yulin, Sun Kun. "Development and prospects of the Non-Aligned Movement". *Contemporary International Relations*, No. 4, 1983, p. 3.

Zhu, Fenglan. "The status of foreign economic aid in Japan's post-war development". *World History*, No. 2, 2003, pp. 34–44.

Part Two

Practice of International Development Cooperation

Chapter 4

Introduction to the Management Systems of International Development Cooperation

Section 1. The Concept of Aid Management System

Aid management system is a set of top-down policies, regulations, institutions, and management arrangements which establish aid guidelines and set objectives to meet them. According to the definition given by UNDP and the Institute of International Trade and Economic Cooperation of the Ministry of Commerce (2016), aid management system is composed of domestic policy framework, institutional arrangements, and development cooperation implementation tools (such as funds, information, and knowledge platform). In short, any arrangement involving foreign aid management can be regarded within the scope of aid management system in general.

The research into aid management system is a very important issue in the field of international assistance. Firstly, it is a basic research. To understand a country's foreign aid, the discussion of its aid management system cannot be avoided. Besides, each country's aid management system is unique with respect to the evolution process and characteristics. Therefore, to probe into a country's foreign aid or to compare it with other countries, we must answer the basic question that what the aid management systems of these countries are. Secondly, as aid management system is a variable of many important issues in the field of international aid, it can affect aid efficiency, aid decision-making mechanism, aid implementation efficiency, aid fund utilization, and other issues of a country. To explain these issues, it is necessary to analyze the construction of aid management system. Consequently, as a variable with important impact on many subtopics in the field of foreign aid, the research into aid management system is essential.

Specifically, the components of aid management system can be divided into three parts: aid guidelines, aid agencies, and internal operation mechanism. Among them, the internal operation mechanism can be further divided into four points, namely, leadership mechanism, funding system, department network, and monitoring and evaluation system (as shown in Figure 4.1).

Aid guidelines, which describe the principles, objectives, priorities, methods, and standards of foreign aid, are the fundamental guide to donor countries' foreign aid. From the perspective of the science of organizational behavior, the guidelines of an organization are the beacon of behavior for the organization and its members, which provide orientation and incentives and act as the internal driving force to unit and stabilize the organization. The guidelines of an organization indicate its orientation, whereas the management system is the means to achieve the objectives. In this sense the guidelines are consistent with the management system. Representative international aid guidelines include Japan's *Development Cooperation Charter*, the UK's *International Development Act*, and Canada's *Official Development Assistance Accountability Act*. However, aid objectives are often diversified and a specific project may have clear aid objectives, but the overall behavior of a country's foreign aid may lack clear aid guidelines. Without aid guidelines, aid projects will lack the overall guidance to coordinate the aid at the macro level. Consequently, due to the inadequate legitimacy, ambiguous status, uncertain functions, and unclear boundary of the foreign aid, it will fail to form an independent

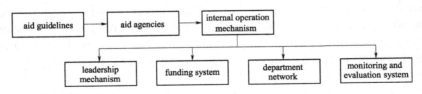

Figure 4.1:   Typical framework of aid management system.

agenda and system and will more than often be temporarily sacrificed to many other key national policies. In addition, the formulation of aid guidelines is of great political significance for a country to carry out foreign aid. First of all, by combing the history of foreign aid practice, summarizing the explicit or unwritten principles, styles, and methods formed in the process of foreign aid, and sorting out the major policies of foreign aid, it is helpful to integrate foreign aid into the national strategy and to gather domestic forces to serve the overall goal of the national strategy. Secondly, by formulating a guiding document with legal effect, making it known to the public, and endorsing its commitments with national credit, it is helpful to respond to the confusion and doubts about a country's foreign aid at home and abroad, establish a good international image, and win worldwide understanding and support. Thirdly, the formulation of aid guidelines is especially important for the emerging donor countries. Currently most emerging donor countries' notion of aid is different from that of the traditional developed countries. Although many emerging donor countries have promoted foreign aid in the name of the broad-sense "South–South Cooperation" and exerted a certain impact on the traditional notions and standards of foreign aid, none of the numerous emerging donors has become a model to set up a set of complete, systematic, and convincing aid guidelines that are unique to emerging donors. Therefore, the countries that take the lead in setting up and disseminating aid guidelines and obtaining international recognition will help to unite the vast number of emerging donors, set a model and a leading position in the emerging donor groups, spread their own development ideas, and even guide the trend of international aid rules.

Aid agencies are the core entities of aid management system. An entity is required to take charge of the various functions of aid such as decision-making, fund, information, coordination, and even implementation. On the one hand, as a window to foreign countries, aid agencies are the first objects of understanding a country's foreign aid at home and abroad. On the other hand, as the administrative center of foreign aid function, one or more aspects of aid decision-making, implementation, fund, information, knowledge, experts, and other resources are contained here. Hence, the quality of foreign aid is directly affected by whether the aid agencies are set up and whether they are reasonably set up. However, due to the diversity of aid functions, the setting of aid agencies often meets with great difficulties. Firstly, from the horizontal perspective, aid cannot be conducted independently but requires the cooperation of different professional organizations. Although foreign aid has its unique expertise and ability requirements, it is classified when specifically implemented. When conducting science and technology aid, the ministries related to science and technology are at the core of knowledge and technology; when conducting medical aid, the ministries related to health and hygiene are at the core of personnel and equipment; and when conducting agricultural aid, the ministries related to agriculture are at the core of patents and personnel. Therefore, when providing foreign aid, instead of running independently, aid agencies need the cooperation of other relevant ministries or organizations with professional talents, technology, and network. And when setting up aid agencies, it is necessary to take into consideration the cross-field cooperation and frictions between aid as an independent field and other fields related to specific aid projects. Secondly, from the vertical perspective, there are often many levels of cooperation involved in aid, so it is difficult to sort out the aid functions at different levels. Besides the state-to-state assistance, many ministries also need to carry out international exchanges and cooperation, which will involve some international assistance. With the continuous development of China's economy, foreign trade and cooperation of many provinces in China are also on the increase, including cooperation with some provincial or state governments of other countries, some of which can be also categorized as international assistance. Even in the international cooperation at the level of many municipal governments or educational institutions such as colleges and universities, a lot of cooperation belongs to the scope of international assistance. International aid at different levels has different priorities and demands, but it ultimately has to serve the overall national aid strategy and objectives, which is hard to obey in the practice of international aid at different levels. This may also cause disorder or even frictions in a country's aid management system or even its diplomacy. Therefore, the integration of international aid at different levels is also an important issue to be considered in the establishment of aid agencies.

From the history of the construction of the OECD countries' aid management systems and the latest measures taken by India, Saudi Arabia, and other emerging donor countries regarding the construction of aid management systems, we can see that, with an increase in the scale, projects, and coordination requirements of a country's foreign aid, especially with the growing strategic and political significance of foreign aid which helps a country shape a good international image and reflect the voice of domestic public opinion, it is the only choice for all countries to promote the construction of governance structure of foreign aid by reforming and constantly improving the setting of aid agencies. Take China as an example. China's core organization of foreign aid in the past was the Department of Foreign Assistance of the Ministry of Commerce. As the strategic significance of foreign aid keeps manifesting itself, when reforming the institutions of the State Council in March 2018, China combined the responsibility for foreign aid of the Ministry of Commerce with the responsibility for foreign aid coordination of the Ministry of Foreign Affairs, and then established China International Development Cooperation Agency, which is directly affiliated to the State Council and takes full charge of China's foreign aid. This is a huge milestone in China's construction of its foreign aid management system.

The internal operation mechanism is the structural relationship and operation mode of aid management system. As far as the leadership mechanism is concerned, a good leadership mechanism should have a clear power structure, distinct boundaries of responsibility, and definite authority and responsibility entities for all affairs. To be more specific, only when the leadership mechanism is clear can the implementation agencies have a clear division of labor and clear interest relations, and the responsibility can be traced back when problems occur. This is especially true for foreign aid, the implementation of which often involves many ministries and organizations and requires their full cooperation due to its strong professionalism. If the leadership mechanism of aid cannot be clearly defined, it will easily lead to the phenomenon that related departments of aid rush for it when it is profitable, and shirk responsibility when problems arise, which will result in the failure of aid. From the perspective of funding system, aid tasks should be supported by corresponding funds, since budget is also an important means to motivate related departments and organizations. However, in terms of the allocation power of funds, it should be properly centralized, and the sources of aid funds of related departments and organizations should be coordinated, arranged, planned, and accounted for. If aid is carried out in the form of simply assigning tasks and requiring related departments and organizations to raise funds by themselves, the binding force and the authority of the aid tasks will be greatly weakened due to the uncontrolled financial resources of the aid agencies, which is not conducive to restricting the subordinate aid implementing agencies to serve the prescribed strategic aid objectives and also easily leads to a free-for-all among aid agencies and related departments. In terms of department network, a good department network should cultivate the sense of responsibility in each department, build trust between departments, and construct a coordinated inter-departmental cooperation mechanism. When there are tasks that need close cooperation of all departments, a good department network can gather all departments to form a joint force, produce the co-integration effect, and promote the tasks to be completed better. In the practice of foreign aid, there exist both cooperation and competition between related departments. At the same time, due to the large number of aid-related departments and organizations, the increase in the number of participants will further aggravate the complexity of inter-departmental competition and cooperation. Therefore, it has become increasingly important to build a coordinated department network, which is also an important part of the internal operation mechanism. In terms of monitoring and evaluation system, a perfect monitoring and evaluation system is an important guarantee of continuous improvement of the quality and efficiency of aid. The establishment of monitoring and evaluation system, through the tracking of the history of aid and systematic monitoring, evaluation and thinking, helps to form the institutional memory of foreign aid, accumulate the best practice of foreign aid, form a unique style, promote the continuous improvement and development of specific aid projects and macro foreign aid policies, realize self-renewal, and form a benign cycle. On the other hand, the collation and disclosure of data can help to improve the transparency of aid, respond to domestic and international confusion and queries, and is also an important way to account for the budget and citizens for public projects.

Section 2. Research on Aid Management System and Aid Effectiveness

Aid effectiveness, an issue of great importance in the field of foreign aid, refers to whether development aid is effective in achieving development goals. The core measurement of aid effectiveness is the difference between aid expenditure and development output and profits.

In fact, for many years, the ODA of developed countries to developing countries has failed to alleviate the widespread wars, poverty, and diseases in developing countries, which makes the issue of aid effectiveness increasingly prominent and also has caused doubts from many people in donor countries about the point of their governments' tremendous foreign aid (Wood *et al.*, 2011). The developed donor countries dominated by the OECD-DAC have also gradually realized this problem and began to pay more attention to aid effectiveness. In 2005, the Paris High Level Forum on Aid Effectiveness held by the OECD formulated the *Paris Declaration on Aid Effectiveness*, which incorporated the concept of aid effectiveness into the connotation of foreign aid and put forward five principles to improve aid effectiveness. In 2008, the OECD held the third High Level Forum on Aid Effectiveness in Accra, capital of Ghana, and drew up the AAA which proposed four guidelines on the further implementation and improvement of the *Paris Declaration on Aid Effectiveness*. The fourth High Level Forum on Aid Effectiveness, held in Busan, Korea, in 2011, formulated the *Busan Partnership Agreement*, which further reinforced the principles in the *Paris Declaration on Aid Effectiveness* and the AAA and established the monitoring framework of the Global Partnership for Effective Development Cooperation to guide and improve aid effectiveness of the DAC (see Table 4.1). These declarations made by those developed countries aimed at improving aid effectiveness are also the principles aimed at improving aid management systems. Moreover, from the perspective of public administration science, when one country provides aid to another, how to reasonably design its internal management system so as to make its aid in the latter more effective is of great significance both in the theory and in the practice of foreign aid.

The traditional research on the relationship between aid management system and aid effectiveness focuses on the domestic political and administrative system of the recipient country. The logic behind this is that only when the recipient country has a good and effective environment and ability to implement aid projects can aid be effective. This view can be traced back to the theory of good governance agenda on international aid in the 1990s. The most remarkable researches include that by Burnside and Dollar (1997) and the World Bank's 1998 research report on foreign aid. Burnside and Dollar's research verifies the positive correlation between aid and the recipient country's own "good" system construction and economic policies (free trade, marketization, tight fiscal, and monetary policies) through empirical research, simultaneously claiming that aid has little effect on those countries with poor system construction. Based on such empirical research, Burnside and Dollar, as economists of the World Bank, draw the conclusion that recipient countries should improve their domestic governance structure and practically adopt the reform policies in line with the "Washington Consensus" in order to improve the efficiency

Table 4.1:   Key points of resolutions on improving aid effectiveness in three OECD high level forums.

Paris high level forum on aid effectiveness	Accra Agenda for Action	Busan partnership agreement
(1) Ownership: Developing countries should set up their own poverty reduction strategies, improve system construction, and punish corruption	(1) Ownership: Developing countries should have more say in the development process, participate more widely in the formulation of development policies, play a stronger leading role in coordination, and use more localized systems in aid implementation	(1) Ownership: Only when developing countries take the lead and implement the methods in line with their own specific situation and needs can the relations of development cooperation be successful
(2) Alignment: Donor countries should provide support based on these objectives and use the recipient country's system	(2) Inclusive partnerships: The OECD-DAC member countries, recipient countries, other donors and civil society should be fully involved	(2) Focus on results: Investment and efforts must have a lasting impact on poverty and inequality reduction, sustainable development, and the improvement of the capacity of developing countries, while closely integrated with the development priorities and policies of developing countries themselves
(3) Harmonization: Donor countries should coordinate and simplify procedures and share information to avoid repetition of aid	(3) Delivering results: Aid should focus on tangible and measurable impact on development	(3) Inclusive development partnerships: In the process of achieving development goals, openness, trust, mutual respect, and learning should be the core of effective partnership, and the different but complementary roles of all participants should be recognized
(4) Results: Developing countries and donor countries should shift their focus to development outcomes and assessment results	(4) Capacity development: Developing countries should enhance their capacity so as to manage their own development future	(4) Transparency and accountability: Accountability to each other and accountability to the target beneficiaries, national citizens, organizations, assignors, and other interested parties of development cooperation are key to achieving development results; transparency is the basis for the constant improvement of accountability
(5) Mutual accountability: Donor countries and their recipient partners should be mutually held accountable for the results of development		

of aid, and that the World Bank should also be selective in providing aid and prioritize aiding those countries with "good governance". "Good governance agenda" has exerted a profound impact on the practice of international aid. International aid agencies, including the World Bank and the IMF as well as some donor countries such as the US, often impose strict domestic reform conditions on recipient countries when offering foreign aid (known as "Governance Intervention"). And the recipient countries' failure to adopt the "good governance agenda" has thus been widely regarded as a common excuse for insufficient aid effectiveness. However, since then, the "good governance agenda" has received criticism both in practice and in theory. Grindle (2004 and 2007) proposes "good enough governance" to replace "good governance agenda". This view also emphasizes the importance of good governance structure in recipient countries for improving aid efficiency, but adopts a more pragmatic approach. It holds that it is unrealistic to conduct aid after a comprehensive, complete, and thorough reform of good governance. The reform of good governance should follow the principle of gradual improvement. The practice of foreign aid can be started when the "good enough governance" is achieved, that is, when the single most critical governance reform that cleared the hindrance to development is completed.

In fact, aid is a two-way interaction. Aid effectiveness also depends on the governance capacity construction of donor countries (Bouorguignon and Sundberg, 2007). The World Bank (2007) points out that government effectiveness and corruption control are the keys to governance ability. Easterly and Pfutze (2008) further point out that the degree of transparency is the most important factor affecting the success of aid.

That the internal operation mechanism of donor countries has an important impact on aid effectiveness has been widely recognized by the academic community. Tendler (1975) holds that the organizational variables within aid agencies have a crucial impact on the result of aid despite being uneasy to detect sometimes. De Renzo (2005) points out that it is of great significance to set up reasonable incentive mechanism at different levels in aid agencies for the effect of aid: reasonable incentive mechanism is conducive to sorting out relations and motivating different levels, whereas unreasonable incentive mechanism will cause internal frictions and negative impact. Many other scholars have also discussed about the impact of the decentralization of aid governance structure on aid effectiveness (Acharya *et al.*, 2006; Arinoto and Kono, 2009; Easterly, 2007). The organizational fragmentation caused by multiple branches in aid agencies will increase the difficulty in implementing, coordinating and communicating aid policies, and lead to high transaction costs in the specific implementation of aid projects. In fact, in the construction of Western administrative system, this fragmentation of management system is partly due to the emphasis on specialization, decentralization, and competition in Western thought of public administration. Some scholars represented by Six (1997, 2002) put forward the theory of holistic governance which tries to solve the fragmentation of administrative system. The fragmentation includes conflicts between policy objectives, conflicts between policy and means, lack of communication and coordination among departments, departments' responsibility shifting, project duplication and waste, and so on. Holistic governance emphasizes the integrated operation of an government's internal departments, which makes the government move from "fragmentation" to "integration". The four major types of governance behavior including policy, regulation, service, and supervision can realize the integration of governance at the same level or different levels within the government, the integration of different governance functions, the integration of the public departments or between public departments and non-profit organizations or private sectors. And then a holistic government in which goals and means can promote and benefit each other can be built through the integration between fragmented responsibility mechanism and information system (Six, 2002). Some scholars put forward the idea of introducing holistic governance to the construction of foreign aid management system so as to improve aid effectiveness of emerging donor countries by building an integrated aid management system (Zhao and Ouyang, 2018).

In terms of the best practice of specific aid governance structure, the OECD has summarized the good practice of some of its member countries (OECD, 2005 and 2008). This is especially true in the OECD report of 2009, in which the internal governance structure of donor countries is divided into four modes according to the characteristics: the first mode is to incorporate foreign aid agencies into the original regional departments of the Ministry of Foreign Affairs and to place the formulation and implementation of aid policies in the hands of the Ministry of Foreign Affairs; the second, still dominated by the Ministry of Foreign Affairs, is to set up a special foreign aid department or agency to fulfill both decision-making and executive functions related to foreign aid and put it under the organizational leadership of the Ministry of Foreign Affairs; the third is to separate the decision-making function from the executive function of foreign aid, in which one ministry (usually the Ministry of Foreign Affairs) is responsible for the formulation of foreign aid policies, while the other executive agency is responsible for the implementation of foreign aid; and the fourth is to establish a new ministry independent of the Ministry of Foreign Affairs so as to be exclusively responsible for the formulation and implementation of foreign aid policies (OECD, 2009).

However, even though many OECD documents have summarized the best practices, these reports do not demonstrate what kind of aid management system is best suited to improve aid effectiveness (see Figure 4.2). Gulrajani (2014 and 2015), Faure and Prizzon (2015), and Choi and Bak (2017) have done pioneering research in this field. By means of case analysis, Gulrajani (2014) points out that the following characteristics of governance structure help to improve aid effectiveness: aid agencies are responsible for both aid policy formulation and implementation; aid agencies have clear aid guidelines; and aid implementers have certain

Mode 1: A regional organization system integrated into the Ministry of Foreign Affairs

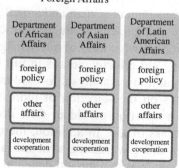

Mode 2: A special department or an agency for development cooperation in the Ministry of Foreign Affairs

Mode 3: A policy making department with independent executive agencies

Mode 4: A department or an agency exclusively responsible for policy formulation and implementation

Figure 4.2:   Organizational structure of aid management.
Source: Gulrajani (2014).

discretion. In addition, among the four aid modes proposed by the OECD, Gulrajani (2015) believes that the first mode and the second mode (i.e. integrating foreign aid policies and implementation dominated by the Ministry of Foreign Affairs) are the most conducive to improving aid effectiveness. By constructing and comparing aid effectiveness index, Faure and Prizzon (2015) believe that the first mode and the fourth mode (i.e. coordinating and leading foreign aid policymaking and implementation at the ministerial level) can help to improve aid effectiveness. By taking the OECD countries as samples and taking the ODA/GNI ratio of donor countries, the proportion of humanitarian aid, the proportion of multilateral aid and the proportion of gratuitous donation in total aid as proxy variables of aid effectiveness, Choi and Bak (2017) further verify the correlation between aid management system and aid effectiveness through empirical analysis and draw the conclusion that the second mode (i.e. a special agency or department responsible for all the functions related to foreign aid and placed under the organizational leadership of the Ministry of Foreign Affairs) among the four aid modes proposed by the OECD is the most helpful to improve aid effectiveness.

On the whole, the view that aid management system and aid effectiveness are inseparable has been widely recognized by the academic community. On the other hand, the research on what kind of aid management system is most conducive to improving aid effectiveness is in full swing. Some scholars have begun to use quantitative analysis to explore their correlation, but there are still disputes on the selection of indicators of aid effectiveness. For example, the proportion of aid in GNI does not necessarily decide the final effectiveness of aid. In addition, the current research on the relationship between aid governance structure and aid effectiveness focuses on the OECD countries and the aid data and evaluation criteria are all subject to the OECD-DAC, which means that the representativeness of the sample is questionable giving the lack of research on emerging donor countries.

References

Acharya, A., A. T. F. De Lima and M. Moore. "Proliferation and fragmentation: Transactions costs and the value of aid". *Journal of Development Studies*, Vol. 42, No. 1, 2006, pp. 1–21.

Arimoto, Y. and H. Kono. "Foreign aid and recurrent cost: Donor competition, aid proliferation, and budget support". *Review of Development Economics*, Vol. 13, 2009, pp. 276–287.

Bourguignon, F. and M. Sundberg. "Aid effectiveness: Opening the black box". *The American Economic Review*, Vol. 97, No. 2, 2007, pp. 316–321.

Burnside, C. and D. Dollar. *Aid, Policies, and Growth.* Washington, DC: The World Bank, 1997.

Choi, Jin-Wook and Jina Bak. "Governance and management for better aid effectiveness: A donor country's perspective". *International Review of Public Administration*, Vol. 22, No. 1, 2017, pp. 45–59.

De Renzo, P., D. Booth, A. Rogerson and Z. Curran. *Incentives for Harmonization and Alignment in Aid Agencies.* Overseas Development Institute Working Paper 248. London: Overseas Development Institute, 2005.

Easterly, W. "Are aid agencies improving?" *Economic Policy*, Vol. 22, 2007, pp. 633–678.

Faure, R., C. Long and A. Prizzon. "Do organisational and political models for development cooperation matter for development effectiveness". ODI Working Paper, 2015.

Grindle, M. S. "Good enough governance: Poverty reduction and reform in developing countries". *Governance*, Vol. 17, No. 4, 2004, pp. 525–548.

Grindle M S. "Good enough governance revisited". *Development Policy Review*, Vol. 25, No. 5, 2007, pp. 533–574.

Gulrajani, N. "Organising for donor effectiveness: An analytical framework for improving aid effectiveness". *Development Policy Review*, Vol. 32, No. 1, 2014, pp. 89–112.

International Bank for Reconstruction and Development. *Assessing Aid: What Works, What Doesn't, and Why.* Oxford: Oxford University Press, 1998.

OECD. *Effective Aid Management: Twelve Lessons from DAC Peer Reviews.* Paris: Organisation for Economic Co-operation and Development, 2008.

OECD. *Managing Aid: Practices of DAC Member Countries.* Paris: Organisation for Economic Co-operation and Development, 2005.

Organisation for Economic Co-operation and Development (OECD). *Managing Aid: Practices of DAC Member Countries.* Paris: France, 2009.

Perri 6, Diana Leat, Kimberly Seltzer and Gerry Stoker. *Towards Holistic Governance: The New Reform Agenda.* New York: Palgrave, 2002.

Perri 6. *Holistic Government.* London: Demos, 1997.

Tendler, J. *Inside Foreign Aid.* Baltimore: Johns Hopkins University Press, 1975.

United Nations Development Programme, Chinese Academy of International Trade and Economic Cooperation. *Mix and Match? How Countries Deliver Development Cooperation and Lessons for China.* Beijing: China Commerce and Trade Press, 2016, p. 5.

Wood, B., J. Betts, F. Etta, J. Gayfer, D. Kabell, N. Ngwira, F. Sagasti and M. Samaranayake. *The Evaluation of the Paris Declaration: Final Report.* OECD: Copenhagen, 2011.

World Bank. *A Decade of Measuring the Quality of Governance.* Washington, DC: World Bank, 2007.

Zhao, Jianzhi and Ouyang Zhe. "An analysis of the dynamic evolution of post-war Japan's foreign aid and international strategy: A comparison with Euro-American perspectives". *Contemporary Asia Pacific*, No. 2, 2018, pp. 92–125.

Chapter 5

Participants in International Development Cooperation

Section 1. Governments or International Development Agencies: Latest Developments

National governments or their international development agencies are the leading providers of foreign aid. According to the statistics of the DAC, 91.7% of the total amount of ODA in 2017 came from national governments, totaling about US $161.15 billion,[1] of which DAC members accounted for 82.5%.[2] Although many countries that provided foreign aid were not DAC members or did not report the aid data to the DAC, the total aid of about US $146.6 billion in 2017 demonstrates the earnest efforts of DAC members in foreign aid (Figure 5.1).[3]

Among the developed countries, the US, Germany, the UK, Japan, and France, with the aid amount of US $35.26 billion, US $24.68 billion, US $17.94 billion, US $11.48 billion, and US $11.36 billion, respectively, in 2017, provided the largest amount of foreign aid in that year. The aid amount of each of the rest countries was far less than US $10 billion, and the status of the top five donors had remained unchanged for a long time.

The US began its foreign aid during World War I by providing food aid to some European countries while carrying out Dollar Diplomacy.

---

[1] The data were based on the OECD-DAC database in 2017.
[2] *Ibid.*
[3] *Ibid.*

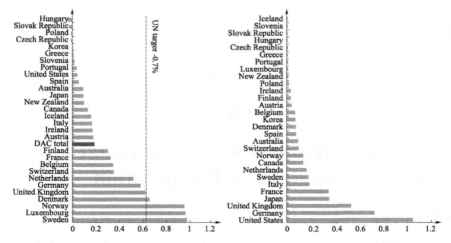

Figure 5.1:   DAC countries' total aid and the proportion of total aid in GNI in 2017.
Source: The OECD-DAC database.

After World War II, the US passed the Foreign Assistance Act of 1948 in 1948 and signed the Marshall Plan to carry out the post-war reconstruction assistance to Europe. In 1961, the US passed the Foreign Assistance Act of 1961 and founded the United States Agency for International Development (USAID) as the administrative agency of its economic assistance program.

In terms of the scale of aid, the US has long been the largest donor country in the world,[4] but in terms of the ODA/GNI ratio, the US in this regard is lower than many other developed countries. Since 1973, the US' ODA/GNI ratio has been lower than 0.3% for a long time, far lower than the 0.7% target promised by the DAC. In 2017, its foreign aid amount was US $35.26 billion, accounting only for 0.18% of its GNI (Figure 5.2).

Germany's foreign aid began in 1952, when the Federal Republic of Germany (i.e. West Germany) joined the UN's "Extended Assistance Scheme", the predecessor of the UNDP. In 1961, Germany founded the Federal Ministry for Economic Cooperation and Development (BMZ), an independent department of the cabinet government to be responsible for its foreign aid.

---

[4]This is the case except from 1991 to 1999, when Japan surpassed the US as the world's largest donor.

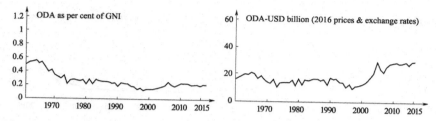

Figure 5.2: The US' ODA scale from 1960 to 2017.

Source: The OECD-DAC database.

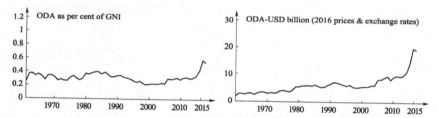

Figure 5.3: Germany's ODA scale from 1960 to 2017.

Source: The OECD-DAC database.

Germany is one of the largest donors in the world. Since 2013, its foreign aid began to grow rapidly. In 2016, its ODA/GNI ratio accomplished the DAC target of 0.7%, which nearly doubled compared with 0.38% in 2013. In 2017, Germany's total foreign aid amount was US $24.68 billion, accounting for 0.66% of GNI (Figure 5.3).

The UK is also one of the leaders in international aid. In 1997, it set up the famous Department for International Development (DFID) to take charge of its foreign aid. This organization is also an independent development aid ministry, which coordinates the UK's multilateral and bilateral aid.

The amount of the UK's ODA had been stable for a long time in history, about US $4 billion. After entering the millennium, it has been gradually increasing, except for a decline in 2007 caused by the global financial crisis. As far as the ODA/GNI ratio is concerned, the UK's foreign aid is relatively higher than many other countries. Since 2013, the UK's ODA/GNI ratio has remained at a high level of 0.7%. In 2017, the amount reached US $17.94 billion (Figure 5.4).

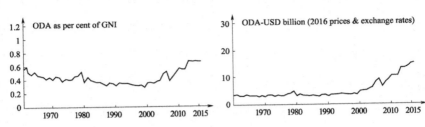

Figure 5.4:   The UK's ODA scale from 1960 to 2017.

Source: The OECD-DAC database.

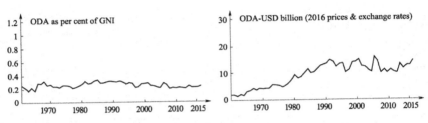

Figure 5.5:   Japan's ODA scale from 1960 to 2017.

Source: The OECD-DAC database.

Japan is the first Asian country to join the DAC and the only non-European-and-American country among the top five DAC donors. As a non-military country, foreign aid is an important diplomatic tool for Japan to safeguard its national interests. The Japanese International Cooperation Agency (JICA) was established in 1974 as a public service group but was in 2003 transformed into a government agency directly under the Ministry of Foreign Affairs of Japan to be responsible for Japan's foreign aid.

From 1960 to 1991 when Japan became the world's largest donor country and entered the "lost decade" at the same time, its ODA had increased steadily and the aid amount has maintained at about US $10 billion annually since then. However, in terms of the ODA/GNI ratio, Japan in this regard is relatively low — below 0.4% — and has remained at the level of 0.2% in the past 10 years. In 2017, Japan's foreign aid amount was US $11.48 billion, accounting for 0.23% of GNI (Figure 5.5).

As a permanent member of the UN Security Council, France is also one of the most important donors in the world. The French Development Agency (AFD) is the core institution of France's foreign aid. Its predecessor is the Central Fund for Free France, which was established by General

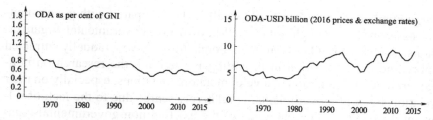

Figure 5.6:   France's ODA scale from 1960 to 2017.
Source: The OECD-DAC database.

de Gaulle in 1941 when he was exiled to the UK. Apart from being the executive agency of ODA, the AFD is also a state-owned enterprise, which has been playing a role similar to that of a development bank in France's foreign aid rather than being an independent ministry like Germany and the UK. In June 2017, the AFD was granted the status of a financial company by the European Central Bank, but this does not affect its status and responsibilities under the French legal system.

The amount of France's ODA had been increasing since 1978, reaching more than US $10 billion in 1994, and had been falling since then, dropping to US $6.17 billion in 2000. However, it has begun to rise unsteadily since 2000. The amount of France's foreign aid in 2017 was $11.36 billion. In terms of the ODA/GNI ratio, the 1980s and 1990s were the peak period of French foreign aid, which maintained at the level of 0.6% for a long time, and then gradually decreased to the level of about 0.4%. In 2017, France's foreign aid accounted for 0.43% of GNI (Figure 5.6).

Section 2. Non-Governmental International Development Organizations: A Perspective of Government Funding

Non-governmental international development organizations are also an important component of international aid. To be specific, some cross-border non-governmental international development organizations actively participate in the practice of international aid, and most of them focus on a specific field to provide assistance, such as medical care or education. However, it is difficult to measure and count them due to their large number, diverse forms, and small scales compared with governmental assistance. Although some well-known non-governmental organizations, such as the Gates-Melinda Foundation, have gradually attracted more and more attention in providing foreign aid, the research on non-governmental international development organizations, especially on their relationship with governments, is relatively scarce due to the lack of relevant data and the fact that most of the existing non-governmental organization studies focus on their domestic affairs.

One of the most important research questions is whether government funding will affect the operation of non-profit organization (NPO) projects. For a long time, people had been worried that government funding would damage or even deflect the mission of NPOs. The current theory and empirical research cannot fully demonstrate the relationship between government funding and NPOs' project expenditure. This section examines this issue by exploring the impact of government funding on the NPOs' expenditure on the projects in the field of international development. Based on the 20-year data of non-governmental international development organizations registered with USAID, we find that NPOs with more government funding have higher project expenditure, which means that government funding seems to have increased the project expenditure of those NPOs, making them more focused on mission-related activities.

1. Introduction

The emergence of new governance, privatization, public–private partnership and cooperative governance provides new prospects for public administration (Ansell and Gash, 2008; Kettl, 2002; Osborne, 2010; Savas, 2000). Today, public administration activities are no longer entirely carried out by traditional government agencies, but often being extended beyond governments (Kettl, 2006). By "hollowing out" the state, NPOs increasingly provide public services in the form of collaborative networks (Brinkerhoff, 2002; Milward and Provan, 2000). In this context, the government is increasingly funding non-profit activities in service provision and policy implementation in various policy areas (Salamon, 1995; Smith and Lipsky, 1993). For government agencies, they do not directly provide public services to meet the needs of the public, but provide funds in the form of contracts and donations for many NPOs and share the responsibility of providing services with them. Therefore, government funds account for a large part of many NPOs' income. According to a recent estimate, direct government funding (i.e. contracts and donations) accounts for one-third of the total revenue of the US non-profit sector (McKeever, 2015). Similar proportion can also be found in many other countries (Salamon *et al.*, 2017; Struyk, 2002).

Although government funding has brought various tangible benefits to NPOs (Salamon, 1995), the serious dependence of NPOs on government funding inclines the public to worry that it may change the operation of NPOs and result in adverse consequences. Scholars have tried to describe the complex relationship between governments and NPOs and to summarize the potential impact of government funding (Salamon and Toepler, 2015; Smith and Grønbjerg, 2006; Young, 2000). The core concern among scholars is that government funds will damage the NPOs' mission and blur their citizenship, which will eventually undermine the civic foundation of the non-profit sector and deprive it of its unique functions in democratic governance (Alexander *et al.*, 1999; Eikenberry and Kluver, 2004). Previous empirical studies have examined the potential impact of government funding on various aspects of non-profit activities, such as governance, decision-making, revenue strategy and advocacy engagement (e.g. Andreoni and Payne, 2003; Edwards and Hulme, 1996; Lu, 2018; Nikolic and Koontz, 2007; Peci *et al.*, 2011; Smith, 2008).

Part of the studies of the relationship between government and NPOs examines the impact of government funding on NPOs' project expenditure (Alexander *et al.*, 1999; Sloan and Grizzle, 2014; Thornton, 2014). Generally speaking, NPOs have three main aspects of expenditure: project operation, internal management, and financing. Project expenditure is important because it represents the organizational resources specifically dedicated to mission-related outputs (Tinkelman and Mankaney, 2007; Weisbrod and Dominguez, 1986). Since NPOs are founded to provide charitable services to advance social progress, the NPOs with higher project expenditure are more welcomed by voters and the society, because they devote more resources to project outputs to support charitable goals, which is the real task of NPOs (Garven *et al.*, 2016). By contrast, lower project expenditure has always been seen as manifestations of inefficiency and waste, because administrative and financing costs are the transition of the organizational resources from project outputs (Bowman, 2006; Gneezy *et al.*, 2014; Sloan, 2009).

The current scholarship provides different answers to the impact of government funding on NPOs' project expenditure. According to the interdependence theory, government funding can bring financial stability and legitimacy to NPOs so as to enable them to focus on accomplishing missions and increasing the numbers of projects (Salamon, 1995; Salamon and Toepler, 2015). On the contrary, the resource dependence theory or institutional isomorphism shows that government-funded NPOs must invest a lot of resources to meet the program and accounting requirements involved in the application and management of government funding, which will result in an increase in administrative expenditure which affects project expenditure (DiMaggio and Powell, 1983; Pfeffer and Salancik, 1978). On the basis of these theories, the conclusions of previous empirical studies are inconsistent (Alexander *et al.*, 1999; Ecer *et al.*, 2017; Grønbjerg, 1993; Sloan and Grizzle, 2014; Thornton, 2014). In fact, the key issue behind the debate is how government funding affects NGOs' ability to perform their missions, which is further related to the fundamental issue of how government actions will affect the role of the non-profit sector in democratic governance. If government funding does reduce the project expenditure of NPOs and the increased non-project expenditure increases the social cost of obtaining the service output produced by the NPOs, then it will damage the social value that the NPOs are expected to create.

This study explores this issue by examining the impact of federal funds on the project expenditure of international development NPOs. Based on the 20-year data of NPOs registered with USAID for financing purposes, we find that NPOs with more government funding have a significant increase in project expenditure. In other words, government funding seems to have increased the project expenditure of NPOs, making them more focused on mission-related activities. In this case, we agree with the interdependence theory, that is, government funding is conducive to increasing the project expenditure of NPOs and helping them further perform their social missions. We call for more relevant research in the future to explore empirically NPOs' mission deviation caused by government funding.

This section is arranged as follows. In the second part, the impact mechanism of government funding on NPOs' project expenditure is discussed theoretically and the related literature is reviewed. The third part introduces the research design, including data and variables. The fourth part is the statistical results. The fifth part discusses the theoretical and management issues involved in the research results and points out some limitations for further research.

2. Literature Review

Project expenditure is the resources of NPOs, used for providing projects and services that support their missions. This is a common criterion adopted by donors, charity supervision organizations, the press and other organizations to assess organizational performance (Garven *et al.*, 2016; Krishnan *et al.*, 2006; Sloan, 2009). The higher the project expenditure, the more valuable the organization will be considered, for it is believed that NPOs with more project expenditure will maximize their project output, thus further enhancing their ability to advance their charitable missions. Administrative and financing efforts do not directly serve output activities, so they are often regarded as the transition of the funds of an organization's core mission function (Weisbrod and Dominguez, 1986). With the government becoming an important source of income to support NPOs, how government funding affects their project expenditure so as to support their missions has become an important subject in research and practice. The literature in this regard provides a comparative prediction of the potential impact. We briefly review the two leading theories widely used in the study of the relationship between government and NPOs.

2.1 *Resource dependence/institutional isomorphism chain*

According to the theory of resource dependence or institutional isomorphism, when an organization relies on external resources, it will inevitably be subject to external control and bear the pressure to meet external expectations (DiMaggio and Powell, 1983; Pfeffer and Salancik, 1978). Accordingly, when NPOs rely on government funding, their operation will be affected by the expectations and preferences of the funding institutions (Nikolic and Koontz, 2007; Verschuere and De Corte, 2014). In the relationship between government and NPOs, NPOs must invest a lot of resources to improve their internal business in order to meet the financial and procedural requirements involved in the application and management of government funding (Smith, 2008). For example, in order to gain a strong position in the competition for government funding, NPOs need to expand their administrative infrastructure (such as professional staff and visible facilities). In addition, while managing government grants and contracts, NPOs must rely on more professional staff with financial expertise to meet the accounting and reimbursement requirements that come with government funding. NPOs also need to formalize their internal control procedures in response to the cumbersome administrative reports and documents related to government assessment and regulation. All of these organizational changes will significantly increase the administrative expenditure of NPOs and squeeze out the resources for project services, resulting in "greater emphasis on management and public relations at the expense of service delivery" (Eikenberry and Kluver, 2004, p. 135).

There is empirical evidence that supports this analysis (Alexander *et al.*, 1999; Ebrahim, 2003; Frumkin and Kim, 2002; Grønbjerg, 1993). For example, the pioneering study of non-profit financing sources by Grønbjerg (1993) finds that non-profit managers generally consider government funding as the most difficult task to undertake compared with other funding sources. She concludes that the guarantees and management of government grants and contracts are complex and very likely to dominate the agency activities (169). According to a recent national survey of the relationship between government and NPOs in the US, more than two-thirds of NPOs point out that the application and reporting procedures required for government contracts and grants are too complex and time-consuming (Boris *et al.*, 2010). Frumkin and Kim (2002) analyze 990 figures from 1985 to 1995 and propose that those NPOs with more government funding had a higher proportion of administrative expenditure, which means that the proportion of project expenditure was reduced. As they claim, the ability of NPOs to operate effectively with government funding faces significant challenges given the costs associated with bidding and winning contracts as well as the corresponding responsibilities and reporting requirements once funding is in place (Frumkin and Kim, 2002, p. 8). Anyway, the increase of investment in administrative infrastructure and the continuous improvement of management regularization will raise the administrative expenditure to a very high level. With the increase of administrative expenditure, the proportion of expenditure on project output in total expenditure will decrease. Therefore, this reasoning assumes that government funding has a negative impact on NPOs' project expenditure.

2.2 *Interdependence chain*

The theory of interdependence chain challenges the concept of the conflict between government and NPOs (Salamon, 1995; Salamon and Toepler, 2015). This theory shows that the interaction between the government and the non-profit sector is mutually beneficial, because they complement each other. In this way, government funding can help increase NPOs' project expenditure in two aspects. Firstly, a common problem faced by many NPOs is they lack sufficient and reliable resources to fulfill their missions (Salamon, 1995). Compared with other sources of funding, government funding is generally more stable and predictable (Grønbjerg, 1993; Lu, 2015; Van Slyke, 2003). Therefore, the financial stability and credibility brought about by government funding will reduce the disruption to organizational activities and give NPOs more time to expand their projects and services (Toepler, 2010). This effect is particularly relevant to NPOs in the field of international development (Kerlin, 2006). Secondly, the quality standards and accountability mechanisms related to government funding will discipline NPOs and make their internal management more effective by cracking down on unprofessional operations, which can check the growth of administrative expenditure and leave more resources for achieving project objectives (Ecer *et al.*, 2017).

There is also empirical evidence that supports this interdependent theory, that is, government funding may benefit the proportion of non-profit project expenditure. For example, the research on art and social service organizations by Andreoni and Payne (2003) as well as the research on symphony orchestras by Hughes *et al.* (2014) show that government funding has led to a significant reduction in NPOs' fund-raising expenditure. Ecer *et al.* (2017) review the income composition and efficiency of NPOs and report that the NPOs receiving more government grants usually have less indirect expenses (i.e. administrative and fund-raising costs). As a result of savings on administrative and funding expenditure, NPOs can devote more resources to mission-related expenditure. In addition, Sloan and Grizzle (2014) and Thornton (2014) directly measure the relationship between government funding and non-profit project expenditure ratio. Sloan and Grizzle find that the faith-based and community-based organizations in Kentucky accepted higher levels of federal funding and the ratio of project expenditure increased. Thornton proves that government funding can stimulate the output of NPO projects in some cases. In short, government funding can bring financial stability and legitimacy to NPOs, which will free them from non-mission-related activities and focus on project services. Therefore, this theory holds that government funding can have a positive impact on NPOs' project expenditure.

In fact, both views have empirical evidence. Although the differences in the literature indicate the complexity of the relationship between government and NPOs (Smith and Grønbjerg, 2006; Young, 2000), it is necessary for scholars to conduct a more thorough analysis of the impact of government funding on NPOs' project expenditure.

3. Research Method

We explore this issue by analyzing the data from a group of international development NPOs registered with USAID for funding purposes from 1995 to 2014. USAID has worked with international development NPOs to address development, humanitarian and health challenges overseas for decades (Lindenberg, 1999; McCleary and Barro, 2008). It uses a variety of financial mechanisms, such as contracts and grants, to obtain services from these NPOs and use their connections and expertise to achieve US foreign policy objectives (Stoddard, 2012). For example, nearly half of USAID's quota went to these NPOs in 2014 (Tarnoff, 2015). The financing relationship between government and NPOs in the field of international development has attracted the attention of a large number of scholars for many years (e.g. Brinkerhoff, 2002; Ebrahim, 2003; Edwards and Hulme, 1996; Gulrajani, 2015; Herzer and Nunnenkamp, 2013; McCleary and Barro, 2008).

To be specific, we collect the data from USAID's *Report of Voluntary Agencies Engaged in Overseas Relief and Development* (VolAg report). The report details the expenditure and income of each NPO registered with USAID based on its self-reported materials during its annual registration process. In fact, the NPOs seeking to cooperate with USAID should first apply to the USAID registry and determine whether they are eligible for most USAID funding through a pre-screening process. In this process, the NPOs are required to submit supporting documents about their legal, governance and financial conditions, which are to be approved by USAID to register with its registry, and then participate in performance-based aid funding competitions. For instance, as of 1 September 2016, 491 American NPOs and 106 international NPOs had been registered with USAID.

After collecting 20 years of data from the VolAg report, we use the following measures to process the data. First of all, to ensure the comparability of NPOs in our sample, we only investigate the NPOs that are governed by US law and headquartered in the US. Second, we delete the observations of which expenditure or income items are negative, such as private donations, government contracts, government grants, program expenditure or financing expenditure, as well as the observations of zero administrative or financing expenditure, because these data are highly controversial in the literature and are considered unusable (Krishnan *et al.*, 2006; Tinkelman and Mankaney, 2007). Third, we also include the observations of zero government revenue in all years in the sample, because it is found that these observations do not affect the change of government funding in the test of their effects on PSRs (Andreoni and Payne, 2003). Fourth, we use the consumer price index to adjust all financial data for inflation. Our final sample consists of 8,537 observations from 1,142 NPOs.

The data we get from the VolAg report have several advantages. First of all, the self-reported financial information provided by NPOs during the annual registration process must be supported by audited financial statements and subject to the review of USAID. Our data seem to be more reliable in this way, especially when previous studies have found that NPOs might manipulate self-reported financial data (Garven *et al.*, 2016; Krishnan *et al.*, 2006; Parsons *et al.*, 2017). Second, the distinction between contracts and grants and other support made by USAID and other federal agencies in the VolAg report enables us to measure government funding for NPOs in more detail. Third, the data include organizations of all sizes, because all NPOs, regardless of their size, must register with USAID and report their financial information before seeking USAID funding. This can redress the selection bias that only large and medium-sized organizations were included in previous studies.

According to the previous literature (e.g. Garven *et al.*, 2016; Sloan and Grizzle, 2014), we set project expenditure as the dependent variable, which is measured by the percentage of (domestic and foreign) project expenditure in total expenditure. The key independent variable, that is, government funding, is measured by the percentage of the funds received from USAID and other federal government agencies in total revenue.[5] In addition, we set up control variables including other income and expenditure items to illustrate the possible interaction. Those control variables include private donations (measured by the percentage of private donations in kind and in cash from all sources in total income), business income (measured by the percentage of business income such as service

---

[5] USAID's funding includes contracts, grants, sea freight covered by Article 123, P.L. 480 freight and the food donated by P.L. 480. Other federal funding includes contracts and grants.

Table 5.1:   Descriptive statistics of variables ($N = 8,537$).

Variables	Mean	Median	The 25th percentile	The 75th percentile	Standard deviation
			Dependent variable		
Project expenditure	85.51	86.58	79.71	93.58	10.67
			Independent variable		
Government funding	29.9	19.14	3.96	51.2	28.16
Private donations	64.87	86.88	32.95	97.62	36.82
Business Income	11.38	2.32	0.21	12.49	25.72
Administrative expenditure	10.2	8.36	3.8	14.11	8.07
Financing expenditure	4.25	2.08	0.12	6.56	5.52
Organizational size	15.44	15.39	14.04	17.03	2.22

fees, membership fees, investment income, etc., in total income), administrative expenditure (measured by the percentage of administrative and management expenditure in total expenditure), and financing. Finally, our variables also include the organizational size, which is measured by the logarithm of total dollar income (see Table 5.1).

Table 5.1 gives descriptive statistics of the variables used in the analysis, including the mean, the median, the 25th percentile, the 75th percentile, and the standard deviation. In particular, the mean of our dependent variable project expenditure is 85.51%, and the median is 86.58%. Its distribution is quite concentrated. The value of the 75th percentile is about 15% larger than that of the 25th percentile. The key independent variable, i.e. government funding, has a mean of 29.9% and a median of 19.14%. There are large differences among organizations. The value of the 75th percentile is about 12 times higher than that of the 25th percentile.

4. Research Results

We start with a preliminary analysis of the relationship between government funding and NPOs' project expenditure. We first made a linear prediction graph between the two variables (Figure 5.7). It can be seen from the figure that there is an obvious positive correlation between the two, which shows that the increase of government funds seems to increase the project expenditure. Then we conducted a correlation analysis, and the

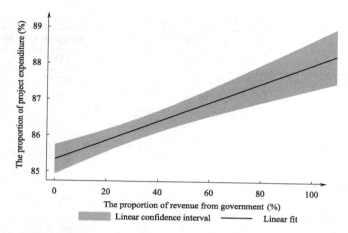

Figure 5.7:   Relationship between government funding and NPOs' project expenditure.

Note: The reason for the high Y-axis is that most of the effective observations exceed 85% of the project expenditure.

Table 5.2:   Correlation of variables.

Variables	(1)	(2)	(3)	(4)	(5)	(6)	(7)
Project expenditure	1.00						
Government funding	0.07	1.00					
Private donations	0.03	−0.63	1.00				
Business income	−0.12	−0.11	−0.56	1.00			
Financing expenditure	−0.54	−0.23	0.22	−0.02	1.00		
Administrative expenditure	−0.85	0.06	−0.17	0.15	0.02	1.00	
Organizational size	0.18	0.18	−0.23	0.08	0.03	−0.29	1.00

coefficients are shown in Table 5.2. It is worth noting that the correlation between project expenditure and government funding is positive ($r = 0.073$), indicating that the former will increase with the increase of the latter. Similarly, NPOs with more government funding tend to focus more on mission-related activities. In short, government funding seems to be able to make NPOs more responsible by pushing them to distribute more resources to mission-related outputs.

To further explore the statistical significance of this relationship, we use panel data for regression analysis. In particular, we use the fixed

Table 5.3:   Regression results.

Variables	Fixed effects model		Random effects model	
	(1)	(2)	(3)	(4)
Government funding	0.03***	0.02**	0.03***	0.02**
	(5.76)	(2.76)	(6.46)	(2.70)
Private donations		0.01*		0.02***
		(1.98)		(5.04)
Business income		0.00		0.01*
		(1.42)		(2.15)
Financing expenditure		−0.3***		−0.66***
		(−16.18)		(−36.49)
Administrative expenditure		−0.27***		−0.46***
		(−24.37)		(−46.34)
Organizational size		1.91***		0.71***
		(18.01)		(13.24)
Constant	85.44***	59.64***	84.72***	80.57***
	(818.77)	(34.37)	(300.11)	(83.77)
R2	0.12	0.17	0.12	0.18
Number of organizations	1,142	1,139	1,142	1,139
Times of observation	8,542	8,537	8,542	8,537

Note: The statistical data of *t* value are in brackets. $*p < 0.05$, $**p < 0.01$, $***p < 0.001$.

effects model and the random effects model to specify the regression model. The results are shown in Table 5.3. Columns (1) and (2) show the regression results with and without fixed effects model for the control variables respectively. Columns (3) and (4) show the regression results using random effects model by the same standard.

The core conclusion is quite clear. In all four cases, the estimated coefficient of government funding is positive; and statistically speaking, the significance level of full specification is 95% and the simpler specification level is 99%. The credibility of the estimates of government funding do not change significantly in the four cases. In terms of the simpler models in Columns (1) and (3), the size of government funding coefficient shows that if government funding increases by 1 percentage point, the project expenditure would increase by 2.74 and 2.85 percentage points. However, as for the complete model in Columns (2) and (4), the values are reduced to 1.98 and 1.59 percentage points.

Generally speaking, our analysis shows that there is a statistically significant positive correlation between government funding and NPOs' project expenditure. This finding is stable in different models.

5. Discussion and Conclusion

Conceptually, NPOs are established to undertake the social mission of providing various services to communities and individuals. With the government becoming an important sponsor of the non-profit sector under the governance mode of the third-party government and hollow state, how government funding affects the operation and identity of NPOs so as to serve their mission has become a prominent issue of common concern among scholars and practitioners. In the literature on the relationship between government and NPOs, scholars have been worried for a long time that government funding will damage NPOs' mission and cause their deviation from the mission. This argument is well documented, although it has been rarely explicitly studied in the broader literature.

We explore this issue from a resource or financial perspective, i.e. the proportion of organizational resources/expenditure spent on mission-related outputs. In fact, NPOs have been always expected to maximize the resources invested in their projects and minimize non-productive costs. The project expenditure of NPOs has become an index to evaluate the value of NPOs.

Clearly, the issue of mission deviation involves other aspects. For example, Toepler (2010) discusses this issue from the customer's perspective. For him, mission deviation occurs when the focus of NPO managers deviates from the original core customers. Lipsky and Smith (1993) also believe that mission deviation refers to changing NPOs' organizational norms from focusing on individuals in the past to treating all customers equally, which is similar to the model of government service agencies.

Section 3. Multilateral Development Banks: A Comparative Perspective

As one of the symbols of China's increasing participation in global economic governance, the establishment of the Asian Infrastructure Investment Bank (AIIB) has attracted much attention from the academic and policy circles at home and abroad, especially whether it is different from the traditional multilateral development banks. However, most of the existing studies use narrative method, lacking micro or macro evidence. This section uses case study method to examine the AIIB and the Asian Development Bank (ADB), a typical traditional multilateral development bank. It conducts an in-depth comparative analysis by selecting their highly comparable projects and pays special attention to the aspects of management structure, procurement, economy, risk, supervision and security that reflect the AIIB's aims — "simplification, integrity and greening". We find that compared with the ADB, the AIIB, while simplifying project system design, emphasizes project efficiency more, which basically confirms its concept of simplification and efficiency. Thirdly, different from the ADB, the AIIB weakens the contents with value preference and additional administrative expenses in the aspects of project procurement, risk, and supervision, and only retains the indicators directly related to the quality and efficiency of project implementation. This section holds that the AIIB, on the basis of conforming to international norms, has both openness and economic sustainability and has higher project operation efficiency, which is thus an innovative transcendence of traditional multilateral development banks. The research results of this section have certain value for the in-depth understanding of China's global governance ideas and demands.

1. Introduction

Under the leadership of the Bretton Woods system after World War II, the World Bank and regional multilateral development banks provided important financial support and technical assistance for the economic development and cooperation of developing countries. However, in recent years, such multilateral development banks dominated by European and American developed countries have been widely criticized for their lagging reform. Take Asia as an example. The ADB is the largest regional multilateral financial institution with a long history in the Asian-Pacific region. However, it has been questioned due to a series of problems caused by its long-term dominance of Japan and the US, such as the loan standard exceeding the development capacity of the borrowing country and the project approval time being too long. These problems make it unable to better meet the expanding infrastructure construction needs of Asian countries. The ADB's own report also points out that the Asian-Pacific region needs US $26 trillion in infrastructure construction by

2030 but the current gap is as high as US \$800 billion a year (ADB, 2017a). In order to improve the backward situation of infrastructure construction in Asian countries, the AIIB led by the Chinese government was set up in 2015. Unlike the ADB, which is involved in many fields, the AIIB would focus on infrastructure construction in Asia.

Since the idea of founding the AIIB was put forward, scholars and policy circles have frequently questioned or even challenged it, such as whether it is necessary for China to build a global economic governance system centered on itself, seeing the AIIB as a direct challenge to the Bretton Woods system (Reisen, 2015); questioning the governance structure of the AIIB, believing that it is merely reorganization based on a set of uncertain systems of rules (Wolf and Rogowsky, 2015); or comparing the AIIB to the contemporary Marshall Plan (Maverick, 2015). On the whole, there are obvious defects in these related researches. First, because their research perspective is constrained by the existing conditions, their research conclusions are basically obtained through concept combing or theoretical discussions and the relevant information, data and materials are not detailed or systematic enough. Second, due to the lack of analysis of specific information at the micro level, some scholars make a predictive argument merely through simple induction and summary, lacking empirical basis, especially micro evidence, which weakens the persuasiveness of their articles.

In view of this, this section attempts to re-examine the above views more scientifically by choosing the representative and comparable road construction projects implemented by the AIIB and the ADB in India respectively as the research cases and then by comparing their policy framework and operation modes in each stage. To be specific, this section attempts to answer the following research questions: is the AIIB a simplified version or a reformed version of the ADB? What breakthrough has it made in the specific project implementation and management mode? Does this represent a new way or a new concept of global governance?

The research on these issues will help us to clarify the different roles of the two banks in global governance, especially the significance of the AIIB for China's participation in international governance. As an innovation of global governance system initiated by China, the AIIB is of great significance to the realization of infrastructure interconnection in Asia and the improvement of global economic governance system. Meanwhile, as a multilateral development bank that provides international public goods, its project operation is an important indicator of its core competitiveness.

This not only helps respond to the international community's query on its governance structure and project standards, but also has great significance for the optimization of China's international development assistance and the Belt and Road Initiative.

The main findings of this section show that the institutional design and operation mode of the AIIB's projects are basically in line with its concept of streamlining and efficiency. Different from the ADB, the AIIB weakens the contents with value preference and additional administrative expenses in the aspects of project procurement, risk, and supervision, and only retains the indicators directly related to the quality and efficiency of project implementation. This section holds that, on the basis of conforming to the international norms, the AIIB has the characteristics of openness, internationality, economic sustainability, and higher project performance, which means that it is are formed version of the ADB. However, while implementing the concept of streamlining, the AIIB should strengthen the openness and transparency of the information of its projects, thus truly achieving its construction goal of "integrity".

The organization of this section is as follows: in the second part, we will systematically sort out the existing literature and then point out the contribution of our research to the existing literature; the third part is the background introduction, which introduces the background of the establishment of the AIIB and the ADB and their governance ideas and then makes a basic introduction to and comparison of the selected cases; the fourth part is the core part of this section, which will make an in-depth study on the respective cases of the AIIB and the ADB. The fifth part summarizes the whole section.

2. Literature Review

Since the idea of the AIIB was brought up, a large number of studies have analyzed it. The existing research is mainly carried out in the following two aspects.

The first type of research focuses on the reasons for the establishment of the AIIB and its impact, which is also the most extensive in the existing literature. The attitudes of the academic circles at home and abroad reveal obvious difference between China and the West. Western academic circles tend to interpret the AIIB from the perspective of power transition and hegemonic politics, believing that the establishment of the AIIB poses a challenge to the US-centered international economic order. For example,

Shintaro Hamanaka (2016) believes that China wants to replace Japan so as to gain the regional leadership by establishing the AIIB without the participation of the US and Japan. Based on this, some scholars hold that the establishment of the AIIB heralds the end of the Western-centered development model and that China will establish an international financial system centered on itself to replace the US hegemony system (Reisen, 2015). In addition, scholars with geopolitical views believe that the AIIB will greatly weaken the dominant position of the ADB in the Asian-Pacific region (Jakupec and Kelly, 2015). On the contrary, most scholars in China adopt a positive attitude. For instance, Jin Liqun (2016), President of the AIIB, views the AIIB as a rebalancing measure of global economic governance, giving emerging economies more rights and opportunities. Besides, some scholars hold that the AIIB will not challenge the existing international economic mechanism; on the contrary, it will promote the sound operation of the world economy by providing "global public goods" (Liu, 2015).

The second type of research focuses on the comparative study between the AIIB and other major multilateral development banks around the world. Perhaps limited by data and methods and other factors, this kind of research is relatively inadequate. Some studies are based on the comprehensive comparison of the world's major multilateral development banks, which are characterized by horizontal comparison method, that is, comparison of macro indicators is made in a certain time span and data scale (IEG, 2010; Himberg, 2015). Other studies focus on the comparative analysis of one or several dimensions. These studies generally summarize and sort out the legal documents of each institution, or conduct quantitative research through independent construction of models and variables. For example, Chris Humphrey (2015) uses four variables to build a model to predict the development prospects of the New Development Bank and the AIIB. He believes that although the AIIB may develop slowly in the initial stage, it would have greater development potential in the later stage. By analyzing the linguistic composition in the agreement terms of the World Bank, the AIIB, and the ADB, Ming Wan (2016) concludes that the governance model of the AIIB is actually embedded in the governance rules of the World Bank and the ADB. Similarly, by summarizing the agreement terms and analyzing the voting rights distribution system, decision-making rules and decision-making institutions of the World Bank, the ADB and the African Development Bank from a legal point of view, Zuo Haicong and An Wenjing believe that the AIIB should draw on the experience of those institutions in its system designing and take efficiency and fairness into account while adhering to the principle of independence of international organizations (Zuo and An, 2015). However, on the whole, scholars in China have done little comparative research on the AIIB and other international development banks, while Western scholars mainly focus on macro level research, lacking micro level evidence. The main reason is that compared with other multilateral institutions with a long history, the AIIB is still in its infancy, its own information, data and materials being far from sufficient. Therefore, in the absence of micro level information, making predictive arguments merely through a simple summary does not hold water.

In view of this, this section believes that the micro level research has a great contribution to the existing literature in terms of the comparative study of the AIIB and the ADB. The AIIB has a lot of project practice since its establishment, and its image has become more well-developed compared with its initial stage. In addition, as a multilateral development bank providing international public goods, project implementation is its core competitiveness. Therefore, this section selects two comparable and representative cases of the AIIB and the ADB, uses case study method to compare the policy framework and operation mode of the two institutions in each stage of the projects, summarizes the similarities and differences between them, and tries to answer the research questions raised at the beginning of this section, hoping to make contributions to the existing literature.

3. Background Introduction

3.1 *Background of the two banks*

The ADB is the largest regional multilateral financial institution in the Asian-Pacific region and one of the four major regional development banks operating in collaboration with the World Bank.[6] Since its establishment, the ADB has been aiming to help developing countries in the Asian-Pacific region eradicate poverty and to promote the economic development and cooperation in the region through development

---

[6]The other major regional development banks are the African Development Bank (AfDB), the Inter-American Development Bank (IDB) and the European Bank for Reconstruction and Development (EBRD).

assistance. The ADB now has 67 member states, 48 of which are from the Asian-Pacific region. The ADB's capital base is US $165 billion and its private sector financing scale reached US $2.6 billion in 2015, with a year-on-year increase of 37% (ADB, 2016). The governance structure of the ADB is divided into three layers. The highest decision-making layer is its council, which meets annually. The council elects 12 executive directors, including 8 from the Asian-Pacific region and 4 from non-Asian-Pacific region. Under the leadership of the president, the board of directors is responsible for the approval of the bank's budget, loan policies, and technical assistance. The third layer is the management, including the president and six vice presidents. In terms of shareholding, Japan and the US are the largest shareholders of the ADB (both 15.6%), followed by China and India (6.4% and 6.3%, respectively) (ADB, 2017b). Since its establishment, the ADB presidency has always been held by people of Japanese nationality.

The background of the establishment of the AIIB is more concentrated. The AIIB, led by the Chinese government, was officially put into operation in January 2016 to help the emerging countries play a bigger role in the world economy and global financial governance, to improve the backward situation of infrastructure construction in Asian countries, and also to act as an important participant in China's Belt and Road Initiative. The AIIB is headquartered in Beijing and has 57 founding members. According to its terms, the regional members have a total of 75% of the voting rights. Its initial capital is US $100 billion, of which 20% is paid in capital and 80% is to be paid in capital. In terms of shareholding, Asian countries, especially the emerging Asian countries, hold more shares. China invested US $50 billion, making it the largest shareholder of the AIIB. India ranked second with US $8.4 billion in investment. The governance structure of the AIIB conforms to the practice of other mainstream international financial institutions, which also adopts a three-tier structure composed of the council, the board of directors, and the management. In terms of governance idea, the AIIB aims to create "the best innovative international practice" that meets the requirements of the 21st century.[7] Under the guidance of the goal of being "lean, clean, and green", the AIIB does not set up a resident executive board. Discussions and decisions are made by the executive directors through

---

[7] Caixin: "Building AIIB with innovative international best standards". URL: http://www.caixin.com/2016-01-15/100900210_all.html.

regular or irregular meetings, video or teleconferences. In terms of project operation, the AIIB and the World Bank have jointly financed 10 projects with a cooperative investment of US $3.7 billion since its operation in January 2016. As of January 2018, the AIIB has invested in 24 infrastructure projects, with a total loan of more than US $4.2 billion.[8]

3.2 Background introduction to the two cases

Due to the fact that the AIIB is still in its infancy and lacks data for quantitative research, this section selects two representative and comparable projects of the AIIB and the ADB to conduct case studies. For the AIIB, this section selects the case of "Gujarat Rural Roads (MMGSY) Project". This project is aimed at the construction of the non-urban roads in Gujarat, India, and was implemented from August 2017 to June 2019. For the ADB, this section selects the case of "Madhya Pradesh District Connectivity Sector Project". This project is aimed at the construction of the non-urban roads in Madhya Pradesh, India, and was implemented from November 2014 to April 2018 (Figure 5.8).

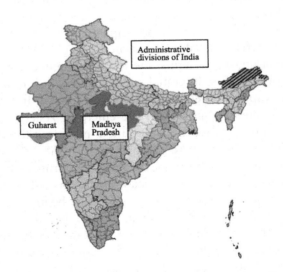

Figure 5.8:   Map of Gujarat and Madhya Pradesh, India.

---

[8]Xinhuanet. "After two years' operation, AIIB presents a proud report card". URL: http://www.xinhuanet.com/fortune/2018-01/16/c_1122268353.htm.

This section selects these two projects as case studies based on the following factors. First of all, the role of infrastructure in economic growth is obvious, huge and comprehensive. It can not only drive economic growth and improve labor productivity but also rapidly create more jobs, partly increase national income and enhance the total demand of society in the short term, and increase supply in the long term. Road construction is representative and extensive in infrastructure construction. As one of the active emerging economies, India is one of the representative countries in Asia that urgently needs investment in infrastructure. Although the Indian government has been increasing road construction in recent years, India's backward road transport capacity still restricts the pace of its economic development. Especially, the lack of transportation roads in rural areas has further widened the gap between urban and rural economic development in India. In its 12th Five-Year Plan for Infrastructure Development (2012–2017), the Indian government also made it clear that increase in its road construction is an important task; and in the following Three-Year Action Plan, it would focus on rural road construction so as to basically realize the full coverage of rural roads nationwide by 2020.[9] Therefore, focusing on non-urban road construction projects in India is both representative and realistic. From the perspective of project implementation sites, Madhya Pradesh and Gujarat have similar situations in road construction. As India's second largest state, Madhya Pradesh's economic growth rate reached 19.7% in 2017.[10] In the meantime, rural population accounts for 70% of the whole population in Madhya Pradesh and agriculture is its leading industry. Hence, road connection in its rural areas plays a key role in promoting the local economic development and poverty eradication. Similarly, Gujarat is an important industrial city in India, with an economic growth rate of about 10% in the past three years.[11] However, while leading the industrial development,

---

[9]Government of India, Planning Commission. "Twelfth Five Year Plan 2012–17". *New Delhi* (2012). URL: http://planningcommission.gov.in/plans/planrel/12thplan/pdf/12fyp_vol1.pdf; Government of India, "Three Year Action Agenda 2017–18 to 2019–20". *New Delhi* (2017). URL: http://niti.gov.in/writereaddata/files/coop/ActionPlan.pdf.
[10]PRS Legislative Research. "Madhya Pradesh Budget Analysis 2018–19". URL: http://www.prsindia.org/parliamenttrack/state-budgets/madhya-pradesh-budget-analysis-2018-19-5135/.
[11]PRS Legislative Research. "Gujarat Budget Analysis 2018–19". URL: http://www.prsindia.org/parliamenttrack/state-budgets/gujarat-budget-analysis-2018-19-5111/.

Gujarat still has nearly 60% rural population, which means that the relatively backward rural road construction has become a major obstacle to its economic development.

Secondly, the two cases selected in this section are representative and comparable in terms of project content and operation modes. From the perspective of project time, both projects represent the two banks' mature project management and operation modes. For example, the Gujarat project was implemented in August 2017 by the AIIB, which had more project management experience than most other projects carried out in its founding year. From the perspective of project areas, both are non-urban road construction projects implemented by Indian provincial governments and multilateral banks. Among them, the Madhya Pradesh project of the ADB is its first regional road project in India, which is of pioneering significance. From the perspective of project funds, the amount of the two projects is similar (AIIB invested US $329 million while ADB US $350 million), and both projects were independently financed by banks. In addition, the Gujarat project is also one of a few independent financing projects by the AIIB, which means that the AIIB can fully display and implement its management ideas. Finally, the two project implementation areas have a certain foundation in road construction. For instance, thanks to the Prime Minister's Rural Road Planning, or PMGSY, 98% villages and towns with a population of more than 500 in Gujarat have realized road coverage. The ADB also carried out provincial highway construction projects in Madhya Pradesh earlier on. Therefore, the two projects selected in this section are similar in operation difficulty. In view of this, this section selects the above two projects for case analysis. Table 5.4 summarizes the basic information of the projects of the AIIB and the ADB.

4. In-depth Comparative Analysis of the Two Cases

In this part, we make an in-depth comparative analysis of the two project cases of the AIIB and the ADB from the aspects of the projects' management structure, procurement, economy, risk, and safeguards and supervision, aiming to summarize their respective characteristics and internal logic deduction. The reasons for choosing these five aspects are as follows.

Table 5.4: Basic information of the projects of the AIIB and the ADB.

Project name	Gujarat rural roads (MMGSY) project	Madhya Pradesh district connectivity sector project
Borrower	India	India
Project executing agency	Gujarat government/Roads and Construction Department	Madhya Pradesh government
Project objectives	The project aims to improve the road traffic capacity by building all-weather rural roads in 4,000 villages in 33 regions of Gujarat.	The project aims to improve the road traffic capacity by maintaining and upgrading the regional roads of about 1,600 km in Madhya Pradesh
Project implementation time	From 1 August 2017 to 30 June 2019	From November 2014 to April 2018
Project expenses	US $658 million	US $500 million
Financing program	AIIB: US $329 million Gujarat government: US $329 million	ADB: US $350 million Madhya Pradesh government: US $150 million
Bank's lending terms	The term of the loan is 13 years, including a 5-year grace period. The loan can be repaid according to the bank's base rate based on sovereign guaranteed loans	The term of the loan is 25 years, including a 5-year grace period. The annual interest rate is subject to LIBOR and 0.15% commission fee is charged
Joint financing	No	No
Environmental and social rating	Environmental and social rating: B	Environmental rating: B Involuntary immigration rating: B Indigenous rating: C
Project risk level (low, medium, high)	Medium	Medium
Main contents of the project	(1) Construction and upgrading of non-planned road (NPR) (2) Upgrading of planned road (PR) (3) Technical assistance (4) Application of innovative technology	(1) Reconstruction and repair of regional roads to meet all-weather and road safety standards (2) Improvement of the level of road maintenance and asset management

First of all, as the core content of project management, the organizational structure of project management is becoming the "secret" for project managers to achieve overall planning (Alie, 2015). Whether or not the project management structure is scientifically and effectively formulated not only directly affects all aspects of the project implementation process but also will manifest itself in the evaluation of project performance.

The second aspect is the procurement policies of projects. Many studies have already discussed the important impact of procurement process and related policies on the performance of construction projects through case studies and other methods (Eriksson and Westerberg, 2009; Khisa, 2015; Laby *et al.*, 2016). Compared with other types of projects, road construction projects are more complex and uncertain, and there is a large demand for procurement of civil engineering and other materials. Therefore, project procurement policies have become the core intermediate link affecting the costs and the implementation efficiency of road construction projects. At the same time, project procurement policies can better reflect the openness and internationalization of multilateral development banks.

The third is the economic analysis of projects. Project economic analysis measures the economic sustainability of a project, and systematically evaluates and predicts the expected return of the project. It is an important reference index for commercial multilateral development banks to decide on investment. Effective integration of resources and economic and feasible suggestions for project decision-making are conducive to improving the efficiency of project implementation and avoiding uncertainty and risks.[12] Therefore, for a road construction project with high uncertainty, it is very important to formulate a set of thorough and appropriate project economic analysis in the early stage of the project.

The fourth is the risk analysis of projects. Project risk analysis provides a set of systematic evaluation indicators and avoidance measures for project implementation and is an important means to ensure the orderly implementation of all the aspects of a project (Lavanya *et al.*, 2008). At the same time, a bank's preference for project risk content and risk type can reflect its governance ideas.

The last aspect is the analysis of project safeguards and supervision system. Project safeguards assess the potential impact of the project on local society and environment and ensure the sustainability of the project

---

[12]URL: https://www.adb.org/data/economic-research-initiatives/economic-analysis-projects.

by preventing or reducing negative effects through institutional design (IEG, 2010). As a means of guaranteeing the quality and efficiency of project implementation, project supervision system involves many aspects of project implementation, such as project fund supervision, compliance supervision, quality supervision, social and environmental supervision, and so on, so its importance is self-evident. By providing a set of solutions to the problems, project supervision system can realize the risk management of the project implementation so as to improve the project performance (Baum, 1982; Kilby, 1995; AfDB, 2010). Due to the large number of contractors and suppliers with different responsibilities at all levels in infrastructure projects, a set of systematic and mature supervision system can effectively integrate resources and ensure the compliance of project implementation progress and quality. In addition, due to the flexibility and subjectivity of the project safeguards and supervision system, the analysis of the system can systematically reflect a bank's hidden preference for values.

4.1 *Analysis of project management structure*

As a framework design, project management structure is very important for the management and operation of loan projects, and can also better reveal the corporate governance and project operation modes of multilateral development banks, the in-depth research on which is thus helpful to better understand those banks' concepts and styles. As for the cases of this section, the AIIB and the ADB's arrangements of their project executing agencies and their responsibility frameworks are as follows (Table 5.5).

Generally speaking, the two projects are similar in project management structure. The main executing agency of the AIIB's project is the Road Construction Department of Gujarat, assisted by a project management consultant. As one of the government agencies in Gujarat, the Road Construction Department of Gujarat has experience in cooperation with international financial institutions including the World Bank and also has sufficient professional staffing and project management capacity. The executing agency of the ADB's project is the government of Madhya Pradesh and is represented by the Madhya Pradesh Road Development Corporation (MPRDC). As a large state-owned enterprise, the MPRDC has a close relationship with the local government — the government's chief minister is at the same time a member of the board of directors of the MPRDC — and has cooperated with the ADB for three times and is

Table 5.5:   Comparison of the project executing agencies and responsibility frameworks between AIIB and ADB.

Variables	AIIB	ADB
Project executing agency	Gujarat Road and Construction Department	Madhya Pradesh Road Development Company
Nature of the project executing agency	Government agency	State-owned enterprise
Responsibilities of the project executing agency	It is responsible for coordinating the project implementation and assigning a project management consultant to assist in the project management and provide daily technical support, including subproject selection, supervision of the project process, review of the project reports, etc.	It is responsible for coordinating the procurement, management, progress, financial report of the project, safeguards supervision, staff assignment, etc.
Management mode of the project executing agency	Flattening	Flattening
Duties of the bank	It conducts regular on-the-spot investigation to ensure that the project progress is in line with the expected planning	It is responsible for supervising and examining the environmental impact, resettlement, procurement and payment, budget allocation and other aspects of the project

quite familiar with the project process and implementation standards of the ADB, which inclines this project to choose it again (ADB, 2014). In addition, the two management modes of the two projects are flat. They are divided into several parallel project groups according to the project requirements, which is conducive to improving the administrative efficiency and ensuring the project progress.

As for the bank's responsibilities, the ADB defines its own responsibilities in the project more clearly and specifically, involving the core areas of the project such as environmental and social safeguards, project procurement and payment, financial budget, etc., and sets deadlines in each stage of the project. On the contrary, the AIIB only generally describes its own responsibilities, stipulating in the project documents that it will conduct regular on-the-spot investigations to ensure that the project progress is in line with the expected plan but not specifying the investigation contents and the time arrangements.

To sum up, the project management structure of the AIIB is characterized by diversity and openness. Comparatively speaking, the project management structure of the ADB is more centralized and specific.

4.2 *Project procurement analysis*

For multilateral development banks, whether or not the project procurement can be carried out economically and effectively not only affects the project costs, but also affects whether or not the expected benefits of the project can be fully obtained. For example, the project procurement policy of the AIIB is closely related to one of its construction objectives, that is, being "clean". Therefore, the analysis of project procurement policy and related systems is of great research value. In the two cases of this section, the arrangements of project procurement by the AIIB and the ADB are as follows (Table 5.6).

The analysis of project procurement mainly involves three aspects: procurement scales, procurement methods and procurement procedure. In general, the AIIB's procurement policy follows the institutional tradition of other multilateral financial institutions (Górski, 2016). By comparing the AIIB's project and that of ADB, it is found that they are generally similar in terms of project procurement. In addition, the ADB has a set of detailed procurement policies and procedures in its official procurement guidelines. Comparatively speaking, the system design of the AIIB in each stage of its project procurement is simplified. For instance, in terms

Table 5.6:   Comparison of the project procurement between AIIB and ADB.

Variables	AIIB	ADB
Content of procurement	goods, construction, consulting services	goods, construction, consulting services
Number of procurement contracts	1,400+	20+
Scale of procurement amount	The contract amount of a single project ranges from US $80,000 to US $3 million.	US $400 million
Method of procurement	– International competitive bidding (ICB) – National competitive bidding (NCB) – Quality and cost based selection (QCBS) – N-procure electronic bidding platform	– International competitive bidding (ICB) – National competitive bidding (NCB) – Quality and cost based selection (QCBS) 80:20
Procurement procedure	(1) Approval of the procurement contents and amount by the Road and Construction Department (2) Technical approval (3) Drafting bidding documents (4) Bidders' confirming the bidding through the N-procure electronic platform after the bidding announcement is issued (5) Opening the bid and announcing the results	(1) Preparing bidding contracts (2) Pre-examining bidders' qualifications (3) Preparing bidding documents (4) Opening the bid (5) Evaluating the bid (6) Awarding contracts

of the scope of application of the procurement policy, all goods, construction, non-consulting services and consulting services in the AIIB's project adopt the same set of procurement policy. The ADB, on the other hand, treats consulting services separately from other services such as goods, engineering and non-consulting services, adopting two different sets of procurement standards and methods.

Specifically speaking, there are some differences between the two banks in terms of procurement scales, procurement methods and procurement procedure. First of all, the number of procurement contracts and the capital scale of the AIIB's project are larger than those of the ADB's project. According to the project delivery report, the AIIB's project involves nearly 1,400 engineering contracts, of which the amount of a single project contract ranges from US $80,000 to US $3 million. However, compared with ADB's more open and detailed procurement information, the AIIB lacks a detailed narrative of the number and amount of its procurement contracts. Secondly, the selection and standard of procurement methods are similar: their procurement of goods and construction is carried out through international competitive bidding and national competitive bidding, while the procurement of consulting services is conducted according to the principle of "selection based on quality and costs", giving consideration to both service quality and costs. In the international competitive bidding, the AIIB conducts global procurement, not being limited to the procurement of member countries. The difference between the two banks is that the ADB has set a clear standard for service quality and cost (80:20), whereas the AIIB's allocation of specific weight in this regard is relatively vague. Besides, in the procurement process, the ADB has more stringent screening criteria for bidders, adding a pre-examination of bidders' qualifications to ensure that the bidding invitations are only sent to bidders with sufficient capacity and resources. Comparatively speaking, the system design of the AIIB in the procurement process is more open. Finally, the AIIB's project adopts the "N-procure" electronic bidding platform to realize the informatization of the whole bidding process, which is innovative and is conducive to improving procurement efficiency, enhancing transparency, and informatization supervision. To sum up, the AIIB's project procurement policy intensively displays its construction objectives — being lean, green, and clean.

4.3 *Project economic analysis*

The cost-benefit analysis and economic risk assessment of a project determine whether or not the project has economic feasibility and sustainability, and are also basic factors on which whether multilateral development banks grant loans is based. In the long run, sound and reasonable project economic indicators and economic risk assessment play an important role in influencing the banks' decision on long-term sufficient and stable financing. Therefore, the project economic analysis is of great significance for understanding the governance ideas of multilateral development banks. The project economic analysis of the AIIB and the ADB is shown in Table 5.7.

In this case, the core of project economic analysis is the analysis of the economic benefits and sensitivity of the projects. Among them, the introduction of the forecast of road traffic analysis is conducive to more

Table 5.7:   Comparison of the project economy and risks between AIIB and ADB.

	AIIB	ADB
Road traffic analysis		
Forecast of future average traffic growth rate	√	√
Calculation of traffic growth rate	×	√
Provincial motor vehicle registration growth	×	√
Project costs		
Capital expenditure	√	√
Road maintenance expenditure	√	√
Project benefits		
Passengers save time and cost	√	√
Vehicles save operation costs	√	√
Agricultural output increases	√	×
Project sensitivity analysis		
Economic internal rate of return (EIRR)	√	√
Subproject internal rate of return (EIRR)	×	√
Project net present value (NPV)	√	√
Conversion value test	×	√
Government revenue and expenditure in recent 5 years	√	×
Project budget allocation	√	×

accurate evaluation of project costs. In terms of research methods, both projects evaluate the economic benefits and risks by quantifying the different situations "with project" and "without project".[13] Table 5.7 shows more directly the specific analysis contents of the two projects.

4.3.1 *Traffic flow analysis and forecasts*

In the evaluation of the traffic of the project construction section, the AIIB classifies the vehicles more carefully and calculates the traffic frequency of eight kinds of vehicles in different road sections. However, the ADB only divides vehicles into "carrying people" and "carrying goods", the classification standard being relatively simple.

In addition, both banks calculate the future average traffic growth rate, but their research methods are different. The AIIB estimates that the traffic growth rate of the project implementation section would be 8–10% in 2017–2020, 7–8% in 2021–2025, and 5–7% after 2026, believing that the traffic growth rate would decrease with time. The ADB, on the other hand, merely predicates that the local traffic growth rate would be 6.5%. However, the AIIB does not explain the calculation method and data source of the growth rate, whereas the ADB synthetically calculates the future traffic growth rate of the project construction road by analyzing the economic growth rate of the province, the number of the motor vehicles registered and the government road construction planning data. Therefore, in terms of data sources, the ADB's information transparency is higher.

4.3.2 *Project income analysis*

The cost structure of the two projects is the same, including capital expenditure and road maintenance expenditure. In terms of project income, the AIIB incorporates the agricultural output growth brought by the road improvement into the calculation scope of the project income, and calculates the expected conservative income based on the local prices.

---

[13] In the evaluation of the situations "with project", the evaluator suggests the predicative value for future growth index based on the local data over the past years, and quantifies it as the project economic income according to the local price level. The evaluation of the situations "without project" only needs to calculate the economic benefits brought by the local natural development trend. This method can measure the economic benefits of the project accurately by quantitative analysis.

Compared with the ADB, the AIIB adopts a more simplified and single calculation method for the project income. Take the calculation of passengers' reduction in time cost as an example. Merely by calculating the annual per capita GDP/hour of Gujarat, the AIIB concludes that the average time cost saved by passengers is 38.72 rupees/hour, which is used to calculate the project income. By contrast, the ADB calculates the hourly labor income of passengers taking buses (47.67 rupees/hour), cars (70 rupees/hour), and tricycles (40 rupees/hour) respectively, and then calculates the final income of the project according to the weight of the three vehicles. Comparatively speaking, the ADB's calculation method of passenger time cost is more scientific.

4.3.3 *Project sensitivity analysis*

Both banks test the sensitivity of their projects according to the EIRR and the NPV through hypothesis tests. On this basis, the ADB also adds the calculation of project switching value (Table 5.8).

Table 5.8:   Comparison of the project sensitivity between AIIB and ADB.

	AIIB (overall data of the project)		ADB (subproject data)		
	EIRR (%)	NPV (million)	EIRR (%)	NPV (million)	Switching Value (%)
Base	15.8	11,350	15.64	142.84	/
Increase in capital investment by 10%	14.5	8,135	/	/	/
Increase in road maintenance investment by 10%	14.6	7,647	/	/	/
Increase in total costs by 10%	/	/	14.22	93.83	29.1
Decrease in total revenue by 10%	13.1	3,297	14.08	79.54	22.6
Simultaneous changes in benefits and costs by 10%	/	/	12.74	30.53	(12.7)
One-year's delay in the completion of the project	13.5	5,020	14.09	87.31	/

Note: The reference discount rate of NPV is 12%, and the currency unit is Indian rupees (RS).

In terms of the overall data of the two projects, the EIRR of the AIIB's project is 15.8% and that of the ADB's project is 20.02%, both of which exceed the minimum standard of 12% of the two banks and thus have high investment value. Among them, the change in the AIIB's project cost (i.e. capital investment and road maintenance investment) has little impact on the economic benefits of the project, but 10% reduction in total income has the greatest negative impact on the project income.

Different from the overall analysis of the AIIB, the ADB conducts sensitivity tests on the four subprojects respectively and the test conditions are more stringent. Apart from making the same analysis as the AIIB, the ADB also adds the test condition of benefits and costs simultaneous changing by 10%. Table 5.8 records the data of "Chitrangi-Kasar Road", a subproject with the highest unit construction cost and the lowest EIRR. Because the initial EIRR of this subproject is similar to that of the AIIB's project, they can be compared to some extent. As shown in Table 5.8, when the benefits and costs change by 10% at the same time, the impact on the project income reaches the maximum, but it is still higher than the minimum standard of 12% set by the bank. Moreover, when the benefits and costs change by 10% respectively and the project is delayed for one year, the sensitivity of the ADB's subproject is lower than that of the AIIB's project. Therefore, based on the analysis of this part, this section believes that the sensitivity evaluation standard of the project by the ADB is more stringent from the perspective of economic risk analysis, so the economic stability may be higher.

4.3.4 *Project risk analysis*

According to the project characteristics, project risk is divided into three parts: public financial management, project procurement, and project safeguards. The following table directly shows the similarities and differences between the two banks in terms of the contents and evaluation standards of project risks. In Table 5.9, "/" indicates that this item is empty.

Both of the two banks assess the comprehensive risk of their projects as "medium" and both carry out risk assessment on the main contents of the projects. Specifically, except for the risk assessment of project safeguards being the same, there are some differences between the two banks in the risk assessment of public financial management and project procurement. The ADB covers more types of risks, especially in public

Table 5.9:   Comparison of project risk assessment between AIIB and ADB.

	AIIB	ADB
Risk description	Risk assessment	
Public financial management		
Public financial management	/	Low
Capital flow	/	Low
Reduction in project importance and limited sources of funds	/	Low
The local economy being in serious recession	/	Low
Executive ability of the project implementation agency	Low	Low
Delay in payment	Medium	Low
Project procurement		
Delay in bidding and procurement	Medium	Medium
Transparency of the bidding process	Medium	Low
Bidders' lack of interest in project engineering	/	Medium
Project safeguards		
Lack of quality supervision	Medium	Medium
Environmental and social impacts of the project	Medium	Medium
Comprehensive risk assessment of the project	Medium	Medium

financial management, such as making a more detailed risk assessment of the local political and business environment and project capital flow. In contrast, the risk assessment by the AIIB is more concise while retaining the main contents of the project, mainly involving project safeguards and procurement. This may also have something to do with the idea of being "lean" that the AIIB claims to achieve.

4.3.5 *Analysis of project safeguards and supervision*

Project safeguards and corresponding supervision and evaluation systems are important factors to ensure the smooth implementation of the project as scheduled. Among them, the project safeguards and supervision measures are complementary and interrelated, which can best reflect the governance ideas and value systems of the two banks conveyed through the projects. Therefore, this part compares the project safeguards and the project supervision framework at the same time.

Table 5.10 summarizes the project safeguards and the corresponding measures of the AIIB and the ADB.

The safeguard policies of the two projects mainly involve environmental safeguard and social safeguard, and there are similar arrangements

Table 5.10: Comparison of project safeguard contents and measures between AIIB and ADB.

Safeguard contents	Bank		Specific measures
Environmental safeguards			
Assessment and management of environmental impact	AIIB	√	Formulating environmental and social management framework (ESMF) and specific management schemes based on different categories
	ADB	√	Formulating environmental management plan (EMP) and environmental assessment and review framework (EARF)
Supervision of environmental impact	AIIB	×	/
	ADB	√	Formulating environmental monitoring plan (EMOP)
Protection of natural resources	AIIB	×	/
	ADB	√	Obtaining the approval of the forest and wildlife protection agency before the construction of the project
Climate change	AIIB	√	Taking into account the potential impacts of climate change in the design of the project
	ADB	×	/
Public health and safety	AIIB	√	Considering the dust, noise and other side effects of road construction, and promoting the local residents and contractors to jointly discuss solutions
	ADB	√	Monitoring soil erosion, water quality, air and other indicators related to public health through EMOP
In total	AIIB	Three items	
	ADB	Four items	

(Continued)

Table 5.10:   (*Continued*)

Safeguard contents	Bank		Specific measures
			Social safeguards
Land acquisition, resettlement and compensation	AIIB	×	/
	ADB	√	Formulating resettlement-policy framework (RF) within the ADB safeguard policy framework
Indigenous people	AIIB	√	Including the assessment and management of indigenous people in the safeguard policy
	ADB	√	Formulating an indigenous people's resettlement plan
Sex	AIIB	×	/
	ADB	√	Giving priority to local women in recruitment and training
Labor standards	AIIB	×	/
	ADB	√	Ensuring all labor contracts are in accordance with local laws and implementing them
Appeal mechanism	AIIB	√	Setting up an appeal bureau at the township level and district level respectively to deal with different complaints at different levels
	ADB	√	Establishing a hierarchical appeal system to receive anti-corruption, abuse, fraud and other appeals related to the implementation of the project from the public
In total	AIIB	Two items	
	ADB	Five items	

in specific safeguard measures. However, it is not difficult to find that the two banks have different preferences. The ADB's classification of safeguard policies is more detailed and its corresponding safeguard measures are more specific. For example, the ADB adds regulatory measures for the environmental assessment of the project, which are responsible for monitoring the environmental quality related to public health such as drinking water, air, noise, soil, and so on. It also clarifies in the specific measures the responsibilities of and relationships among the project executing agency, the contractors, and the environmental consulting experts in the specific implementation of environmental protection policies. In the field of social safeguard, the ADB covers five items, adding policies and measures for gender sensitivity and labor standards. For example, in road design and personnel recruitment, women's rights and interests should be guaranteed to the maximum extent, all labor contracts should be in line with the local laws and regulations, and the specific implementation of labor contracts should be supervised. In contrast, the AIIB's project safeguard framework is more simplified, focusing on the safeguard contents directly related to the project. Figure 5.9 shows the institutional framework of project supervision between the AIIB and the ADB.

As shown in Figure 5.9, the supervision measures of the AIIB project are composed of five aspects, while the supervision measures of the ADB's project are carried out in three aspects. According to their functions, the role of the "project result framework" of the AIIB is similar to that of the "project performance monitoring" of the ADB. They are listed as the first layers. The "project compliance monitoring" of the ADB equals the integration of the "quality supervision system", "bank supervision" and "project management consultation" of the AIIB. They are listed as the second layers. In addition, the "electronic supervision system" of the AIIB and the "project safeguard monitoring" of the ADB have their own characteristics, which are listed as the third layers.

The first layer of monitoring system records the implementation data and performance indicators of each stage of the project so as to monitor

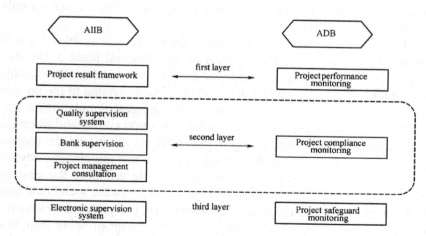

Figure 5.9:   Comparison of the project regulatory institutional frameworks between AIIB and ADB.

the project's implementation progress. The implementing agency of the ADB's project obtains the feedback of the project progress information by formulating annual evaluation questionnaire. The AIIB's project realizes the information supervision of the whole process of the project implementation through the electronic supervision system.

The second layer monitoring system mainly involves the quality monitoring and financial audit of the project. The AIIB pays more attention to the quality monitoring of the project implementation, while the ADB pays more attention to the compliance of the project funds. For example, the AIIB independently sets up a quality supervision system and tries to ensure the project quality meeting the specifications through the three-tier quality inspection institutions from top to bottom. On the other hand, the ADB ensures the use of the funds by the project borrowers being in accordance with the loan agreements through mid-term project review.

The third layer monitoring system reflects the different preferences and characteristics of the two banks. The electronic supervision system developed by the AIIB realizes the real-time supervision of project engineering and financial situation. The engineers of each construction site can upload the photos of the project progress in real time, and the road construction department can timely understand and adjust the specific scheme of the project so as to speed up the implementation efficiency of the project. Different from the AIIB, the ADB focuses on project safeguards and formulates detailed and specific regulatory policies in the areas of environmental safeguard, social safeguard, and women's rights and interests protection.

The above comprehensive analysis of the project safeguard and supervision can clearly reveal the different preferences and ideas of the two banks. The AIIB pays more attention to the efficiency and quality of project implementation, as well as the contents directly related to the project implementation progress, such as financial management and climate factors. For example, the hierarchical quality inspection system and informatization monitoring system set up by the AIIB are all around the project quality and efficiency. Informatization operation has the obvious advantages of being convenient and transparent while reducing the cost of information. Moreover, the AIIB weakens its output in the social field and adopts a relatively streamlined and centralized project governance system. To sum up, the AIIB not only implements its concept of being lean, but also helps to improve the performance level of the project. In contrast, the ADB focuses on the use of project funds and diversified project safeguards. For instance, the ADB's project safeguards involve relatively complex social safeguard contents such as the resettlement of indigenous people, women's rights and interests, and NGO's participation. This reflects that the ADB's project also has a strong preference for the so-called "good governance" values and the output of corresponding social effects in addition to project construction. However, the corresponding policies reflecting the ADB's values also result in cumbersome administrative processes and high implementation costs.

According to the above comparative analysis of the two projects in terms of management structure, procurement, economy, risk, safeguard and supervision, this section summarizes the characteristics and styles of the two banks in different aspects of the project (Table 5.11).

Table 5.11: Comprehensive comparison of the project characteristics between AIIB and ADB.

Variables	AIIB	ADB
Project management structure	Pluralism and openness	More concentrated and specific
Project procurement	Having a large scale of procurement; realizing the informatization platform operation of the whole process of project procurement	More specific and open procurement information; more stringent selection criteria in procurement process
Project economic analysis	Covering the main contents involved and making an overall analysis of the sensitivity of the project	Higher information transparency of project economic benefits, relatively stricter evaluation standard of project sensitivity, and stronger economic stability of the project
Project risks	Relatively simple contents of risk assessment	Covering a wide range of risks
Project safeguard and supervision	Paying more attention to the efficiency and quality of project implementation	More attention to the use of project funds and social safeguard contents with values preference

5. Conclusion

By selecting representative project cases of the AIIB and the ADB, this section sorts out and compares the policy frameworks and operation modes of the two banks in terms of project management structure, procurement, economy, risk, safeguard and supervision, and so on. This section holds that the institutional design and operation mode of the AIIB's project are in line with the international norms of the existing multilateral development banks and reveal its concept of simplification and pragmatism. Moreover, the AIIB's policy on project safeguard and supervision clearly reflects its preference for the quality and efficiency of project implementation, resulting in weakening other contents with additional administrative costs brought by values preference. Furthermore, compared with the ADB, the AIIB scales down the links in project procurement and risk analysis but covers the main evaluation indicators directly related to project performance.

To sum up, on the basis of conforming to the international norms, the AIIB has the characteristics of openness, internationality, economic sustainability and higher project performance. It is a reformed version of the ADB.

Based on the above comparative analysis, this section proposes the following suggestions on the future planning of the AIIB project implementation. First, while continuing to implement its concept of simplification and pragmatism, the AIIB should strengthen the openness and transparency of the project implementation information. For example, up to now, the AIIB has failed to announce the information such as the contents and amount of project procurement and bidding, which is likely to incline the outside world to question the transparency and integrity of its project implementation. Second, it should strengthen the implementation of its "green" concept. In this case, the utilization of paperless office is one of the highlights of the AIIB project implementation, which reflects the bank's concern about its two major goals of being green and clean. In the long run, the AIIB should actively implement the green concept in more aspects of the project and form an institutionalized model that can be followed as soon as possible. Third, a set of systematic and institutionalized policy framework and institutional standards should be formulated as soon as possible. Compared with the ADB's mature and integrated system, the institutional design and evaluation criteria of the AIIB in terms of project procurement and supervision are too scattered, not systematic and coherent enough. In the future, the AIIB should further improve the construction of monitoring and evaluation systems, strengthen the top-level design, and improve the level of standardized system construction.

Section 4. International Cooperative Governance: A Global Governance Perspective — Cooperation between G20 and DWG

1. Background of Development Working Group (DWG) and Its Financial Inclusion Field

1.1 *Background of financial inclusion*

The Great Recession triggered by the US financial crisis in 2008 can be said to be the deepest, longest and most extensive crisis since the Great Depression. The impact of the crisis was far beyond the expectations of experts and policy makers, especially in its early stage, when most views believed that the subprime crisis would only be limited to countries and regions with more subprime products, such as the US and some Western European countries. However, with the rapid spread of the crisis, experts and policy makers gradually realized that the Great Depression would repeat itself unless effective, forceful and globally coordinated intervention was conducted. Therefore, at the end of 2008, the US proposed to hold a meeting of central bank governors and finance ministers from 20 countries to jointly discuss strategies for coping with the financial crisis for the first time, and finally upgraded it to the G20 Summit.

Although the G20 was born in a period of financial crisis, its function has evolved from a financial crisis response platform at the early stage to a long term coordination platform for economic growth and global development with the global economy gradually being out of recession. At the G20 Summit in 2009, the leaders of its members announced that the G20's goals are realizing strong, sustainable and balanced growth and improving the living standards of emerging market and developing countries.[14] Subsequently, at the Summit in 2010 in Toronto, it confirmed again and

---

[14]The G20 Seoul Summit Leaders' Declaration. URL: http://online.wsj.com/public/resources/documents/G20COMMUN1110.pdf.

emphasized that development should be put in the G20 agenda as an important issue, and it stated that "narrowing the development gap and reducing poverty are integral to achieving our broader framework objectives of strong, sustainable and balanced growth by generating new poles of growth and contributing to global rebalancing".[15]

The Toronto Summit made clear the importance of development, and then the G20 Seoul Summit in 2010 specified it. As a representative of the East-Asia miracle, Korea realized the transformation from a developing country to a developed country within a generation, therefore, the establishment of the G20 DWG in Korea would help to enhance its legitimacy. At the Seoul Summit, based on the Seoul Development Consensus for Shared Growth and the Multi-Year Action Plan on Development, the DWG established guidelines for its work, which contain six core principles and nine key areas, including financial inclusion. Although the working areas of the DWG have undergone several adjustments since then, the status of financial inclusion as one of its key areas has never changed.

1.2 *Evolution of overseas remittances and Global Partnership for Financial Inclusion (GPFI)*

Although the G20 is an important forum for dialogue between traditional developed countries and emerging economies, the emerging economies in theG20 are basically middle-income countries and above. The financial systems of these countries are not among the least developed, and their residents also enjoy basic financial resources. However, according to World Bank estimates, more than 2 billion adults are excluded from formal financial systems, and millions of micro and small and medium enterprises face severe financial constraints and have difficulty in obtaining formal financial resources. Most of these individuals and enterprises are located in countries that are not G20 members.[16] Given the importance of the availability of financial resources for the economic development and living standards of families, businesses and countries, how to help these groups that are excluded from formal financial systems has become an important global development issue, not just for G20 members.

---

[15] G20 2010. DWG URL: https://g20.org/about-g20/past-summits/2010-seoul/.
[16] Seoul Development Consensus for Shared Growth, 2010. URL: http://www.g20dwg.org/documents/#ul_t_1.

At the Seoul Summit, the DWG made three action plans for financial inclusion, which laid the foundation for the following work. First of all, the DWG decided to launch the GPFI in November 2010 as an inclusive platform to promote inclusive finance and at the same time to strengthen its cooperation with the Alliance for Financial Inclusion, the International Finance Corporation (the private business unit of the World Bank), and other platforms. Secondly, the finance challenge faced by small and medium enterprises (SMEs) is also one of the concerns of the DWG. Considering that the lack of financial resources of the SMEs in developing countries has seriously restricted the economic development and the improvement of living standards, the Seoul Summit selected 14 winning SME financing challenge projects as its financial innovation models for promotion. Finally, the Financial Inclusion Action Plan was developed based on the G20 Principles for Innovative Inclusion. These include the establishment of the Standard Setting Bodies to further strengthen the integration of financial inclusion and financial innovation principles so as to prevent inappropriate financial innovation. In addition, at the Seoul Summit, the issue of overseas remittances was also mentioned. Although it was not listed as a separate field, its importance as one of the two actions in the field of Growth with Resilience can be seen. The Summit proposed that the existing multilateral financial institutions should take the lead to coordinate the implementation of the General Principles for International Remittance Services by the G20 and non-G20 members in the Global Remittances Working Group.[17]

The G20 Summit in Cannes, France in 2011 further strengthened the importance of financial inclusion and overseas remittances as part of achieving strong, sustainable and balanced growth, especially overseas remittances. For the first time, the issue of overseas remittances was proposed by the DWG as a separate area of work. According to the report, overseas remittances are particularly important to the economic well-being of families in low-income countries: if the cost of cross-border remittances can be reduced by 5% (relative rather than absolute), the income of families in the receiving countries will be additionally increased by US $15 billion, which is very significant and direct welfare improvement. Therefore, the DWG should urge G20 countries to play a

[17]The G20 Seoul Summit Leaders' Declaration. URL: https://www.oecd.org/g20/summits/seoul/G20-Seoul-Summit-Leaders-Declaration.pdf; The Seoul Summit Document. URL: https://www.oecd.org./gzo/summits/seoul/Seoul-Summit-Document.pdf.

greater role in reducing the cost of overseas remittances, because more than 50% of cross-border remittances come from or flow to G20 countries. Moreover, the Cannes DWG also suggested that the World Bank should play a role in monitoring and assessing the cost of overseas remittances so as to effectively reduce it. It also agreed to further promote and support the business of GPFI. There are several points that deserve particular attention. Firstly, the DWG reiterated the principle of promoting the innovation of financial inclusion by providing financial innovation models. Secondly, while concerning about the availability of financial resources for SMEs in low-income countries, special attention would be paid to the SMEs owned by female entrepreneurs and those related to agriculture. Finally, it would help governments to more scientifically formulate the implementation goals of financial inclusion and evaluate its implementation by integrating relevant resources and promoting and establishing cross-border measurement indicators and databases of financial resource accessibility.[18]

Although the G20 DWG in Los Cabos, Mexico in 2012 failed to include financial inclusion and overseas remittances into its three key areas, it continued to recognize their importance as part of the Multi-Year Action Plan on Development. The Los Cabos DWG did not continue the Cannes DWG's way of separating overseas remittances from finance. Instead, it referred to the Seoul Summit model and listed it as part of the Growth with Resilience area. It re-emphasized the importance of reducing the cost of overseas remittances to improve the welfare of low-income countries and families, and proposed that G20 members adopt the tool of reducing the cost of overseas remittances put forward by France, Australia and Italy at the 2011 Summit. It continued to suggest that the World Bank report to it every six months on the latest progress in reducing the cost of overseas remittances worldwide. In the area of financial inclusion, the DWG continued the practice of previous years and listed it as one of the main areas. It reiterated the importance of maintaining consistency between the Sub-group on Principles and Standard Setting Bodies (SSBs) and the Principles for Innovative Financial Inclusion. Additionally, the SSBs should be committed to serving as a "library" of financial innovation cases and best practices. In order to maintain the coordination

---

[18]Cannes Summit Final Declaration — Building Our Common Future: Renewed Collective Action for the Benefit of All. URL: http://www.g20.utoronto.ca/2011/2011-cannes-declaration-111104-en.html.

between the SSBs and the GPFI platform, the DWG assisted in hosting the global financial inclusion working conference hosted by the Bank for International Settlements on 29 October 2012. Moreover, in terms of the access to financial resources for SMEs, the DWG continued to emphasize strengthening the ties with the global partners in financial inclusion, especially with the SMEs related to agriculture and women entrepreneurs. Furthermore, it set up a data and assessment subgroup dedicated to establishing the G20 basic system of financial inclusion indicators so as to track the progress of countries in the world in achieving financial inclusion.[19]

In 2013, the DWG of St. Petersburg, Russia, combined financial inclusion with overseas remittances for the first time and included them in the five priority areas of development work. It continued the tradition of attaching importance to financial inclusion with overseas remittances for low and middle-income countries. It proposed two specific and key action plans. The first was to maintain its coordination with the GPFI and to promote financial inclusion from two specific aspects: making full use of the existing emerging financial instruments to help families in low-income countries get access to financial resources, such as electronic and mobile payment systems, and strengthening the financial knowledge reserve, education, and consumer protection of the low-income groups, especially the vulnerable groups like women, youths, and immigrants. The second plan was to accelerate financial innovation to reduce the cost of overseas remittances, especially the remittances to developing countries. The DWG also proposed to further strengthen the role of the G20 SME Forum in improving the financial accessibility of the SMEs in developing countries.[20]

In 2014, the DWG of Brisbane, Australia proposed for the first time for an accountability framework to supervise and track the completion of projects in various work areas. This framework effectively integrated the work of previous G20 development working groups. The report held that the DWG had begun to implement most of the announcements in the field of financial inclusion and overseas remittances, including implementing

---

[19]2012 Progress Report of the Development Working Group. URL: https://www.oecd.org/g20/summits/los-cabos/2012-0619-dwg.pdf.

[20]2013 St Petersburg Accountability Report G20-Development Commitments. URL: https://www.oecd.org/g20/summits/saint-petersburg/St-Petersburg-Accountability-Report-G20-Development-Commitments.pdf.

the recommendations of the GPFI, promoting financial education, identifying the barriers to the financial accessibility for women and youths, and establishing SME finance compact. In addition, in view of the fact that the target of reducing the rate of remittances to 5% at previous meetings had not been fully achieved, the DWG proposed that the GPFI should further explore the solutions at the technical level.[21]

In 2015, the DWG of Antalya, Turkey, continued the 2014 DWG's accountability framework and assigned each G20 member tasks on the completion of projects in various working areas in 2015. The annual report mainly included two aspects in the field of financial inclusion and overseas remittances. The first was to renew the commitment to reducing the cost of overseas remittances. In 2015, the governments of G20 members formulated the implementation plans to achieve the 5% target, and then the Markets and Payments System Subgroup under the GPFI would be responsible for supervision and tracking the progress. The second was to accelerate the promotion of the innovative programs to reduce the cost of overseas remittances and establish a "library" of innovative programs so as to provide knowledge reserves for the DWG to further reduce the cost of overseas remittances in the future.[22]

2. Progress of GPFI and Overseas Remittances

Given the importance of access to financial resources for SMEs and families, especially in developing countries, and given that the G20 Seoul Summit held that "narrowing the development gap and reducing poverty are integral to achieving our broader framework objectives of strong, sustainable and balanced growth by generating new poles of growth and contributing to global rebalancing", the GPFI platform was officially established at the G20 Summit in Seoul in 2010. The purpose of the GPFI is to provide "an inclusive platform for all G20 countries, interested non-G20 countries and relevant stakeholders to carry forward our work on financial inclusion". The meeting was co-hosted by Korea, France, and

[21]2014 G20 Brisbane The G20 and Global Development Agenda. URL: https://us.boell.org/sites/default/files/downloads/DWG_Mandate__4-14_1.pdf.
[22]G20 and Low Income Developing Countries Framework. URL: http://www.g20.utoronto.ca/summits/2015antalya.html; G20 Development Working Group — 2015 Annual Progress Report. URL: https://www.oecd.org/g20/topics/development/G20-Development-Working-Group-Annual-Progress-Report-2015.pdf.

Mexico, deciding to strengthen the cooperation with the Alliance for Financial Inclusion, the Consultative Group to Assist the Poor (CGAP) and the International Finance Corporation (IFC). At that year's meeting, the GPFI identified five major areas to report to the Leaders of the Summit. The first was to continue to implement the Principles for Innovative Inclusion, especially to promote the work of other countries by sorting out financial innovation models. The second was to propose establishing the SSBs and promote them to consider the GPFI White Paper and the case studies of five relevant countries in promoting financial inclusion so as to improve their standards and guidelines. The third was to establish the SME Finance Forum. The International Finance Corporation (IFC) of the World Bank would be responsible for the operation of the forum. The forum should pay special attention to the accessibility of financial resources for women entrepreneurs and young entrepreneurs. The fourth was to mobilize the funds, including donations and private venture capital, to participate in the operation of the SME Financial Forum to enhance its capital scale and operation mode. The fifth was to request the IMF to establish and strengthen the measurement and data of financial inclusion so as to effectively track the progress of the work and make cross-border comparisons. It also decided to set up three groups: the group of Financial Inclusion Principles and Engagement with the Standard-Setting Bodies, the group of SME Finance, and the group of Data and Measurement.[23]

In 2014, the work of the GPFI was further divided into ten major areas of work while retaining the three major areas of work from previous years.

(a) The SME forum:
  (1) To accelerate and replicate successful policy experience to G20 members;
  (2) To build the forum into a platform for sharing and publicizing the best practices of the global SMEs' financial development;
  (3) To improve the accessibility of financial resources through SME Finance Compact and SME Finance Initiative.

---

[23]The G20 Seoul Summit Leaders' Declaration. URL: https://www.oecd.org/g20/summits/seoul/G20-Seoul-Summit-Leaders-Declaration.pdf; The G20 Seoul Summit Leaders' Declaration. URL: https://www.oecd.org/g20/summits/seoul/Seoul-Summit-Document.pdf.

(b) Regulations and SSBs:
  (1) To improve the protection of financial inclusion and financial stability and integrity and consumers' rights and interests through the setting of standards;
  (2) To set financial inclusion and financial accessibility as one of the dimensions of financial institutions' evaluation and supervision.

(c) Financial consumer protection and financial literacy:
  (1) To protect consumers and improve their financial literacy by strengthening the functions and capacity of financial supervision departments;
  (2) To propose for the first time strengthening digital products and services to better supervise and protect consumers' rights and interests, identifying effective digital products, and improving financial literacy.

(d) Markets and payment system:
  (1) To help analyze and identify alternatives to the money transfer operator;
  (2) To reduce the cost of sending remittances;
  (3) To expand opportunities to improve financial inclusion through innovation.

In addition, the GPFI also determined to focus on innovation, women's economic empowerment, data assimilation, and cooperation with the private sector.

At the 2015 Turkey Summit, the GPFI summarized its work over the past years and reported to the Leaders of the Summit. The report recommendations are[24]:

(a) To call upon the Financial Stability Board and the relevant SSBs to continue to integrate financial inclusion in their work, strengthen their interaction with the GPFI, and give attention to emerging issues in financial inclusion of relevance to multiple SSBs.
(b) To call upon the Financial Stability Board and the relevant SSBs to participate in the work of the GPFI White Paper as well as the Global

---

[24]GPFI Report to the Leaders: G20 Summit, Antalya, 2015. URL: http://www.gpfi.org/publications/gpfi-report-leaders-g20-summit-antalya-2015.

SSBs and Financial Inclusion under the Chinese G20 Presidency in 2016.

(c) Considering the crucial role of SMEs for employment, investment, innovation and economic growth, to endorse the Joint Action Plan of the GPFI SME finance Sub-group and the IIWG which aims to promote financial markets infrastructure, as well as to expand the joint knowledge and policy agenda on Drivers and constraints for innovative SME finance policies and instruments, in particular with regard to digital finance, long term finance and the construction of the SME finance data.

(d) To consider the role and importance of dealing with the topic of youth entrepreneurship specifically, given global demographic developments and worldwide youth unemployment rates.

(e) To urge countries to address the recommendations of the new report on innovative approaches in agricultural finance which focuses on agricultural insurance, ICT solutions for agricultural finance, smallholder demand and agri-financing for women to promote access to finance in the agricultural sector.

(f) To stress the central role of private sector in financing smaller companies, including financial institutions, financial markets infrastructure providers, larger firms in supply/value chains, etc. To welcome the conversion of the SME Finance Forum into a global membership network. And to encourage the creation of strong public–private sector partnerships for setting priorities and implementing reforms to promote SME finance and financial inclusion in G20 and non-G20 countries.

(g) To call on G20 countries to strengthen their efforts to develop evidence-based policies and practices (based on existing G20 principles, guidelines and tools) aimed at improving the financial literacy of individuals and MSMEs and protecting them in their dealings with financial services in a changing and increasingly digital environment.

(h) Given the critical importance of global remittances in reducing poverty and enabling economic development in societies where it is particularly needed, to call upon all actors, including SSBs, regulatory and policy making authorities, banks, money transfer operators, and other remittances service providers, to ensure that the approach to the provisioning of remittances services is proportionate to the actual risks involved and that remittances are used as an on-ramp for the responsible use of other appropriate financial services.

3. Coordination between DWG and GPFI in Financial Inclusion and Overseas Remittances

From the analysis of the above two parts, we can see that the purposes of the DWG and the GPFI were not exactly the same at the initial stage of overseas remittances. The former focused on how to better let G20 countries help non-G20 countries — especially low-income countries — develop their economies, while the latter mainly aimed to improve the financial inclusion of G20 countries. However, with the recovery of the global economy, the focus of the G20 has shifted from economic growth to economic development. G20 Leaders have recognized the importance of non-G20 countries, especially low-income countries, to global economic recovery and sustainable economic growth. As a result, effective cooperation between the DWG and the GPFI has become more important and timely.

3.1 *DWG's coordination in financial inclusion and overseas remittances and its integration with UN 2030*

There is a consensus between G20 and non-G20 countries on the importance of the cost of sending remittances in family welfare, especially for residents in low-income countries. According to the World Bank's estimation, the current global average cost of sending overseas remittances is 10%. If it can be reduced by 5% (relative rather than absolute value), it will increase the income of the families in receiving countries by US $15 billion, which is very significant and direct welfare improvement. Article 10 of the UN 2030 Agenda emphasizes that by 2030, the transaction costs of migrant remittances should be reduced to less than 3% and remittance corridors with costs higher than 5% should be eliminated.[25] It means that the international community has reached a consensus on reducing the costs of sending remittances. However, due to the differences in the development level of various countries as well as the differences in various domestic interest demands, there are inconsistencies in the specific implementation by both G20 and non-G20 countries. Therefore, as one of the most important global economic governance mechanisms, the G20 is crucial in the overall coordination of the reform in the field

---

[25] UN 2030 Agenda. URL: https://sustainabledevelopment.un.org/post2015/transforming ourworld.

of overseas remittances. At present, it can try to coordinate by the following ways.

3.1.1 *To set up a cross-border platform of data, evaluation, and standards*

It is suggested that the DWG should take the lead to set up a global cross-border data platform for overseas remittance costs, including standard setting and long-term follow-up evaluation. The specific operation can be commissioned to related international organizations, such as the World Bank, because it has a lot of relevant research and talent support. Up to now, the international community has made a lot of assessment of the costs of overseas remittances, such as the average costs of overseas remittances in the international scope. However, the existing assessment is mainly limited to the global average value, lacking detailed cross-border and cross-time data. Therefore, in order to better track the efforts and achievements of countries and the international community in reducing the costs of overseas remittances, a detailed dynamic database of transnational data will be able to solve this problem. It is suggested that, by considering the Tax Working Group model, the DWG should cooperate with related international organizations to implement the "Working Group + 1 (international organization)" model and establish a unified standard and supervision system, so as to better monitor and track the achievements of the DWG and the GPFI in the implementation of G20 goals. In the long run, Article 10 of UN 2030 Agenda that the transaction costs of migrant remittances should be reduced to less than 3% can be better realized. In addition, as the 2030 Agenda suggested that any remittance corridors with costs higher than 5% should be eliminated and that the relevant legal system should be authorized by the international community and supervised by relevant international organizations, it also can guarantee the realization of the goal (Qureshi, 2014).

3.1.2 *Set up a case-study center*

It is suggested that the DWG should initiate the establishment of a case-study center for digital finance in reducing global costs. In recent years, with the popularity of the Internet in developed and developing countries, emerging Internet companies have made great progress in reducing the costs of remittances and transfer. For example, developed countries have made great progress in smart phone payment and the transfer cost has been reduced. However, some developing countries have also made remarkable achievements. For instance, the mobile payment system M-PESA in Kenya effectively reduces the costs of domestic transfer, especially makes it easier for some remote areas and low-income families to access financial resources, and greatly improves the convenience and economic welfare of low-income groups (Jack and Suri, 2011). However, due to the differences in economic development and national conditions of different countries, different countries do not have a systematic sample database when looking for models to follow. Moreover, until now, the relevant research of the GPFI has focused on the successful experiences and practices of G20 countries in relevant fields, lacking case studies on non-G20 countries, especially low-income countries. Therefore, it is suggested that the DWG coordinate with the GPFI and the related international organizations to establish a case-study center including innovative tools such as digital finance in reducing transfer costs both from G20 countries and non-G20 countries. From this perspective, the DWG has more comparative edge and broader knowledge reserves than other working groups (Van den Bergh, 2015).

3.2 *Coordination between DWG and GPFI in financial inclusion and DWG's integration with UN 2030*

Financial inclusion is very important for SMEs and families, especially in developing countries. As the G20 Seoul Summit held that "narrowing the development gap and reducing poverty are integral to achieving our broader Framework objectives of strong, sustainable and balanced growth by generating new poles of growth and contributing to global rebalancing", the GPFI platform was officially established at the G20 Summit in Seoul in 2010. Its purpose is to provide "an inclusive platform for all G20 countries, interested non-G20 countries and relevant stakeholders to carry forward our work on financial inclusion". Both UN 2030 Agenda and Addis Ababa Action Agenda also emphasize that financial inclusion should be promoted as an important agenda of sustainable development.[26]

---

[26]Addis Ababa Action Agenda of the Third International Conference on Financing for Development. URL: http://www.un.org/esa/ffd/wp-content/uploads/2015/08/AAAA_Outcome.pdf.

At present, the coordination between the G20 DWG and the GPFI can be promoted from the following aspects.

3.2.1 *SME finance forum*

It is suggested that the DWG should strengthen its participation and coordination in the work of the SME Finance Forum, especially in the work related to SME financing in developing countries, and strive to transform the G20 SME Financial Forum from a forum dominated by G20 members into a global forum. SMEs are essential for promoting global economic growth, employment, and innovation. Therefore, the UN 2030 Agenda has a number of objectives that address the issue of the financial accessibility of the SMEs, especially women entrepreneurs, young entrepreneurs and women related enterprises. Sustainable Development Goal (SDG) 2, that is, "hunger eradication", mentions ensuring equal access to "financial services" for women, indigenous people, farmers, pastoralists and fishermen by 2030. In SDG 8, i.e. to "promote sustained, inclusive and sustainable economic growth, full and productive employment and decent work for all", the issue of SME owners' financing is mentioned twice: 8.3 is to "promote development-oriented policies that support productive activities, decent job creation, entrepreneurship, creativity and innovation, and encourage the formalization and growth of micro-, small- and medium-sized enterprises, including through access to financial services"; and 8.10 is to "strengthen the capacity of domestic financial institutions to encourage and expand access to banking, insurance and financial services for all". In SDG 9, i.e. to "build resilient infrastructure, promote inclusive and sustainable industrialization and foster innovation", 9.3 is to "increase the access of small-scale industrial and other enterprises, in particular in developing countries, to financial services, including affordable credit, and their integration into value chains and markets".[27] In addition, the Addis Ababa Action Agenda specifically discusses the importance of development finance in the realization of UN 2030 Agenda. Hence, the DWG can fully participate in the G20 SME Finance Forum while maintaining close integration with the UN 2030 Agenda. In view of the fact that the SME Finance Forum has been

---

[27]UN 2030 Agenda. URL: https://sustainabledevelopment.un.org/post2015/transforming ourworld.

dominated by G20 countries, the DWG should strive to turn it into a global forum.

3.2.2 *Data and policy research center*

It is suggested that the DWG initiate the establishment of Financial Inclusion Data and Policy Research Center, which can be achieved through the establishment of informal subgroups by the DWG. Due to the different development stages of different countries, there is a wide difference in financial accessibility in different countries, which means that one of the biggest challenges in promoting financial inclusion lies in the replicability and popularization of financial experience. Although the proposal on financial inclusion data has been listed as one of the working areas of the GPFI for many years, the relevant work progress has been quite slow. Besides, the GPFI's data and policy research center focuses on G20 members, which may result in insufficient attention to the data and experience of non-G20 countries. Therefore, the DWG's proposal of establishing a data and policy research center for both G20 and non-G20 countries will make up for this deficiency. Specifically, it can be conducted from three aspects. The first is to continue to strengthen the global financial inclusion data measurement indicators. The World Bank has set up a financial inclusion database and made great progress in data and indicators, especially at the transnational level. However, if a dedicated data and policy research center is established, it will be able to integrate the relevant research around the world and avoid the current situation of data fragmentation. The second is for the research center to include worldwide financial inclusion cases studies. At present, many non-G20 developing countries, especially low-income countries, lack case studies that are applicable to their national conditions. For example, in terms of micro finance, is the Yunus micro finance in Bangladesh suitable for the Sahara countries? And what are the applicability and institutional premises of micro finance? These problems need further study. The third is to strengthen policy research, especially the integration of academic and evidence-based policy study in the field of financial inclusion. At present, there is no integrated knowledge bank in the field of financial inclusion. Many research institutions and centers related to development have conducted some research about financial inclusion, so the issue of information fragmentation is relatively serious. If the research center can integrate worldwide academic and policy research on financial inclusion into a unified platform, it will greatly promote the integration of information and enhance the relevance of the DWG, and the cost of this work will not be very high, because what it needs is only a website or platform to integrate other resources.

3.2.3 *Global SSBs and financial inclusion*

The G20 DWG should actively formulate global standards that meet the national conditions of low and middle income non-G20countries. Both the UN 2030 Agenda and Addis Ababa Action Agenda mentioned that they are committed to creating a harmonious and responsible financial standard. The core content of the G20 DWG is to facilitate the dialogue and communication between G20 and non-G20 countries (especially the low-income countries among them), so that the G20 can better promote the global sustainable development.[28] At present, a prominent problem in international governance is that developed countries are responsible for setting standards while developing countries complying with them. However, in the process of formulating standards, developed countries often act in their own interests, whether intentionally or unintentionally, which often brings about the result that these standards formulated by developed countries are not suitable for the national conditions of developing countries. Therefore, the G20 DGW should fully learn from the experience, understand its position in the G20, fully realize the differences between the G20 DWG and other G20 working groups, actively participate in and formulate the work of the global standard setting and financial inclusion, strive to help the low-income countries of non-G20 countries obtain the standard setting suitable for their development level, and promote the G20's role in promoting the global financial inclusion so as to strengthen its relevance in international development work.

References

ADB. "ADB private sector financing tops $2.6 billion in 2015, up 37% year-on-year". 2016. URL: https://www.adb.org/news/adb-private-sector-financing-tops-26-billion-2015-37-year-year.

---

[28] *Ibid.*

ADB. *Meeting Asia's Infrastructure Needs: Highlights*. Asian Development Bank: Manila, 2017a. URL: https://www.adb.org/sites/default/files/publication/227496/special-report-infrastructure-highlihigh.pdf.

ADB. "Members, capital stock, and voting power". *Annual Report*, 2017b. URL: https://www.adb.org/sites/default/files/page/30786/ar2017-oi-appendix1.pdf.

ADB. *Project Administration Manual. Madhya Pradesh District Connectivity Sector Project (No. 47270)*. Manila: Asian Development Bank, 2014.

AfDB. "Project supervision at the African development bank 2001–2008". *Final Report. Operation Evaluation Department*. Tunis: Africa Development Bank, 2010. URL: https://www.oecd.org/derec/afdb/47064891.pdf.

Alexander, J., R. Nank and C. Stivers. "Implications of welfare reform: Do nonprofit survival strategies threaten civil society?" *Nonprofit and Voluntary Sector Quarterly*, Vol. 28, No. 4, 1999, pp. 452–475.

Alie, Salina S. "Project governance: #1 critical success factor". Paper presented at PMI® Global Congress 2015 — North America, Orlando, FL. Newtown Square, PA: Project Management Institute, 2015.

Andreoni, J. and A. A. Payne. "Do government grants to private charities crowd out giving or fund-raising?" *American Economic Review*, Vol. 93, No. 3, 2003, pp. 792–812.

Ansell, C. and A. Gash. "Collaborative governance in theory and practice". *Journal of Public Administration Research and Theory*, Vol. 18, No. 4, 2008, pp. 543–571.

Baum, Warren C. *The Project Cycle*. Washington, DC: World Bank, 1982.

Boris, E. T., E. de Leon, K. L. Roeger and M. Nikolova. *Human Service Nonprofits and Government Collaboration*. Washington, DC: Urban Institute. 2010.

Brinkerhoff, J. M. "Government–nonprofit partnership: A defining framework". *Public Administration and Development*, Vol. 22, No. 1, 2002, pp. 19–30.

DiMaggio, P. J. and W. W. Powell. "The iron cage revisited: Institutional isomorphism and collective rationality in organizational fields". *American Sociological Review*, Vol. 48, No. 2, 1983, pp. 147–160.

Ebrahim, A. "Accountability in practice: Mechanisms for NGOs". *World Development*, Vol. 31, No. 5, 2003, pp. 813–829.

Ecer, S., M. Magro and S. Sarpça. "The relationship between nonprofits' revenue composition and their economic-financial efficiency". *Nonprofit and Voluntary Sector Quarterly*, Vol. 46, No. 1, 2017, pp. 141–155.

Edwards, M. and D. Hulme. "Too close for comfort? The impact of official aid on nongovernmental organizations". *World Development*, Vol. 24, No. 6, 1996, pp. 961–973.

Eikenberry, A. M. and J. D. Kluver. "The marketization of the nonprofit sector: Civil society at risk?" *Public Administration Review*, Vol. 64, No. 2, 2004, pp. 132–140.

Eriksson, Per Erik and Mats Westerberg. "Effects of procurement on construction project performance". *International Conference on Management of Technology*, 2009.

Frumkin, P. and M. T. Kim. *The Effect of Government Funding on Nonprofit Administrative Efficiency: An Empirical Test*. Cambridge, MA: Ash Institute for Democratic Governance and Innovation, John F. Kennedy School of Government, Harvard University, 2002.

Garven, S. A., M. A. Hofmann and D. N. McSwain. "Playing the numbers game: Program ratio management in nonprofit organizations". *Nonprofit Management and Leadership*, Vol. 26, No. 4, 2016, pp. 401–416.

Górski, Jędrzej. "An update on AIIB's procurement regulations. procurement policy and co-operation with other multilateral development banks". Working Paper No. 17, 2016.

Grønbjerg, K. A. *Understanding Nonprofit Funding: Managing Revenues in Social Services and Community Development Organizations*. San Francisco: Jossey-Bass, 1993.

Gulrajani, N. "Dilemmas in donor design: Organisational reform and the future of foreign aid agencies". *Public Administration and Development*, Vol. 35, No. 2, 2015, pp. 152–164.

Herzer, D. and P. Nunnenkamp. "Private donations, government grants, commercial activities, and fundraising: Cointegration and causality for NGOs in international development cooperation". *World Development*, Vol. 46, 2013, pp. 234–251.

Himberg, Harvey. "Comparative review of MDB safeguard systems". 2015. URL: https://consultations.worldbank.org/Data/hub/files/consultation-template/review-and-update-world-bank-safeguard-policies/en/phases/mdb_safeguard_comparison_main_report_and_annexes_may_2015.pdf.

Hughes, P., W. Luksetich and P. Rooney. "Crowding-out and fundraising efforts". *Nonprofit Management and Leadership*, Vol. 24, No. 4, 2014, pp. 445–464.

Humphrey, Chris. "Developmental revolution or Bretton Woods revisited? The prospects of the BRICS New Development Bank and the Asian Infrastructure Investment Bank". Working Paper 418, 2015, pp. 30–31.

IEG (Independent Evaluation Group). *Safeguards and Sustainability Policies in a Changing World*. The World Bank: Washington, DC, 2010.

Jack, William and Tavneet Suri. *Mobile money: The economics of M-PESA*. No. w16721. *National Bureau of Economic Research*, 2011.

Jakupec, Victor and Dr. Max Kelly. "The relevance of Asian Development Bank: Existing in the shadow of the Asian Infrastructure Investment Bank". *Journal of Regional & Socio-Economic Issues*, Vol. 5, No. 3, 2015, pp. 42–44.

Kerlin, J. A. "U.S.-based international NGOs and federal government foreign assistance: Out of Alignment". In E. T. Boris and C. E. Steuerle (Eds.),

Nonprofits and Government: Collaboration and Conflict. Washington, DC: The Urban Institute Press, 2006, pp. 373–398.

Kettl, D. F. "Managing boundaries in American administration: The collaboration imperative". *Public Administration Review*, Vol. 66, No. S1, 2006, pp. 10–19.

Kettl, D. F. *The Transformation of Governance: Public Administration for Twenty-First Century America.* Baltimore: Johns Hopkins University Press, 2002.

Khisa, Nekesa R. "Influence of procurement process on completion of road construction projects in Kenya: A case of Bungoma south sub-county". *University of Nairobi. Kenya*, 2015.

Kilby, Christopher. "Supervision and Performance: The Case of World Bank Projects". *Discussion Paper 1995–45*, 1995.

Krishnan, R., Yetman, M. H. and Yetman, R. J. "Expense misreporting in nonprofit organizations". *The Accounting Review*, Vol. 81, No. 2, 2006, pp. 399–420.

Laby, Nikhil C. *et al.* "Analysis of factors influencing procurement process and proposing a decision making module for construction projects on multi-site context". *International Journal of Applied Engineering Research*, Vol. 11, No. 9, 2016, pp. 66–89.

Lavanya, N. *et al.* "Risk analysis and management: A vital key to effective project management". Paper presented at PMI® Global Congress 2008 — Asia Pacific, Sydney, New South Wales, Australia. Newtown Square, PA: Project Management Institute, 2008. URL: https://www.pmi.org/learning/library/risk-analysis-project-management-7070.

Lindenberg, M. "Declining state capacity, voluntarism, and the globalization of the not-for-profit sector". *Nonprofit and Voluntary Sector Quarterly*, Vol. 28, No. S1, 1999, pp. 147–167.

Liu, Junhong. "The US and Japan's disregard for the AIIB reflect their stale understanding of the world". *Modern International Relations*, No. 5, 2015.

Lu, J. "Fear the government? A meta-analysis of the impact of government funding on nonprofit advocacy engagement". *The American Review of Public Administration*, No. 3, 2018, pp. 203–218.

Lu, J. "Which nonprofit gets more government funding?" *Nonprofit Management and Leadership*, Vol. 25, No. 3, 2015, pp. 297–312.

Maverick, Tim. "TPP versus AIIB: Obama's uphill battle". *Wall Street Daily*, 2015.

McCleary, R. M. and R. J. Barro. "Private voluntary organizations engaged in international assistance, 1939–2004". *Nonprofit and Voluntary Sector Quarterly*, Vol. 37, No. 3, 2008, pp. 512–536.

McKeever, B. S. *The Nonprofit Sector in Brief 2015.* Washington, DC: The Urban Institute. 2015.

Milward, H. B. and K. G. Provan. "Governing the Hollow State". *Journal of Public Administration Research and Theory*, Vol. 10, No. 2, 2000, pp. 359–380.

Ming Wan. *The Asian Infrastructure Investment Bank: The Construction of Power and the Struggle for the East Asian International Order*. Palgrave Macmillan, 2016, pp. 78–79.

Nikolic, S. J. S. and T. M. Koontz. "Nonprofit organizations in environmental management: A comparative analysis of government impacts". *Journal of Public Administration Research and Theory*, Vol. 18, No. 3, 2007, pp. 441–463.

Osborne, S. P. *The New Public Governance?: Emerging Perspectives on the Theory and Practice of Public Governance*. New York: Routledge, 2010.

Parsons, L. M., C. Pryor and A. A. Roberts. "Pressure to manage ratios and willingness to do so: Evidence from nonprofit managers". *Nonprofit and Voluntary Sector Quarterly*, Vol. 46, No. 4, 2017, pp. 705–724.

Peci, A., J. Figale and F. Sobral. "The 'invasion' of manufactured civil society: Government–nonprofit partnerships in a Brazilian state". *Public Administration and Development*, Vol. 31, No. 5, 2011, pp. 377–389.

Pfeffer, J. and Salancik, G. R. *The External Control of Organizations: A Resource Dependence Perspective*. New York: Harper & Row, 1978.

Qureshi, Zia. *G20 Growth Agenda, Framework for Strong, Sustainable and Balanced Growth*. Lecture Slides, 2014.

Reisen, Helmut. "How the New AIIB Dwarfs the Asian Development Bank". *The Globalist*, 2015. URL: https://www.theglobalist.com/aiib-to-dwarf-adb-loan-portfolio/.

Salamon, L. M. and S. Toepler. "Government–nonprofit cooperation: Anomaly or necessity?" *VOLUNTAS: International Journal of Voluntary and Nonprofit Organizations*, Vol. 26, No. 6, 2015, pp. 2155–2177.

Salamon, L. M. *Partners in Public Service: Government-Nonprofit Relations in the Modern Welfare State*. Baltimore, MD: Johns Hopkins University Press, 1995.

Salamon, L. M., S. W. Sokolowski and M. A. Haddock. *Explaining Civil Society Development: A Social Origins Approach*. Baltimore, MD: Johns Hopkins University Press, 2017.

Savas, E. S. *Privatization and Public-Private Partnerships*. New York: Chatham House, 2000.

Shintaro Hamanaka. "Insights to great powers' desire to establish institutions: Comparison of ADB, AMF, AMRO and AIIB". *Global Policy*, Vol. 7, No. 2, 2016, pp. 291–292.

Sloan, M. F. "The effects of nonprofit accountability ratings on donor behavior". *Nonprofit and Voluntary Sector Quarterly*, Vol. 38, No. 2, 2009, pp. 220–236.

Sloan, M. F. and C. Grizzle. "Assessing the impact of federal funding on faith-based and community organization program spending". *Public Budgeting & Finance*, Vol. 34, No. 2, 2014, pp. 44–62.

Smith, S. R. "The challenge of strengthening nonprofits and civil society". *Public Administration Review*, Vol. 68, No. S1, 2008, pp. 132–145.

Smith, S. R. and K. A. Grønbjerg. "Scope and theory of government-nonprofit relations". In W. W. Powell (Ed.), *The Nonprofit Sector: A Research Handbook*. New Haven, CT: Yale University Press, 2006, pp. 221–242.

Smith, S. R. and M. Lipsky. *Nonprofits for Hire: The Welfare State in the Age of Contracting*. Cambridge, MA: Harvard University Press, 1993.

Stoddard, A. "International Assistance". In L. M. Salamon (Ed.), *The State of Nonprofit America*. Washington, DC: Brookings Institution Press, 2012, pp. 329–361.

Struyk, R. J. "Nonprofit organizations as contracted local social service providers in eastern Europe and the Commonwealth of Independent States". *Public Administration and Development*, Vol. 22, No. 5, 2002, pp. 429–437.

Tarnoff, C. *U.S. Agency for International Development (USAID): Background, Operations, and Issues*. Washington, DC: Congressional Research Service, 2015.

Thornton, J. P. "Flypaper nonprofits: The impact of federal grant structure on nonprofit expenditure decisions". *Public Finance Review*, Vol. 42, No. 2, 2014, pp. 176–198.

Tinkelman, D. and K. Mankaney. "When is administrative efficiency associated with charitable donations?" *Nonprofit and Voluntary Sector Quarterly*, Vol. 36, No. 1, 2007, pp. 41–64.

Toepler, S. "Government funding policies". In B. Seaman and D. R. Young (Eds.), *Handbook of Research on Nonprofit Economics and Management*, Northampton, MA: Edward Elgar, 2010, pp. 320–334.

Van den Bergh, Paul. "Overview of international and national initiatives to promote financial inclusion and its measurement". *IFC Bulletins chapters* 38, 2015.

Van Slyke, D. M. "The mythology of privatization in contracting for social services". *Public Administration Review*, Vol. 63, No. 3, 2003, pp. 296–315.

Verschuere, B. and J. De Corte. "The impact of public resource dependence on the autonomy of NPOs in their strategic decision making". *Nonprofit and Voluntary Sector Quarterly*, Vol. 43, No. 2, 2014, pp. 293–313.

Wolf, Alan and Robert A. Rogowsky. "The Asian Infrastructure and Investment Bank: Questions that should be asked". *The E15 Initiative*, 2015. URL: http://e15initiative.org/blogs/asian-infrastructure-and-investment-bank-questions-that-should-be-asked/.

Young, D. R. "Alternative models of government-nonprofit sector relations: Theoretical and international perspectives". *Nonprofit and Voluntary Sector Quarterly*, Vol. 29, No. 1, 2000, pp. 149–172.

Zuo, Haicong and An Wenjing. "An analysis of the decision-making mechanism of multilateral development banks and the enlightenment for the AIIB". *Social Sciences of Chinese Universities*, No. 4, 2015.

Chapter 6

A Comparison of the Aid Management Systems of Traditional Donor Countries

Section 1. The United States' Aid Management System

The history of the US foreign aid can be traced back to World War I. In 1917, the US passed a statute to establish US Food Administration which controlled domestic food affairs in wartime to ensure supply and provide assistance to other *entente* countries. This wartime agency was preserved after the war and continued to play its role. During World War II, the US passed the Lend-Lease Act to provide military assistance to other allies. After World War II, it signed the Marshall Plan in 1948 to provide assistance for European reconstruction and established the Economic Cooperation Administration (ECA) in charge of the implementation of the Plan. In 1949, US President Truman further proposed the "Point Four Program" to further reinforce national assistance and established the Technical Cooperation Administration (TCA) in 1950. In 1952, the ECA was renamed as the Mutual Security Administration (MSA), which also incorporated the TCA. In 1955, the International Cooperation Administration (ICA) was established to be in charge of the foreign aid and "non-military security" projects of the US. In November 1961, the US passed the Foreign Assistance Act and officially established the US Agency for International Development (USAID), which incorporated the previous foreign economic assistance functions scattered in USAID, the

Export-Import Bank, and other organizations, and became the core executive agency of the US' foreign aid. In 1961, the US also passed the Peace Corps Act and established the "Peace Corps", which provided assistance in the form of officially sponsored volunteer services and promoted American culture and values. Since then, the US guided the establishment of Pan American Development Foundation, African Development Foundation, and other organizations to step up its foreign aid. In 2003, the US passed the Millennium Challenge Act and established the Millennium Challenge Corporation to provide assistance to global development, aiming at promoting economic growth, eliminating extreme poverty, strengthening good governance, economic freedom, and investment in individual development. In the same year, the US also set up the US President's Emergency Plan for AIDS Relief (PEPFAR) to strengthen its assistance to AIDS groups. In 2006, the US set up the Office of US Foreign Assistance Resources under the Department of State to coordinate the US foreign aid projects and resources (see Figure 6.1).

In the current foreign aid management system of the US, USAID remains the most important aid executing agency, which manages the vast majority of bilateral aid projects and funds and cooperates with many other ministries and aid agencies. Since the US Department of State is the leading institution of USAID, the director of USAID reports directly to the Secretary of State. At the same time, the Department of State itself also takes charge of some assistance tasks, such as immigration and refugee

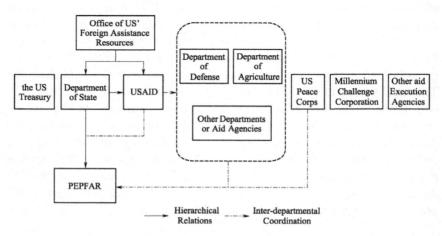

Figure 6.1:   The US foreign aid management system.

assistance. Moreover, it also carries out some assistance tasks jointly with other aid agencies. For instance, the Office of the US Global AIDS Coordinator under the Department of State is in charge of the PEPFAR, but USAID undertakes its actual implementation, while other departments such as the Department of Defense and the Department of Health and Human Services will also take part in this plan. Established in 2006, the Office of Foreign Assistance Resources is responsible for the aid functions of the Department of State and the aid work of USAID, managing in total more than 90% of the US' aid resources.[1] It plays a key role in the formulation of the annual aid budget of the US, and comprehensively arranges the coordination between the foreign aid and foreign policy of the US, the coordination of the aid projects between the Department of State and USAID, the formulation of aid policies, and the evaluation of aid projects. The Department of Defense, mainly responsible for US military aid projects, will coordinate with USAID and the Department of State in the process of aid implementation. Food aid is also an important component of US foreign aid, which is mainly dealt with by the Department of Agriculture, with some of the implementation work being completed by USAID. The US Treasury, as the representative of the US in the World Bank, the IMF, and other international multilateral organizations, is an important participant in international multilateral assistance. The Peace Corps mainly provides human assistance to other countries through volunteers, mainly in the fields of education, medical care, and community development. The aid projects of the Millennium Challenge Corporation are implemented in accordance with the long-term aid plans agreed by the recipient countries and the US, whereas these aid plans are concentrated on developing countries with "good governance" as recognized by the US. In addition, other aid agencies such as the US Trade and Development Agency, Overseas Private Investment Corporation, Pan American Development Foundation, and African Development Foundation also play a certain role in US foreign aid.

Section 2. Japan's Aid Management System

The history of Japan's foreign aid after World War II can be traced back to 1954, when it joined the Colombo Plan led by the UK to provide aid to

---

[1] US Office of Foreign Assistance Resources. URL: https://www.state.gov/f/about/index.htm.

Southeast Asian countries and began to carry out technical cooperation projects. In 1961, Japan's Overseas Economic Cooperation Fund (OECF) was launched, mainly responsible for its assistance loan projects. In 1962, Japan's Overseas Technical Cooperation Agency (OTCA) was officially established to manage its technical cooperation assistance. In 1965, Japan Overseas Cooperation Volunteers (JOCV) was established to undertake human resources management for Japan's foreign assistance in technical cooperation. In 1974, Japan International Cooperation Agency (JICA) was established by merging OTCA and the Immigration Services Bureau of Japan. It was a public organization in charge of Japan's technical cooperation assistance under the guidance of the Ministry of Foreign Affairs. In 1999, OECF merged with the Export-Import Bank of Japan to establish Japan Bank for International Cooperation (JBIC), which is responsible for the execution of Japan's assistance loan programs. JBIC is administratively subordinate to the Ministry of Finance of Japan, but other ministries and commissions also participate in its specific policies of assistance loans. In 2003, JICA was transformed into a government agency under the Ministry of Foreign Affairs of Japan, with the same name Japan International Cooperation Agency. In 2008, Japan's aid management system underwent major reforms, whereby the functions of JICA were greatly enhanced: the assistance loan functions of JBIC together with most of the free donation programs undertaken by the Ministry of Foreign Affairs of Japan were transferred to JICA (Figure 6.2).

For a long time, Japan's foreign aid management system has been lacking in a unitary leading institution. Historically, Japan's aid management system was known as "yonshotaisei", that is, a negotiation mechanism involving the Ministry of Foreign Affairs, the Ministry of Finance,

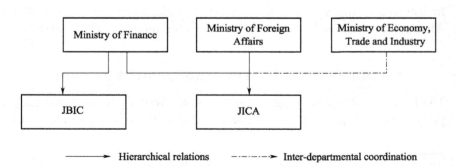

Figure 6.2:   Japan's foreign aid management system.

the Ministry of International Trade and Industry (MITI), and the Economic Planning Agency (EPA). Japan's foreign aid mainly comprises three aid tools: technical cooperation aid, free donation aid, and Japanese yen loan aid. Historically, JICA under the guidance of the Ministry of Foreign Affairs was in charge of technical cooperation assistance and the Ministry of Foreign Affairs was directly in charge of free donation assistance with JICA mainly being responsible for the implementation, while the funds for these two kinds of assistance need to be negotiated by the Ministry of Foreign Affairs and the Ministry of Finance. For a long time, Japanese yen loan aid has been the most important aid tool for Japan, which was originally undertaken by OECF and then transferred to JBIC when it was established. As the most important aid tool, the implementation of Japanese yen loan aid requires the negotiation of multiple ministries and commissions: Japanese yen loan projects need to be negotiated with the Ministry of Foreign Affairs on foreign policy, the Ministry of Finance on financial quota, and the MITI and the EPA on commerce, economy, and investment. In 2001, the MITI and the EPA merged to form the Ministry of Economy, Trade and Industry (METI); thus, the four-ministry/agency agreement mechanism became the three-ministry agreement mechanism. However, the three ministries differ greatly on the starting point of foreign aid. The Ministry of Foreign Affairs attaches great importance to Japan's diplomatic interests and is the main department responsible for Japan's free donation assistance. Since Japan's acts of providing a large amount of Japanese yen loans and emphasizing economic interests for a long period in history have provoked much criticism in the world, the Ministry of Foreign Affairs is the principal supporter in Japan to promote the proportion and quality of free donation assistance and follow the DAC specifications. The Ministry of Finance, placing emphasis on the sustainability of Japanese finance, takes charge of the allocation of aid budget. With all loan projects under its approval and supervision, the Ministry of Finance prefers assistance loan projects because it means the recovery of financial funds. The METI, attaching importance to economic and commercial interests, receives support from Japan's domestic private sector to expand overseas economic interests; thus, it stresses the promotion of tied aid, especially the Japanese yen loan aid with conditions for purchasing Japanese labor and products, which has long been dominant in Japanese history. All the three ministries have a certain say in foreign aid, and each of them is justified to participate; hence, Japan's foreign aid decision-making is complex and competitive to some extent. After the reform of

Japan's aid management system in 2008, the foreign aid loan functions of JBIC under the Ministry of Finance were transferred to JICA; except for the free donation aid retained in the Ministry of Foreign Affairs for the purpose of achieving foreign policy, most of the free donation aid was also allocated to JICA. Consequently, in terms of the policy tools and implementation of Japan's foreign aid, the technical cooperation aid, free donation aid, and Japanese yen loan aid have been unified to a large extent, all of them being incorporated into JICA. In terms of decision-making, JICA further enhances its independence in implementation after taking over Japanese yen loan functions; nevertheless, it is still under the leadership and supervision of both the Ministry of Foreign Affairs and the Ministry of Finance in decision-making and finance and still needs to negotiate with the METI in Japanese yen loan projects.

Section 3. The United Kingdom's Aid Management System

The UK's foreign aid originated from its aid to the colonies. In 1929, the UK passed the *Colonial Development Act* and began to provide certain aid to the colonies, but its main purpose was to promote its own industrial and trade development. In view of the constant social unrests in the colonies during World War II, it passed the *Colonial Development and Welfare Act* in 1940, which increased the expenditure on social welfare projects in the colonies. After World War II, the Labor Party passed the new *Colonial Development and Welfare Act* in 1945 and the *Overseas Resource Act* in 1947 and established two development corporations — the Colonial Development Corporation and the Overseas Food Corporation — in order to support the UK's aid to the colonies. The passage of the two Acts and the establishment of the two companies constituted the earliest foreign aid management system of the UK. In 1964, the newly elected Labor Party established the Ministry of Overseas Development, an independent agency which aimed to exercise the UK's functions of foreign aid at the ministerial level that were once scattered in the Department for Technical Cooperation, the Foreign, Commonwealth Relations and Colonial Offices, and so on, and the earliest ministers were among the cabinet members. In 1970, the Conservative Government demoted the Ministry of Overseas Development to the Overseas Development Administration, which was brought under the leadership of the Ministry of Foreign Affairs. Subsequently, during the alternation of the two parties in power, from time to time this agency was either promoted to be an independent ministry or demoted to be a subordinate administration under the Ministry of Foreign Affairs, with its power and status fluctuating in the British government. Nevertheless, its main purpose remained to serve the economic and commercial interests of the UK, maintain the UK's relationship with the Commonwealth or its influence in its former colonies, cooperate with the Cold War strategy of the US, and maintain its position in the UN. In 1997, great changes took place in the UK's aid management system, whereby the new Labor Party established the Department for International Development (DFID), reestablished the UK's management system of coordinating foreign aid at the ministerial level, and passed the *International Development Act* in 2002, which further standardized and instituted the UK's aid management system (Figure 6.3).

The management system of the UK's DFID falls into the category of the fourth model of aid management system summarized by the OECD in 2009: a unitary government agency at the ministerial level taking charge of the policy and implementation of foreign aid. In the case of the UK, the DFID is independently responsible for the UK's bilateral aid and multilateral aid, which is supported by four subordinate divisions, namely, the Country Programmes, Policy & Global Programmes, Finance & Corporate Performance, and Economic Development and International.

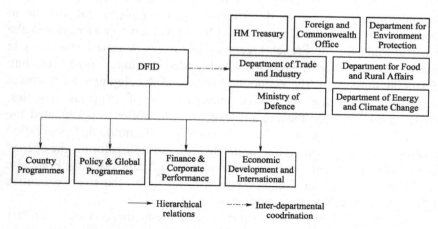

Figure 6.3: The United Kingdom's foreign aid management system.

In 2000, the UK issued a white paper which systematically expounded the concept and policy of its foreign aid, which was legally instituted in the form of *International Aid Act* in 2002. In the Act, the UK established the foreign aid principle of poverty reduction, that is, all aid should be aimed at reducing local poverty (except for aid to the UK overseas territories, humanitarian aid, and funding to multilateral development banks); otherwise the aid is illegal. In addition, in the Act, the UK formally instituted the principle that the UK's aid should not be attached with any conditions for purchasing UK goods and services; thus becoming the first country in the world to shift to untied aid. In specific business, the DFID still needs to cooperate with many other ministries and commissions to achieve the government's unified goals and policy coordination. For instance, the UK launched a departmental committee presided by the minister of the DFID to manage the African Conflict Prevention Pool, with members from the Ministry of Defence and the Foreign and Commonwealth Office. For specific foreign aid areas and matters, the UK coordinates aid affairs through interdepartmental committees to make full use of the expertise, resources, and networks of all the departments.

Section 4. France's Aid Management System

France's foreign aid can be traced back to 1941, when de Gaulle's French government in exile established the Central Fund for Free France (Caisse Central de la France Libre in French) in the UK, with main functions of issuing bills and acting as the Treasury for the government in exile in wartime. In 1944, the Central Fund for Free French was renamed the Central Fund for the French Overseas Territories (Caisse Centrale de la France d'Outre-mer in French), which added the function of providing financial support for the economic and social development of overseas territories. With the successive independence of overseas colonies, the Central Fund for the French Overseas Territories was renamed the Central Fund for Economic Cooperation (Caisse Centrale de Coopération Economique in French). Afterwards, through multiple reforms, the agency eventually turned into the French Development Agency (Caisse Française de Développement in French), which came to be the main executive agency of France's foreign aid (Figure 6.4).

In France's foreign aid management system, there is not a unitary agency responsible for foreign aid, and the highest decision-making

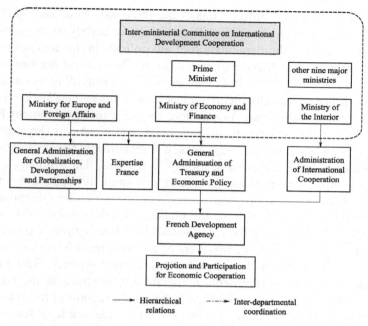

Figure 6.4:   France's foreign aid management system.

body is the Inter-ministerial Committee on International Development Cooperation (Comité interministériel de la coopération internationale et du développement in French), the chairman of which is the Prime Minister. The committee comprises 12 ministries, of which the Ministry for Europe and Foreign Affairs, the Ministry of Economy and Finance, and the Ministry of the Interior together act as joint chairmen. The aid-related policies are implemented by their respective subordinate departments: the General Administration for Globalization, Development and Partnerships (Direction Générale de la Mondialisation, du Développement et des Partenariats in French), the General Administration of Treasury and Economic Policy (Direction Générale du Trésor et des Politiques Economiques in French), and the Administration of International Cooperation (Direction de la Coopération Internationale in French). The General Administration for Globalization, Development and Partnerships is at once responsible for multilateral and bilateral assistance. Multilateral assistance mainly includes donations and contributions to the European Development Fund, the Global AIDS Prevention Fund and the UN.

When classified by policy areas, the General Administration for Globalization, Development and Partnerships is mainly responsible for the formulation and implementation of aid policies in the areas of governance, culture, research and higher education. The General Administration of Treasury and Economic Policy takes charge of providing assistance to most multilateral development agencies, including the World Bank's International Development Association, the African Development Fund, the Pan American Development Bank Fund, and the Asian Development Fund. When classified by policy areas, it is responsible for assistance and cooperation related to debt and monetary policies. The Ministry of the Interior is directly responsible for a relatively small aid budget, mainly in the area of immigration aid. The General Administration for Globalization, Development and Partnerships, the General Administration of Treasury and Economic Policy, and the Administration of International Cooperation jointly take charge of the management of France's most important agency for aid implementation, the French Development Agency. The French Development Agency represents a special aid structure in the field of international aid. On the one hand, it is the main executor of the aid policy of France. On the other hand, it is an enterprise under the legal framework of France and the European Union. To be exact, its legal status is a development bank. Therefore, it has dual status of a public agency for aid implementation and a development bank. Due to such a status, the means of aid provided by it mainly includes preferential and development loans, subsidies, equity investment, and risk guarantee. Besides receiving funds from the Ministry for Europe and Foreign Affairs, the Ministry of Economy and Finance and the Ministry of the Interior, the French Development Agency can also issue bills to raise funds from the capital market. Promotion and Participation for Economic Cooperation (Promotion et Participation pour la Cooperation Economique in French, abbreviated as PROPARCO) is a subordinate of the French Development Agency. In terms of shareholding, the PROPARCO has also brought in many investors from developed and developing countries apart from its major shareholder of the French Development Agency, thus the PROPARCO is also an important handle for the French Development Agency to achieve its aid goals in promoting growth and sustainable development mostly through encouraging and attracting private sector investment. In the meantime, the French Development Agency is also an important organization of France in the field of global environmental assistance, which manages and provides financial assistance to the French Global Environment Facility, and cooperates with the Ministry for Europe and Foreign Affairs, the Ministry of Economy and Finance, and the Ministry for the Ecological and Inclusive Transition to jointly guide the work of the French Global Environment Facility. However, the French Development Agency is not the only aid executing agency in France. For instance, the Expertise France under the Ministry for Europe and Foreign Affairs and the Ministry of Economy and Finance serves as the main executing agency of France's foreign technical assistance.

Chapter 7

A Comparison of the Aid Management Systems of Emerging Donor Countries

Section 1. Introduction to the Aid Management Systems of Emerging Donor Countries

1. Introduction

In recent years, the influence of emerging economies has increased day by day in the field of foreign aid, with continuous increase in the number of participant countries and the amount of foreign aid. In particular, such BRICS countries as China, India, Brazil, and South Africa have increased their foreign aid significantly. According to estimates by the OECD-DAC, from 2011 to 2014, the amount of foreign aid from 30 non-OECD countries and regions increased from US $14.1 billion to US $31.7 billion, accounting for 18.7% of the world's total foreign aid in 2014. On the one hand, this provides the recipient countries with more choices in funding and cooperation; on the other hand, it intensifies the fragmentation of the international aid system as well as the competition among the donor countries.

The growth of China's foreign aid is particularly noticeable, which has resulted in impressive achievements. For example, the UN maintains that China's international assistance has played an important role in the rapid economic growth and effective poverty alleviation of African countries in the past 15 years. Meanwhile, with the rapid growth in its amount of aid funds, there also exist problems such as repeated aid with some other countries, excessive number of aid projects in some certain areas, emphasis on short-term economic benefits, and the lack of effective management in certain projects. Though stemmed from various causes, these problems indicate that there is still much room for improvement in the governance structure of China's foreign aid. Thus, how to conduct in-depth research into and learn from the aid governance structure of other countries is of great significance for optimizing China's foreign aid.

Research into the aid governance structure of donor countries is a key issue of great significance for achieving foreign aid goals and promoting the development of recipient countries. In fact, the ODA provided by developed countries over the years has had limited effects on changing the developing countries' poverty and backwardness and improving the people's living standards, which has made the issue of "the effectiveness of donor countries" increasingly prominent and provoked skepticism about the significance of external aid in the recipient countries. From the perspective of public administration, when one country provides assistance to another country, how to reasonably design the country's internal governance structure to make its assistance to another country more effective is very important in terms of foreign aid theory and practice.

In recent years, many emerging donor countries have adjusted their aid governance structure to coordinate their decision-making process or implementation in foreign aid. For example, Mexico established the Mexican Agency for International Development Cooperation (AMEXCID), Turkey established the Turkish Cooperation and Coordination Agency (TİKA), and Thailand established the Thai International Cooperation Agency (TICA). In addition, countries such as India and Saudi Arabia have also improved their aid governance structures to enhance their aid efficiency. In 2011, China formally established an interministerial coordination mechanism for foreign aid, with the Ministry of Commerce, the Ministry of Foreign Affairs and the Ministry of Finance as the mainstay so as to make overall plans for the formulation and implementation of China's foreign aid strategy.

At present, there is little research in the academic circles into systematic comparison of the characteristics of the aid governance structures of the emerging donor countries like BRICS and analyzing their respective advantages and disadvantages. To this end, this section will introduce the "holistic governance" idea in the second part to establish a preliminary analysis framework for the aid governance structure based on the existing research into aid governance structure. The third part will analyze the public documents and data of the BRICS countries' foreign aid.

The fourth part will compare the characteristics of the aid governance structures of Brazil, India, South Africa, and China and their respective strengths and weaknesses. The fifth part will further explore the directions of improving China's foreign aid governance structure.

2. Theoretical Framework of Aid Governance Structure

The existing literature on international aid has acknowledged the important impact of aid governance structure on aid efficiency, but the relevant literature on the aid governance structure of the BRICS countries is relatively scarce. By summarizing and comparing the existing literature, this part proposes an analysis framework of aid governance structure.

Traditional research on aid governance structure and aid efficiency focuses on the domestic political and administrative system of the recipient country, the logic behind which is that efficient aid can only be achieved when the recipient country is equipped with sound institutional environment for implementing aid projects. This view can be traced back to the "good governance agenda" of international aid in the 1990s. Burnside and Dollar (2000) validate the positive correlation between the recipient countries' domestic policies and aid efficiency through empirical studies, believing that the recipient countries should optimize their domestic governance structure to improve aid efficiency. The "good governance agenda" has exerted profound impact on international aid in practice: international aid agencies, including the World Bank and the IMF, often attach strict domestic reform strings to the recipient countries when providing aid, which is called "governance interference". Afterward, the "good governance agenda" encountered enormous criticism in the practice and theory of foreign aid and was replaced by the "good enough governance". The latter believed that foreign aid could be provided after the single most critical governance reform that cleared the hindrance to development was completed, that is, the realization of "good enough governance", whereas it is unrealistic and unnecessary to provide aid after achieving thorough and fulfilled good governance reform.

As a two-way interaction, aid efficiency also depends on the governance capacity building on the part of the donor countries. The World Bank points out that government effectiveness and corruption control are critical to governance capacity. Relevant studies find that, though the internal organizational variables of aid agencies are sometimes not easy to detect, they have crucial impact on aid results. In addition, it also improves the aid results to set reasonable incentive mechanisms at different levels within the aid agencies. Some studies also find that the internal decentralization of aid governance structure could influence aid efficiency, and the fragmentation within the aid agencies would lead to high transaction costs during the implementation of aid projects.

Some institutes and scholars have tried to develop the best practice for aid governance structure. For instance, through case studies, it is concluded that the governance structure that is conducive to aid efficiency has some of the following characteristics: the aid agencies are responsible for aid policy-making and implementation management; and the aid agencies have clear aid guiding principles or the aid executants have a certain right of discretion. In addition, the model of coordinating and leading foreign aid policies and implementation at the ministerial level through the construction of aid efficiency index is also considered helpful for improving aid efficiency. The empirical analysis with OECD countries as samples indicates that the model of setting up a dedicated functional department of foreign aid under the leadership of the Ministry of Foreign Affairs is most helpful for improving aid efficiency. Owing to differences in national situations, it is obvious that the so-called best practice usually must be tailored according to the practical situations and policy needs of each country.

Based on the above analysis framework, this part will analyze the historical changes and current status of the foreign aid governance structures of Brazil, India, South Africa, and China, with a focus on the development of integrated aid agencies in these countries.

Section 2. India's Aid Management System

India's foreign aid system construction originated from its aid to Nepal. In 1954, India established the Indian Aid Mission Agency to monitor and coordinate its aid projects in Nepal. In 1966, it was replaced by the Indian Cooperative Mission Agency, which was subsequently replaced by the New Economic Cooperation Agency in 1980. During this period, India also set up the Department of Economy and Cooperation, the Joint Action Plan and other aid agencies and projects, most of which were promoted by the Ministry of External Affairs. In 2003, India put forward the Indian

Development Initiative, calling for the integration of its complex domestic aid system, and eventually established the Indian Development Partnership Administration in 2012.

The Ministry of External Affairs plays an absolutely dominant role in India's foreign aid (Figure 7.1), as it controls the vast majority of the foreign aid budget, and its affiliated Development Partnership Administration carries out the overall management of India's foreign aid, with the aim of "comprehensively improving the efficiency of India's foreign aid projects at the stages of concept, launch, implementation and commission". In addition, the Ministry of Finance also plays an important role in supervising the credit loans of the Export-Import Bank of India. Hence, the credit loan projects proposed by the Ministry of External Affairs to other countries shall be completed through communication with the Department of Economic Affairs under the Ministry of Finance.

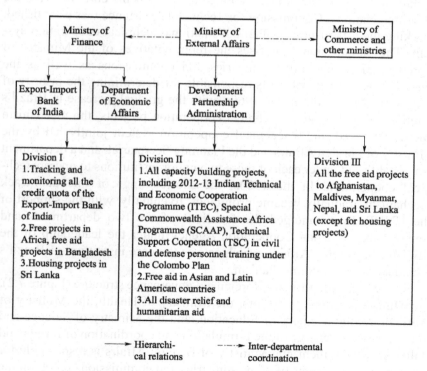

Figure 7.1:   India's foreign aid governance structure.

Other ministries and commissions, such as the Department of Commerce, also have a place in providing business relations consulting and agricultural or health services and support.

From the perspective of holistic governance, India has integrated all previous foreign aid projects and related departments into the Development Partnership Administration as the core, incorporated the functions of other departments such as credit loans into the aid system, and also integrated the relevant private sectors and other information channels involved in the Department of Commerce and other ministries, which has greatly improved the holistic governance proficiency of India's foreign aid.

Section 3. Brazil's Aid Management System

The history of Brazil's foreign aid can be traced back to the 1950s, with technical cooperation with developing countries as the core. In 1959, the Brazilian National Commission for Technical Assistance was established, marking the establishment of Brazil's national technical cooperation system. The commission comprises the representatives of the Ministry of Foreign Affairs and other ministries and commissions as well as the Planning Secretariat, which is responsible for determining the priority of technical cooperation. In the 1960s, with the gradual increase in Brazil's multilateral and bilateral technical cooperation projects, the mechanism was reorganized into a technical cooperation system jointly led by the Ministry of Foreign Affairs and the Planning Secretariat, and a department was established under each of these two major institutions to operate technical cooperation. In the 1980s, the shortcomings of this dual-track mechanism gradually became prominent. Eventually, with the support of the UNDP, Brazil merged the functions of the two departments and founded the Brazilian Cooperation Agency under the leadership of the Ministry of Foreign Affairs, which acts as the core institution of Brazil's technical cooperation mechanism.

Currently, within Brazil's foreign aid governance structure (Figure 7.2), the Ministry of Foreign Affairs, the Ministry of Health, the Ministry of Agriculture, the Ministry of Education, and the Ministry of Science and Technology take charge of the formulation and coordination of foreign aid policies. Among them, the Ministry of Foreign Affairs is responsible for expounding the actions of other ministries and commissions based on the

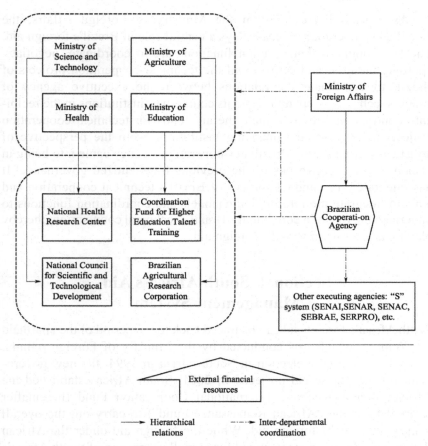

Figure 7.2:   Brazil's foreign aid governance structure.

emphasis of foreign policy. The sources of external funding are very important in Brazil's foreign aid, which reflects the key position of tripartite cooperation in Brazil's foreign aid. A large number of Brazilian aid projects are carried out through cooperation with third-party developed countries or international aid agencies, thus forging a tripartite cooperative relationship of "Brazil-the third-party aid agency-the recipient country". Owing to the leverage of a large amount of third-party funds and resources, Brazil's national budget constitutes only part of the sources of foreign aid funds.

As a subordinate body of the Ministry of Foreign Affairs, the Brazilian Cooperation Agency plays a central role in Brazil's foreign aid. The law stipulates that its main functions are to coordinate, negotiate, approve, monitor, and evaluate all the technical cooperation projects of Brazil, to coordinate the relations between the executive agency of Brazil's technical cooperation and its counterpart institutions in the recipient countries, and to coordinate the aid funds for technical cooperation projects as an auxiliary financing institution. From the perspective of holistic governance, the Brazilian Cooperation Agency came into being in response to the drawbacks of the previous fragmentized governance. It has integrated the funding sources of Brazil's technical cooperation and aims to integrate the information channels and coordination functions to undertake the role of a core hub for Brazil's technical cooperation, thereby playing a key role in Brazil's foreign aid.

Section 4. South Africa's Aid Management System

South Africa's foreign aid can be traced back to the period of the apartheid government, which was conducted by the Ministry of Foreign Affairs. After the democratic election in South Africa in 1994, the new government retained these aid projects. In 2001, South Africa established the African Renaissance and International Cooperation Fund (hereinafter referred to as the "African Renaissance Fund") to carry out the overall management of its foreign aid. While the foreign aid under the African Renaissance Fund only accounted for a small proportion of South Africa's foreign aid, a large amount of foreign aid was carried out independently by other national ministries and commissions within their respective budgets. When the foreign aid acts of various government-funded institutions, parastatal organizations, and other statutory institutions were taken into consideration, the foreign aid under the African Renaissance Fund accounted for an even smaller proportion. Owing to the lack of coordination and integration, all aid agencies went their own way, which resulted in serious fragmentation. In 2007, South Africa put forward an initiative to integrate its foreign aid system, which resulted in the final establishment of the South African Development Partnership Agency in 2012 to carry out the overall management and coordination of South Africa's foreign aid.

According to the ideal state specified in the original design, the South African Development Partnership Agency will solve the problems in the operation of aid governance structure dominated by the African Renaissance Fund and fully integrate and manage the development aid at all levels and of all departments of South Africa while administering the operation of the funds. However, the actual situation is far from the case (Figure 7.3). Currently, the South African Development Partnership Agency only undertakes the functions of communication, coordination, and contact, while the actual operation still needs to be completed by various ministries and commissions with relevant expertise, capabilities, and networks, and the African Renaissance Fund still plays a major role. Administratively, the Fund is affiliated and reports work to the Ministry of International Relations and Cooperation (formerly the Ministry of Foreign Affairs of South Africa), whereas in practical operation it needs to be reviewed and approved by the Ministry of Finance, which has seriously undermined its efficiency.

The Ministry of Finance is another core department in charge of South Africa's foreign aid. Besides partly guiding the African Renaissance Fund, a number of state-owned enterprises under the guidance of the Ministry of Finance also play an essential role in South Africa's foreign aid. Among these enterprises, the most important is the South African Development Bank which is responsible for providing development loans or sovereign loans to other countries and serves as one of the most

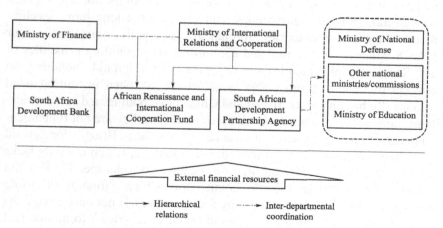

Figure 7.3:   South Africa's foreign aid governance structure.

important policy tools of South Africa's foreign aid. In addition, the Ministry of Finance has been the representative of South Africa on the international stage of multilateral aid. Other national ministries and commissions represented by the Ministry of National Defense and the Ministry of Education also play an important role in South Africa's foreign aid. Besides their own independent aid budgets, these ministries and commissions can also obtain additional aid funds and resources from third-party aid agencies with the increase in tripartite collaboration.

Although South Africa has not attained the ideal state in terms of holistic governance, the establishment of the South African Development Partnership Agency has improved the coordination of South Africa's foreign aid and demonstrates progress in its aid governance structure.

Section 5. A Comparison of Aid Management Systems between China and Other Emerging Donor Countries

1. Construction of Integrated Aid Guiding Principles

The guiding principles of foreign aid approved by the legislative branch or with extremely high legal significance constitute a fundamental document that elaborates the principles, objectives, priorities, methods, and standards for the donor countries' implementation of foreign aid, and also helps to dispel domestic and foreign skepticism about the donor countries' foreign aid, enhance transparency, and promote the long-term development of the donor countries' foreign aid. Currently, none of the four BRICS countries has formulated a complete set of guiding principles of aid. Some official principles and objectives of foreign aid, including the concept of "South–South Cooperation", have not been institutionalized into legally binding texts. Brazil and China have both issued some guidelines, manuals, or white papers on foreign aid, but they are not fundamental programmatic documents in essence. Among them, Brazil's foreign aid guidelines are more like a project operation manual, which not only lacks a basic introduction to the aid framework but also lacks specific data and statistics of its foreign aid. By comparison, China's foreign aid white paper is the most detailed among the four countries. It not only covers the basic objectives of China's foreign aid but also includes information and data on its funding, methods, and distribution. However, it falls short of an introduction to China's domestic aid governance structure and the foundation for decision-making, and the relevant data are also called into question.

One manifestation of the lack of complete aid guiding principles is that the foreign aid of the four countries is invariably "needs-driven", that is, the partner countries first propose their specific needs of foreign aid, and then determine the final aid plans through evaluation and negotiation. The donor countries rarely initiate or jointly design comprehensive assistance plans with their partner countries, which is neither conducive to integrating aid projects in different fields or for different goals to help the recipient countries achieve more comprehensive and coordinated development nor conducive for the donor countries to integrating foreign aid into their countries' development or to proactively communicating their aid concepts and extending their influence in the field of international aid.

2. Establishment of Integrated Aid Agencies

All the four countries have established special foreign aid agencies. Due to historical, institutional, and national conditions, the functions of these institutions are significantly different. The Brazilian Cooperation Agency and the South African Development Partnership Agency emphasize the comprehensive coordination structure for foreign aid, which are both based on the fact that aid agencies are scattered and the related ministries and commissions have their own budgets. With such institutional legacy and divided departmental interests, the two agencies are not positioned for specific decision-making and implementation of foreign aid, but for the communication and coordination of various aid departments and agencies. In theory, these two agencies have comparative advantages in information collection, diplomatic guidance, and monitoring and evaluation. Nevertheless, in practice, though the Brazilian Cooperation Agency controls the allocation of Brazilian technical cooperation funds and the South African Development Partnership Agency exerts certain influence on the African Renaissance Fund, the long-time practice of various ministries and commissions conducting foreign aid separately has been difficult to change. As they lack the necessary authority in aid affairs, the Brazilian Cooperation Agency and the South African Development Partnership Agency are far from becoming integrated aid agencies.

India's Development Partnership Administration, similar to China's Department of Foreign Assistance, is deeply involved in the aid policy and implementation. The three divisions under India's Development Partnership Administration are directly responsible for India's aid projects, while China's Department of Foreign Assistance gives direct business guidance to the agencies implementing China's aid projects. To some extent, the policy and implementation of these two countries' foreign aid has been integrated, which results in better performance in communication and coordination as well as policy implementation.

3. Internal Operating Mechanism

Since the dedicated foreign aid agencies of the four countries attach more emphasis to aid practice, it is more important to do in-depth analysis of the leadership mechanism behind the foreign aid, which is central to the decision-making and implementation of foreign aid. In this regard, the performance of the four countries is not satisfactory. India's performance is slightly better in that its Ministry of Foreign Affairs is responsible for leading the foreign aid work and controls most of the aid projects. Although there are other ministries and commissions involved in foreign aid, the Ministry of Foreign Affairs undertakes a fixed leading position; hence, the leadership mechanism of India's foreign aid is relatively clear. The leadership mechanism of Brazil's foreign aid is embodied in the loose coordination between its Ministry of Foreign Affairs and other ministries and commissions. The Brazilian Cooperation Agency under the Ministry of Foreign Affairs is essentially a comprehensive coordination agency that does not command the necessary authority to perform the functions of comprehensive coordination. The situation in South Africa is similar, where the South African Development Partnership Agency is merely a comprehensive coordinating agency. The long-term competition and the overlapping and separation of businesses between the Ministry of Finance and the Ministry of International Relations and Cooperation in the field of foreign aid have further complicated South Africa's leadership mechanism. The situation in China is not ideal either. Though the Ministry of Commerce of China is authorized by the State Council to be in charge of China's foreign aid matters, it needs to negotiate and communicate with the Ministry of Finance and the Ministry of Foreign Affairs in practical implementation of foreign aid. While the Ministry of Finance is less involved in the specific matters of bilateral foreign aid, the Ministry of Foreign Affairs has a greater say, aiming at ensuring that China's aid plans are in line with China's foreign policies and interests. The two ministries differ greatly in their foreign aid goals: the Ministry of Foreign Affairs focuses on safeguarding China's diplomatic interests, while the Ministry of Commerce focuses on promoting China's economic interests; thus, the two ministries sometimes have frictions and competition over China's foreign aid agenda. Therefore, China's leadership mechanism of foreign aid needs to be further straightened out.

Fund allocation is another important factor affecting the operation of foreign aid. In this regard, China and India have performed slightly better. Most of India's foreign aid funds are allocated by the Ministry of External Affairs, and the credit loans provided by the Export-Import Bank of India are also subject to negotiations with it. The foreign aid budgets and funds of other Indian ministries and commissions are small in proportion. Therefore, India is more concentrated in the allocation of funds. The situation in China is similar to that of India. The Ministry of Commerce is responsible for drafting the draft aid budget and has received most of the bilateral aid funds. Meanwhile, the preferential credit loans of the Export-Import Bank of China are also subject to negotiations with the Ministry of Commerce. International cooperation funds from other ministries and commissions are small in proportion. Brazil's federal funds for technical cooperation are mainly distributed through the Brazilian Cooperation Agency, but the related ministries and commissions and other agencies have independent aid budgets or funds as well as third-party resources obtained through tripartite collaboration; therefore, Brazil does not have a unified outlet of foreign aid funds, which means scattered financial resources of foreign aid and great difficulties in project coordination and communication. The situation in South Africa is not ideal either. In addition to the capital dispersion resulted from the independent aid budgets of various ministries and commissions and third-party resources, the preferential loans of the South African Development Bank under the guidance of the Ministry of Finance also constitute a major outlet of South Africa's foreign aid funds. Hence, the allocation of South Africa's foreign aid funds is also relatively scattered.

Coordinated departmental network relations are also vital to the effective operation of foreign aid. In Brazil and South Africa, different ministries and commissions play independent roles in foreign aid, thus the interdepartmental network is loose and fragmented. There are huge barriers and conflicts of interest derived from the separation of old projects and institutions among the three divisions under the Indian Development Partnership Administration. Although the Development Partnership Administration nominally carries out the overall management of India's foreign aid, the aid plans are in fact operated in a decentralized way, which is due to the lack of mutual assistance and coordination among the divisions. China's foreign aid interministerial coordination mechanism, more symbolic than practical, is conveyed in the form of annual meeting, but seldom plays a coordinating role in routine work. Despite the fact that the Ministry of Commerce leads China's foreign aid, its competition with the Ministry of Foreign Affairs makes it difficult to integrate the aid forces and achieve synergy.

A sound monitoring and evaluation system serves as the guarantee for the continuous improvement of aid project quality and aid efficiency. In terms of the records of aid data monitoring, Brazil, which has been engaged in more tripartite collaboration, performs better with relatively complete data tracking and records. South Africa has no government agency responsible for monitoring and recording the aid data, while India features poor data quality due to confusion and inconsistencies in its accounting system. China has some data records that have not been made public yet, so its operation and data quality are not known to outsiders. In terms of project monitoring and evaluation, there is monitoring and evaluation for specific aid projects but relatively scarce long-term evaluation of aid policies. Relying on the embassies and personnel of the Ministry of Foreign Affairs in the recipient country, the donor country can monitor and evaluate the aid projects in the recipient country at a lower operating cost. However, with numerous tasks, multiple functions, and greater mobility, the assigned officials do not regard the monitoring and evaluation of foreign aid as the focus of their work and they lack relevant professional knowledge and capabilities; therefore, it is not feasible to rely on them to make arrangements for long-term evaluation of the aid to the recipient country. The difficulty mentioned here is shared by the four countries and even by almost all the countries that rely on the diplomatic departments to monitor and evaluate their aid projects.

Based on the four-dimensional analysis of the aid governance structures and an overview of the situations of the four BRICS countries, this part hereby summarizes the evaluation of the aid governance structures of the four BRICS countries as follows (Table 7.1).

Table 7.1: Comparison of the aid governance structures of the BRICS countries.

		Brazil	India	South Africa	China
Establishment of integrated aid agencies		Normal	Good	Normal	Good
Construction of integrated aid guiding principles		Good	Normal	Normal	Good
Integrated internal operating mechanism	Definite leading mechanism	Normal	Good	Normal	Normal
	Integrated fund system	Normal	Good	Normal	Good
	Coordinated departmental network	Normal	Normal	Normal	Normal
	Sound monitoring and evaluation system	Very good	Normal	Normal	Good

4. Conclusions and Suggestions

Through combing and comparing the aid governance structures of the four emerging BRICS donor countries, this part finds that there is still much room for the four countries to improve and perfect their own aid governance structures. Although they have established dedicated aid agencies, China and India have better performance in integrated functions, while Brazil and South Africa are relatively weaker. None of them has managed to form a programmatic document to guide their countries' foreign aid. In terms of the internal operating mechanism, India's leadership mechanism is comparatively clearer. India and China have more centralized control of the aid funds with stronger binding force, while Brazil and South Africa have more fragmented control due to the scattered sources of funds. The foreign aid departmental network relations of the four countries are relatively loose or even harbor major conflicts of interest. Brazil, which is involved in more tripartite assistance, performs relatively better in the construction of the monitoring and evaluation system, followed by China, whereas South Africa and India have serious problems in this respect.

Based on the above comparative analysis, this part puts forward the following suggestions regarding the development directions of China's aid governance structure.

Firstly, strengthen the establishment of integrated aid agencies. At present, the Department of Foreign Assistance, as a department under the Ministry of Commerce, is mainly responsible for the foreign aid projects belonging to the Ministry of Commerce. Although it enjoys certain rights to know the foreign aid of other ministries or units, the Department is far from being able to undertake the important task of coordinating and integrating the foreign aid at all levels of government and various departments across the country. Therefore, it is necessary to further integrate the institutional framework for foreign aid by breaking up the barriers between all levels, functions, and departments, and to strengthen the coordination and communication mechanisms to fully integrate multiparty aid forces to complement each other, so as to improve the efficiency of China's foreign aid and form a sound situation of cooperation and mutual progress.

Secondly, formulate and promulgate programmatic documents guiding China's foreign aid. Foreign aid has become a critical component of China's foreign policy, having attracted more and more attention from the domestic public and the international community. In its long-term foreign aid practice, China has actually formed certain principles, styles, and methods of foreign aid, yet it still needs to formulate legally binding guiding principles of foreign aid in written and institutional form. It is very important to form a set of guiding principles of foreign aid, which is not only helpful to integrate foreign aid into the country's comprehensive national strategic considerations, thus uniting domestic forces to serve the overall national strategic goals, but also helpful to respond to domestic and foreign skepticism about China's foreign aid, build a good international image, and gain understanding and support at home and abroad. Moreover, as a representative of emerging donor countries, it helps to spread China's ideas about development, unite with the vast majority of emerging donor countries, and guide the direction of international aid rules.

Thirdly, straighten out the internal operating mechanism of foreign aid. In view of the current situation that the foreign aid inter-ministerial coordination mechanism centering on the Ministry of Commerce, the Ministry of Foreign Affairs and the Ministry of Finance does not produce evident effects, the leadership mechanism needs to be straightened out, the departmental network relationship needs to be coordinated, and the monitoring and evaluation system needs to be further strengthened, China may establish a deliberative coordination agency analogous to the

"Central Leading Group for Foreign Development Aid" at an appropriate time to streamline the leadership mechanism from a higher level, strengthen the mutual trust and coordination among foreign aid departments, reinforce performance evaluation and accountability, and elevate the level of standardized system construction.

Section 6. China's Aid Management System: A Path-Dependence Perspective

As China has rapidly become one of the major donor countries on the stage of international development, how to manage foreign aid along with how to improve its governance system has become an urgent problem. However, there are few theoretical studies on the governance system and the obstacles to its reform. This section first explores the differences in aid management system between China and traditional donors. Therefore, this section makes an in-depth study on the evolution of China's complex aid management system and employs the path dependence theory to explain the underlying reasons. Furthermore, this section analyzes the administrative arrangements at the ministerial and provincial levels and explains why the current system would hinder the effectiveness of China's foreign aid. Finally, this section attempts to discuss the impact of the newly established China International Development Cooperation Agency (CIDCA) on China's aid management system and to improve the current system in accordance with the path dependence theory.

1. Introduction

Since World War II, international development aid has evolved from developed countries to developing countries mainly in the form of ODA. However, since the beginning of this century, the Great Recession in particular has accelerated the shift of the engine of economic growth from the traditional developed countries to the emerging economies, and the development assistance from emerging countries has increased on a daily basis, thus the pattern of international development has entered a new stage. There is no doubt that China is leading this trend. According to official data generally considered to be underestimated, the total amount of China's foreign aid was RMB 250.63 billion from 1994 to 2009 and RMB 89.34 billion (US $12.8 billion) from 2010 to 2012. AidData even estimates that between 2000 and 2014, China provided more than US $350 billion of such aid and investment. At the same time, China's aid management system has been constantly evolving. For instance, the recently established CIDCA is one of the products of the most profound reforms in government structure in the past 20 years. However, how the Agency will play a role and exert its impact remains to be investigated, which entails more in-depth understanding of China's foreign aid.

There are generally three types of research on China's development assistance. The first type includes the calculation and prediction of China's actual development assistance (Kitano, 2014; UNDP, 2015; Kitano and Harada, 2016; AidData, n.d.). The second type studies the impact of China's aid on the recipient countries, with special attention to the differences between China's aid and the traditional donors' aid (Diamond, 2008; Foster *et al.*, 2009; Reilly, 2012; Bräutigam, 2015). The third type weighs the most for the present study, because it focuses on China's domestic aid management, especially on the formulation process of China's aid policy and the interaction of relevant government institutions therein (Cheung *et al.*, 2014; Xu and Carey, 2015; Varrall, 2016; Zhang and Smith, 2017).

In recent years, there have been three different views on the third type of research. The first view holds that development aid constitutes an important diplomatic tool for China's foreign policy. More importantly, since China's development aid management system is dominated by the Ministry of Commerce, China's aid centers on economy, which is different from the traditional ODA (Bräutigam, 2011). Contrary to the traditional view of seeing Chinese government institutions consistent and systematic, the second view in the literature maintains that China's aid policy lacks strategic considerations in a comprehensive way, thus leading to inconsistent strategies and premature aid projects (Varrall, 2016). The third view, investigating these problems in a more systematic way, believes that China's aid management system, under the leadership of the Communist Party of China, results in competing for influence among various actors through continuous and even fierce competitions. In other words, the Ministry of Commerce, the Ministry of Finance, and the Ministry of Foreign Affairs and other institutions act as the ultimate designers and decision makers of China's aid management structure (Zhang and Smith, 2017). Despite detailed analysis of the participants' decision-making and interaction model from the perspective of international politics by the existing studies, there is still a lack of theoretical reasoning behind the present aid system setting and its historical evolution.

This section attempts to analyze the underlying reasons and raises several research questions to illustrate why the existing literature and theory are not sufficient enough. Why is China's aid management system so different from the traditional donation system and from the major emerging donor countries? For instance, China is not only vastly different from the developed donor countries, but also different from the major emerging donor countries, that is, the Ministry of Commerce instead of the Ministry of Foreign Affairs acts as the main executing agency of foreign aid. In addition, why have many establishments and arrangements, obviously considered ineffective and inefficient, not been adjusted yet? For instance, the development financing provided by China Development Bank to the recipient countries has been operated and funded by its provincial offices rather than its headquarters. What is the driving force behind China's current development aid system? How can it evolve and make progress? With the ever-expanding scale of China's development aid, the root causes behind these problems or puzzles become more prominent. This section attempts to answer these questions from the perspective of public administration with detailed evidence and reveals its underlying logic by resorting to the theory of path dependence.

The remaining part of this section is structured as follows. The second part conducts a detailed analysis of the current management system of China's aid agencies. The third part discusses the development of China's foreign aid system and the fourth part introduces an analytical framework, which illustrates in detail how to use the path dependence theory to explain the current arrangements between the ministries and the provinces. The fifth part discusses the implications of the newly established CIDCA for China's foreign aid management system and puts forward some suggestions to improve the policies of the current aid management system based on the path dependence theory. The sixth part sums up the whole section.

2. The Governance System of China's Foreign Aid

China has a history of more than 70 years in foreign aid. During this period, the world has undergone the tremendous transformation from planned economy to market economy; and China has transformed from a major recipient country to a major donor country, especially after the implementation of the Belt and Road Initiative. However, China's aid management system has not changed in accordance with the rapid development of economy. In fact, we hold that China's aid management agencies, like those in other parts of the world, are more often than not inertia institutions.

In China's foreign aid management system, as shown in Figure 7.4, the Ministry of Commerce, the Ministry of Finance, and the Ministry of Foreign Affairs are the most important actors, with the Ministry of Commerce playing a central role so far. Most of the bilateral foreign

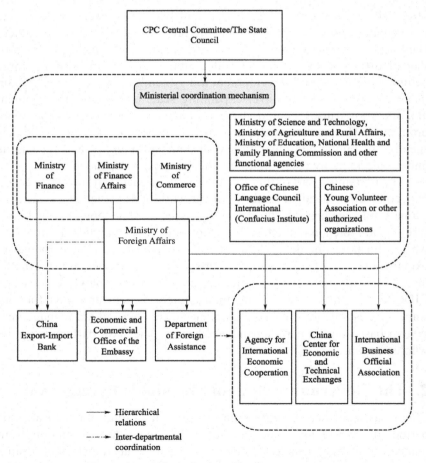

Figure 7.4: China's foreign aid governance system.

aid budget is allocated to the Ministry of Commerce. The Department of Foreign Assistance (DFA) under the Ministry of Commerce is the core institution for China's foreign aid, which is responsible for drafting and organizing the implementation of foreign aid policies and plans, promoting the reform of aid forms, organizing foreign aid negotiations and signing agreements, handling intergovernmental aid affairs, drafting foreign aid plans and organizing their implementation, supervising and inspecting the implementation of foreign aid projects, and so on. The Ministry of Commerce has also established an international economic cooperation agency to manage completed projects and technical cooperation projects. For instance, the China International Center for Economic and Technical Exchanges is responsible for in-kind donations and the Academy for International Business Officials is responsible for cooperation projects on human resources development. The specific implementation of these foreign aid projects was initially carried out under the funding of the DFA and later directly transferred to those subsidiary agencies under the Ministry of Commerce. The DFA has gradually focused on the long-term planning of China's foreign aid. The Economic and Commercial Office of the Chinese Embassy in the recipient country is responsible for the direct coordination and management of the recipient country's foreign aid projects. The Ministry of Commerce also works closely with the China Export-Import Bank on preferential loans and export buyer's credit to help the recipient countries.

The Ministry of Foreign Affairs also plays an important role in China's foreign aid decision-making process. It regularly negotiates with the Ministry of Commerce to ensure that China's foreign aid policy is in line with China's national foreign policy. It even has the power of veto on some specific diplomatic interests, such as the Taiwan issue. In addition, it occasionally has discretion over a small proportion of the foreign aid budget. It can also provide suggestions on the planning and implementation of the aid projects through embassies and economic and commercial consultants.

As the source of foreign aid funds, the Ministry of Finance is also crucial to China's foreign aid. The budgets and aid projects drafted by the Ministry of Commerce must be approved and incorporated into the national budget by the Ministry of Finance, which is also in charge of China's multilateral assistance and provides assistance to development agencies such as the World Bank, UN agencies and the Asian Development Bank. In addition, it is the sole shareholder of the state-owned policy lender, China Export-Import Bank. Despite no inter-ference in its business, the Ministry of Finance is responsible for compen-sating the interest rate difference between the Bank's preferential loans and the commercial loans.

The ministerial coordination mechanism was established in 2011 to strengthen coordination among these departments. However, the fact that the director comes from the Ministry of Commerce and the deputy direc-tors come from the Ministry of Foreign Affairs and the Ministry of Finance not only enhances the role of the Ministry of Commerce as a *de facto* leader but may also undermine the effectiveness of the ministerial coordination mechanism, although the information about the role of the ministerial coordination mechanism is not readily available. The mecha-nism seems to be a symbolic entity with little discussion or cooperation except for holding annual meetings.

The Ministry of Science and Technology and other ministries and commissions, the Office of Chinese Language Council International (Confucius Institute) and other government agencies, and the Chinese Young Volunteers Association and other authorized institutions have also played a certain role in China's foreign aid. The Ministry of Commerce has the right of assignment in the implementation of specific aid projects. With its approval, aid projects can be handed over to other organizations and the relevant aid budget can also be transferred. Under some circum-stances, the State Council decides which ministries or organizations are directly responsible for connecting with international aid organizations. For instance, the Ministry of Agriculture is responsible for cooperating with the Food and Agriculture Organization of the United Nations and the World Food Program, including providing assistance to a third country. In addition, many ministries and commissions have international coopera-tion budgets available for foreign aid, but such projects do not have to be notified to the Ministry of Commerce, despite its right to know.

The Central Committee of the CPC and the State Council do not directly take part in the specific implementation of foreign aid, but major changes in aid policies and practices still require approval from the Central Committee of the CPC. Large scale construction projects require approval from the State Council. The white paper on China's foreign aid, though drafted by the Ministry of Commerce, needs to be audited and released by the State Council. Meanwhile, the Central Committee of the CPC and the State Council shall make the final decision in case of further coordination among different foreign aid departments.

To sum up, compared with other BRICS countries, China's aid management is quite different from that of other countries. The most important difference is that China is the only major emerging country with the Ministry of Commerce and relevant economic departments leading the aid management system. China has been criticized for relying too much on the economic interests of foreign aid, which is partly justifiable. Nevertheless, we believe that the Chinese government has realized the shortcomings of the current system. For instance, some scholars have argued whether China should give the Ministry of Foreign Affairs more say and power in foreign aid to better match its national interests, probably with less attention to the economy, which can be very difficult: as a matter of fact, we have seen that the Ministry of Commerce has expanded its role and power in China's aid management. We think that this unique system and its evolution can be explained in accordance with the path dependence theory, which will be discussed further.

3. Evolution of the Governance System

China's foreign aid started upon the founding of new China in 1949 and accelerated its pace of development after the reform and opening up in 1978. Since China joined the WTO in 2001, the development of China's foreign aid has been further accelerated. Although China's aid governance system has been evolving over the past 60 years, the Ministry of Commerce or its predecessor has retained the most critical role in aid operation and management. For this issue, the historical path can provide some plausible explanations.

3.1 *The early stage of foreign aid management (1950–1960)*

In the early 1950s, China began to provide foreign aid to countries in the same "alliance" (Communist regimes). The top-down approach was adopted in aid decision-making, that is, the central government formulated the policies and all departments were responsible for implementation. On 7 August 1952, the 17th meeting of the Central People's Government Committee announced the establishment of the Ministry of Foreign Trade, which has been responsible for the implementation of foreign aid ever since. At the same time, the Ministry of Finance was responsible for allocating foreign exchange. It was the first time that China

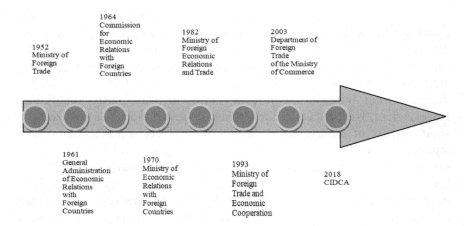

Figure 7.5:   The historical evolution of China's foreign aid system.

institutionalized its aid management. In 1954, China began to provide foreign aid in the form of large-scale and complete sets of equipment under the administration of the Ministry of Foreign Trade and the State Planning Commission. The former was responsible for negotiating with the recipient countries, while the latter was responsible for dealing with the projects and equipment components with relevant ministries or agencies. However, this trend was reversed when the Ministry of Foreign Trade set up subordinate agencies such as the Bureau of Technical Cooperation, the Bureau of Complete Sets of Equipment and the Ministry of Economic Relations with Foreign Countries, all of which were responsible for foreign aid (Figure 7.5).

3.2 *The development stage of foreign aid management (1961–1982)*

Under the background of political events such as the Great Leap Forward, the Cultural Revolution, and the reform and opening up. This period can be divided into three stages.

The first stage was from 1961 to 1964. In 1961, the General Administration of Economic Relations with Foreign Countries was established, which was in charge of the Bureau of Technical Cooperation and the Ministry of Economic Relations with Foreign Countries. Aid-related affairs were transferred from the Ministry of Foreign Trade to the Administration, with the Ministry of Finance being responsible for allocating funds.

The second stage was from 1964 to 1970, when the General Administration of Economic Relations with Foreign Countries was replaced by the newly established agency, the Commission for Economic Relations with Foreign Countries, which was responsible for all the foreign aid to socialist countries, Asian countries, and African countries. In addition, the Bureau of Equipment and Materials and the Technical Office were set up to supplement the Commission. In 1965, the Commission expanded its jurisdiction through the establishment of four regional offices of East China, North China, Northeast China, and Central China. The responsibilities of the Commission includes purchasing aid equipment, selecting and dispatching experts for technical assistance, training foreign interns from the recipient countries, and receiving the delegates of the recipient countries.

The third stage was from 1970 to 1982, when China's foreign aid increased significantly with the development and extension of foreign affairs. In order to improve the management level and efficiency, the Chinese government decided in 1970 to restructure the Commission for Economic Relations with Foreign Countries into a larger department, the Ministry of Economic Relations with Foreign Countries. The new Ministry was composed of six bureaus, which were responsible for foreign aid work regarding socialist countries, African countries, the interns from recipient countries, planning, finance, and economic cooperation.

3.3 *The system construction stage of foreign aid management (1982–)*

With the gradual advancement of economic reform in the early 1980s, the Chinese government carried out major administrative reforms, including the increasingly systematic establishment of its aid governance system. This period can be divided into three stages.

From 1982 to 1993, as the predecessor of the Department of Foreign Trade under the Ministry of Commerce, the Ministry of Foreign Economic Relations and Trade launched a series of major foreign aid initiatives. In 1982, entrusted by the central government, it merged the major agencies related to foreign trade and economic relations, including the Ministry of Foreign Trade, the Ministry of Economic Relations with Foreign Countries, the Import & Export Regulatory Commission and the Foreign Trade and Investment Regulatory Commission. The Ministry of

Foreign Economic Relations and Trade became the administrative body of official foreign aid. Its main tasks and responsibilities include three aspects: the first is the formulation and implementation of the policies, regulations, rules, and assistance plans; the second is to review and supervise the progress of China's foreign aid; and the third is to manage and review the distribution of foreign aid funds and propose China's reform plans of foreign aid.

The second stage was from 1993 to 2003, when the Ministry of Foreign Economic Relations and Trade was renamed the Ministry of Foreign Trade and Economic Cooperation, which played a leading role in China's foreign aid. During this period, China's foreign aid responsibilities and projects had increased significantly, such as macroeconomic supervision and capacity-building for the recipient countries. Therefore, the Department of Foreign Assistance, a special agency under the Ministry, was designated to be a dedicated agency responsible for foreign aid management.

The third stage started since 2003, when the Department of Foreign Trade of the Ministry of Commerce was officially established, replacing the Ministry of Foreign Trade and Economic Cooperation as the administrative organ of China's aid system. With China's joining the WTO in 2001, China's exports and foreign direct investment (FDI) have expanded rapidly, making the Ministry of Commerce play a greater role and assume the leading role in China's foreign economic cooperation, including foreign aid. As China's aid began to increase significantly, this stage was of great significance.

4. Path Dependence of the Foreign Aid System

The path dependence theory in the field of public administration is often used as a framework to analyze the historical role of the evolution of public administration, and has proved that there is no significant change due to the historical lock-in effect, which is just the case with regard to China's aid management system.

Although China's aid management system is sometimes considered inefficient or even defective, the lack of necessary reform can be attributed to path dependence. These institutions are used to the vested interests and the way of project examination. In addition, we also attempt to apply the two dimensions of "increasing returns" and "exogenous vs. endogenous variables" in path dependence proposed by Pierson (2000) to explain China's interministerial administrative arrangements. Moreover, the case study of development finance, an important component of China's international development cooperation, can explain the relationship between the central and the provincial aid agencies.

4.1 *Inter-departmental administrative arrangements*

4.1.1 *Increasing returns*

The concept of increasing returns points to two important characteristics of path dependence (Pierson, 2000). First, it emphasizes how the cost of switching to another alternative method increases over time in the course of path dependence. Second, it emphasizes the importance of time, sequence, and formative events (Pierson, 2000). In the course of increasing returns and path dependence, early events are more important than later events (Pierson, 2000). This concept is also applicable to China's foreign aid management system.

At the level of the central government, the Ministry of Commerce or its predecessor remains a central participant despite many changes in the past 60 years, which is mainly a matter of time. At the initial stage, most of China's international aid involved economic goods implemented in the form of Soviet style friendship. As China has gradually been expanding its international aid, this model remains unchanged, or even gets further enhanced. This leads to the "increasing returns" of the Ministry of Commerce as a major aid participant. Though foreign aid plays an important role in foreign policy, it becomes more difficult to change with the passage of time. Unlike most traditional donor countries and emerging donor countries, the importance of the role of the Ministry of Foreign Affairs in China's international aid is far lower than that of the Ministry of Commerce. The cost of switching systems gradually increases, as can be explained by the path dependence theory.

4.1.2 *Endogenous vs. exogenous*

How an institution or system adopts a path in the first place and how to change the path fundamentally depend on the endogenous and exogenous variables. Exogenous changes are caused by variations in external parameters — in other words, these are changes outside the institution. For instance, changes in the international geopolitical pattern may bring about significant impact on foreign policy decisions, including foreign aid. On the other hand, endogenous changes refer to the changes brought about by changes in the system itself — in other words, these are changes within the system. Endogenous variables are considered to be self-reinforcing, which will drive the institutions to adhere to the current path. In most cases, as Thelen has concluded, destructive processes are exogenous, while reinforcing processes are endogenous (Thelen, 1999, pp. 397–399). This may well explain the evolution of China's aid governance system.

We try to divide it into exogenous and endogenous variables to explain the current system and its trend of evolution. As far as the exogenous variables are concerned, geopolitical variables such as the socialist camp are the main factors to define the path dependence equilibrium of China's foreign aid management system. The original purpose of China's foreign aid was to provide aid to countries of the socialist camp on the basis of friendship. Under the principle of "non-interference in internal affairs", this variable interacts with China's foreign policy to shape the tradition of China's foreign aid that focuses on economy rather than politics. Moreover, because the planned economy is usually centered on material objects rather than money, the Ministry of Economic Relations and Trade has become an ideal organization for foreign aid. Other exogenous policies, such as the "going global", the Belt and Road Initiative, also have the possibility of deviating from equilibrium, but their impact remains to be observed. In other words, a more powerful exogenous variable is needed to reshape China's aid governance system. On the other hand, some endogenous variables may reinforce the current aid management system. For example, the Ministry of Commerce, facing the competition with other ministries and commissions, may be impelled to focus more attention on the economic interests with comparative advantages so as to consolidate its status. Besides, the competition within major institutions, such as the competition between the Department of Foreign Assistance and the Department of Foreign Investment and Economic Cooperation under the Ministry of Commerce, makes the Ministry of Commerce more prominent in the foreign aid management system. This is largely due to the competition between the two departments for the voices and resources of foreign aid. With the exponential growth of China's overseas capital and trade, the expansion and growth of China's Ministry of Commerce has further amplified this effect. Just because of this, the evolution of China's foreign aid management system can be explained by the interaction of exogenous factors and endogenous factors.

4.2 *The relationship between central and provincial aid agencies: A case study of development finance*

Although there is a large body of literature on the relevant departments of China's foreign aid, research on the relationship between the central and provincial foreign aid agencies remains inadequate. Therefore, we try to supplement the existing literature with cases of development finance. The development finance in foreign aid of the Chinese government is regarded as one of the most important ways of international development cooperation (Xu and Carey, 2015). Development finance is mainly provided by two official "policy banks", namely, China Export-Import Bank and China Development Bank, with the former providing more preferential loans than the latter. At present, most of the literature on development finance concentrates on its quantity, including AidData. However, there are few studies on the operation model and historical evolution of the management system of China's development finance. We will take the cooperation between China Development Bank and Ethiopia as an example to illustrate how to apply the path dependence theory to understand the management of development finance.

China Development Bank is the world's largest development bank, with total assets more than 10 times that of the World Bank. Different from the foreign aid dominated by the central government, the development funds of China Development Bank are mainly executed by provincial branch institutions. For instance, the loans and project execution for Ethiopia are provided by the Qinghai Branch of China Development Bank, which is located in the relatively remote, low-income province of Qinghai. The following two reasons render this arrangement somewhat abnormal.

The first reason points to a possible mismatch between Qinghai Province and Ethiopia in terms of donation funds. Qinghai, a province in Northwest China with underdeveloped industrialization, is not an ideal institution to provide technical assistance and expertise to Ethiopia. For instance, according to a news report on *Qinghai Daily* on 7 July 2011, Qinghai Central Business District signed an agreement with the Sugar

Corporation of Ethiopia to provide the Corporation with a loan of US $150 million. Nevertheless, Qinghai Province is a place with virtually no sugar production, nor a major place of sugar consumption, which makes the contract more like a commercial loan than what China Development Bank calls an international development assistance project. The Guangxi Branch of China Development Bank, located in Guangxi which is a major producer of sugar, may be the best loan provider because it can provide more professional technical assistance while providing loans. Another mismatch is the difference in weight between Ethiopia and China Development Bank. Ethiopia is one of the most important partners of China in Africa, which far outweighs the Qinghai Branch of China Development Bank. This situation is mainly attributed to historical reasons. When China Development Bank began to grant international development loans, the Headquarters mainly assigned branch banks to the target customers or recipient countries based on the matching of their economic development stages. However, as the weight of Ethiopia for China grows rapidly, the arrangement of matching Ethiopia with Qinghai Branch of China Development Bank remains unchanged, even though other branches with equivalent donation funds or better expertise and capabilities can provide development assistance to Ethiopia.

If it is reasonable to designate the Ministry of Commerce as the core executive agency considering economic factors or binding aid, then the arrangement of development finance would not be the best choice. To a large extent, there is a mismatch in the arrangement whereby Qinghai Branch of China Development Bank manages the development finance for Ethiopia. However, as is pointed out by the path dependence theory, an institution or arrangement can remain on the suboptimal path only because it merely considers the choices adjacent to its current path. With more and more increasing returns, it is unlikely for China Development Bank to assign a more suitable branch to provide optimized policy loans and capacity building to Ethiopia.

In summary, the factor of increasing returns proposed by the path dependence theory can well explain the evolution of China's foreign aid management and the setting of development finance. This is a typical case that can be explained by the path dependence theory, that is, when the past has impact on the future, the "lock-in" effect of the system makes it difficult to change or restructure. More importantly, as Pierson (2000) puts it, "in the long run, the locked-in results may generate lower returns than the abandoned choices".

5. CIDCA: An Attempt to Break Through Path Dependence?

At the first session of the 13th National People's Congress in 2018, China announced the establishment of CIDCA, which is a part of the largest restructuring plan of the central government in 20 years with the aim of streamlining departments. It is one of the few departments that are newly established rather than merged or abolished, which demonstrates that the central government attaches great importance to international development. According to the official statement, CIDCA will integrate some functions of the Ministry of Commerce and the Ministry of Foreign Affairs, taking charge of strategic planning, policy and foreign aid coordination, and supervising the implementation. Compared with the former ministerial coordination mechanism, CIDCA has significantly changed the relationship between the central government and the ministries. The ministerial coordination mechanism is only a symbolic coordination mechanism led by the Ministry of Commerce, while CIDCA is directly under the State Council of China. There are two differences between CIDCA and the ministerial coordination mechanism.

First of all, compared with the ministerial coordination mechanism with no official entities, the head of CIDCA, with the rank of vice minister, reports directly to the State Council. Secondly, CIDCA is responsible for formulating strategies, policies, coordinating, and supervising foreign aid, rather than holding annual meetings. Although it seems like a major reform and deviates from the previous system, the change can still be explained by the path dependence theory. The problem is how to break through the path dependence theory and emphasize the exogenous factors. Since President Xi Jinping took office in 2017, the Belt and Road Initiative has become the most important foreign policy of China in the coming years, which requires more strategic planning and coordination of foreign aid. This Initiative is regarded as more distinct and ambitious than the "Going Global" strategy. Therefore, the establishment of CIDCA can be explained by the path dependence theory. According to the theory, the emergence of strategic objectives is likely to dissolve the existing path, because internal forces would be generated due to the absence of strategic choice and being locked in a specific path (Wang *et al.*, 2016). Moreover, it is widely believed that President Xi Jinping commands more power than his predecessors, which could be an exogenous impact on the foreign aid governance system centering on the Ministry of Commerce in the past decades. This can also be explained by the path dependence theory which holds that path dissolution may be driven by external forces, thus possibly shaking the system and leading to deviation of the organization from the path (Arthur, 1994). In summary, though the call for the establishment of an independent aid agency has emerged for a long time, it was only realized during Xi's term of office, indicating that the institutionalization of dissolving the existing path involves momentous political strategy, power, and will.

Although the senior leadership of the central government harbors bold reform ambition for the aid governance system, the actual function and evolution model of it are yet unknown. Based on the information available, the present study argues that the central government is more likely to pursue the minimization of transaction costs or reform costs than the maximization of overall efficiency. Besides, given the Ministry of Commerce has taken charge of most assistance, the implementation of assistance may also remain unchanged. Though the efficiency of China's foreign aid may be improved by permitting special agencies, the excessively high transaction costs may also force ambitious reformers to take prudent measures to reduce the transaction costs. For instance, USAID or Japan International Cooperation Agency (JICA) takes charge of the formulation of aid strategy and policy as well as the implementation and supervision. Wang Xiaotao, a former deputy director of the National Development and Reform Commission in charge of foreign investment, overseas investment and trade, was appointed as the first director of CIDCA. The appointment indicates that China's foreign aid in the form of economic development and infrastructure construction may remain the focus of China's agenda on international development.

In view of China's expansion of foreign aid while developing financing, it is imperative to improve the effectiveness and efficiency of foreign aid. As a matter of fact, the central government has been aware of this problem and authorized CIDCA to monitor and evaluate China's foreign aid. Accordingly, we are equally interested in how to improve the new system to fully optimize its effectiveness and efficiency. First of all, it is essential to strengthen the leadership of CIDCA, which requires a lot of political resources and funding. Though CIDCA acts as the core force in charge of China's foreign aid, it remains a considerable challenge to make the policies come true duly and influence other agencies. One obvious reason is that CIDCA is a vice-ministerial organ, not as powerful as the Ministry of Commerce or the Ministry of Foreign Affairs. As is indicated by the path dependence theory, with the Ministry of Commerce and the Ministry of Foreign Affairs getting increased returns as the main body of China's foreign aid, the extent to which CIDCA can play a central role and integrate the functions of those two ministries in China's foreign aid management largely depends on the political will of the central government. Secondly, it is helpful to improve the quality of aid projects by improving the transparency of China's management system and aid projects. As was pointed out by Sydow *et al.* (2009), the lack of transparency among

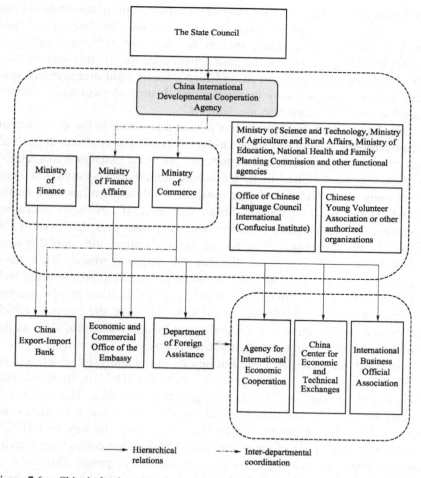

Figure 7.6:   China's foreign aid governance structure after the establishment of CIDCA.

organizations makes it unrealistic to think that the development of organizations is completely under the control of the management. Consequently, improving the transparency of the management system and aid projects can not only make the level administrators better control the affiliated institutions related to China's foreign aid but also better supervise and evaluate the projects (Figure 7.6).

6. Conclusion

As China has rapidly become one of the major donor countries on the international development stage, how to manage its foreign aid and improve its aid management system has become an urgent problem. Through the introduction of the path dependence theory, this section contributes to the existing research on China's foreign aid management system, which enables us to understand its historical evolution, current situation, and the interaction mechanism.

We have found that history has played a key role in the evolution of the governance system of China's aid management institutions. It derived from the exogenous historical factors and provided assistance to socialist countries in kind. Since then, the whole governance system has been developing along this path. Up to now, the whole system has been established on the basis of "South–South Cooperation", with its operation centering on the Ministry of Commerce. We also find that even if the system is sometimes searching for the optimal option, the control system still fails to switch to a more effective alternative approach. We believe that, under the background of the dynamic political patterns and the Belt and Road Initiative, China's foreign aid system will usher in a pioneering situation with the establishment of CIDCA. However, the extent to which the system can be improved depends on a host of variables, such as the transaction costs, political will, and transparency.

In addition, there are some limitations in the analysis, which will be studied in the future. First, limited research on CIDCA restricts our prediction of the evolution of China's aid governance system. This is not only due to the lack of public information but also due to the dynamic evolution of the political pattern which may also affect the role of CIDCA. Secondly, our analysis of the relationship between the central and provincial governments primarily focuses on the development financing of China Development Bank, which is not only owing to the importance of development financing in China's foreign aid structure but also because of the availability of information. However, whether the findings are applicable to other aid agencies necessitates further study. Therefore, we call for more empirical studies to further explore these issues as the reference information and materials necessary for the research are gradually made public.

References

African Renaissance and International Cooperation Fund. *Annual Report for 2015/16 Fiscal Year*, Pretoria. URL: http://www.dirco.gov.za/department/african_renaissence_2015_2016/african_renaissance_fund_2015_16.pdf.

Arimoto, Y. and H. Kono. "Foreign aid and recurrent cost: Donor competition, aid proliferation, and budget support". *Review of Development Economics*, Vol. 13, 2009, pp. 276–287.

Arthur, W. B. *Increasing Returns and Path Dependency in the Economy*. Ann Arbor: University of Michigan Press, 1994.

Bourguignon, F. and M. Sundberg. "Aid effectiveness: Opening the black box". *The American Economic Review*, Vol. 97, No. 2, 2007, pp. 316–321.

Bräutigam, D. "Aid 'with Chinese characteristics': Chinese foreign aid and development finance meet the OECD-DAC". *Aid Regime*, Vol. 23, 2011, pp. 752–764.

Bräutigam, D. *Will Africa Feed China?* New York: Oxford University Press, 2015.

Burnside, C. and D. Dollar. *Aid, Policies, and Growth*. Washington, DC: *The World Bank*, 1997.

Cabral, L. and J. Weinstock. *Brazilian Technical Cooperation for Development. Drivers, Mechanics and Future Prospects*. ODI, 2010.

Chaturvedi, S., A. Chenoy, D. Chopra *et al*. *Indian Development Cooperation: The State of the Debate*. IDS, 2014.

Cheung, Y. W., De Haan, J., Qian, X. and Yu, S. "China's outward direct investment in Africa". *Review of International Economics*, Vol. 20, No. 2, 2012, pp. 201–220.

De la Fontaine, D. and J. Seifert. The role of South-South cooperation in present Brazilian foreign policy: Actors, interests and functions. *Stockholm Papers in Latin American Studies*, 2010.

De Renzo, P., D. Booth, A. Rogerson and Z. Curran. *Incentives for Harmonization and Alignment in Aid Agencies*. London: Overseas Development Institute, 2005.

Decreto No 8.817, de 21 de Junho de 2016. URL: http://www.planalto.gov.br/ccivil_03/_ato2015-2018/2016/decreto/D8817.htm.

Department of International Relations & Co-operation. *Establishment of South Africa Development Partnership Agency (SADPA) (Presentation to the NCOP Select Committee on Trade and International Relations)*, 3 August 2011. URL: http://pmg-assets.s3-website-eu-west-1.amazonaws.com/docs/110803sadpa-edit.pdf.

Diamond, L. "The democratic rollback: The resurgence of the predatory state". *Foreign Affairs*, Vol. 87, No. 2, 2008, pp. 36–48.

Faure, R., C. Long and A. Prizzon. "Do organizational and political models for development cooperation matter for development effectiveness". ODI Working Paper, 2015.

Foster, V., Butterfield, W. and Chen, C. *Building Bridges: China's Growing Role as Infrastructure Financier for Africa*. The World Bank, 2009.

Government Gazette. The African Renaissance and International Co-operation Fund Act (Act No 51 of 2000). URL: http://saflii.org/za/legis/num_act/araicfa2000479.pdf.

Grindle, M. S. "Good enough governance revisited". *Development Policy Review*, Vol. 29, No. S1, 2011, pp. 533–574.

Gulrajani, N. "Organising for donor effectiveness: An analytical framework for improving aid effectiveness". *Development Policy Review*, Vol. 32, No. 1, 2014, pp. 89–112.

Histórico da Cooperação Técnica Brasileira, Agência Brasileira de Cooperação. URL: http://www.abc.gov.br/SobreAbc/Historico.

Ighobor, Kingsley. "China in the heart of Africa: Opportunities and pitfalls in a rapidly expanding relationship". *Africa Renewal*, 2013. URL: http://www.un.org/africarenewal/magazine/january-2013/china-heart-africa.

International Development Research Center. *Emerging Donors in International Development Assistance*. IDRC-Partnership & Business Development Division, Ottawa: IDRC, 2008.

Jin-Wook Choi and Jina Bak. "Governance and management for better aid effectiveness: A donor country's perspective". *International Review of Public Administration*, Vol. 22, 2017, No. 1, pp. 45–59.

Kauffman, D., A. Kraay and M. Mastruzzi. *A Decade of Measuring the Quality of Governance*. The International Bank for Reconstruction and Development. Washington: The World Bank, 2006.

Kitano, N. "China's foreign aid at a transitional stage". *Asian Economic Policy Review*, Vol. 9, No. 2, 2014, pp. 301–317.

Kitano, N. and Harada., Y. "Estimating China's foreign aid 2001–2013". *Journal of International Development*, Vol. 28, No. 7, 2016, pp. 1050–1074.

Lancaster, C. *The Chinese Aid System*. Centre for Global Development, 2007.

Ministry of Commerce of the People's Republic of China. "Rules on the Main Functions of the Interior Institutions and the Personnel Composition of the Ministry of Commerce". 2008. URL: http://www.mofcom.gov.cn/aarticle/ae/ai/200808/20080805739577.html.

Ministry of External Affairs. Annual Report 2012–2013. New Delhi, 2013. URL: http://www.mea.gov.in/Uploads/PublicationDocs/21385_Annual_Report_2012-2013_English.pdf.

OECD-DAC. *Development Finance of Countries Beyond the DAC. Development Co-operation Report 2017.* Paris: Organization for Economic Co-operation and Development, 2017. URL: http://www.oecd.org/development/stats/non-dac-reporting.htm.

Parliamentary Monitoring Group. *South African Development Partnership Agency (SADPA) Progress Report*, 17 February 2016. URL: https://pmg.org.za/committee-meeting/22022/.

Perri 6, Diana Leat, Kimberly Seltzer and Gerry Stoker. *Towards Holistic Governance: The New Reform Agenda.* New York: Palgrave, 2002.

Perri 6. *Holistic Government.* London: Demos, 1997.

Reilly, J. "A norm-taker or a norm-maker? Chinese aid in Southeast Asia". *Journal of Contemporary China*, Vol. 21, No. 73, 2012, pp. 71–91.

State Council of the People's Republic of China. "China's Foreign Assistance (2011) White Paper". 2011. URL: http://www.gov.cn/zwgk/2011-04/21/content_1850553.htm.

State Council of the People's Republic of China. "China's Foreign Assistance (2014) White Paper". 2014. URL: http://yws.mofcom.gov.cn/article/m/policies/201412/20141200822172.shtml.

Sydow, J., Schreyögg, G. and Koch, J. "Organizational path dependence: Opening the black box". *Academy of Management Review*, Vol. 34, No. 4, 2009, pp. 689–709.

Tang Luping. "India's Foreign Aid and its Management". *International Economic Cooperation*, 2013, No. 9, pp. 50–56.

Tendler, J. *Inside Foreign Aid.* Baltimore: Johns Hopkins University Press, 1975.

Thomas Ching-peng Peng. "Holistic Governance: Theory and Institutional Strategies". *Taiwanese Journal of Political Science*, No. 23, 2005, pp. 61–100.

United Nations Development Programme, Chinese Academy of International Trade and Economic Cooperation. *Mix and Match? How Countries Deliver Development Cooperation and Lessons for China.* Beijing: China Commerce and Trade Press, 2016.

United Nations Development Programme. Fast Facts on China's South–South and Global Cooperation, 2015. URL: http://www.cn.undp.org/content/china/en/home/library/south-south-cooperation/fast-facts-on-china-s-south-south-and-global-cooperation-.html, 3 June 2018.

Varrall, M. Domestic actors and agendas in Chinese aid policy. *The Pacific Review*, 2016, Vol. 29, No. 1, pp. 21–44.

Wang, J., J. Hedman and V. K. Tuunainen. "Path creation, path dependence and breaking away from the path: Re-examining the case of Nokia". *Journal of Theoretical and Applied Electronic Commerce Research*, Vol. 11, No. 2, 2016, pp. 16–27.

Wood, Bernard *et al. Evaluation of the Implementation of the Paris Declaration: Phase One; Synthesis Report.* Ministry of Foreign Affairs of Denmark, 2008.

Xu, J. and R. Carey. (2015). "China's international development finance: Past, present, and future". No. 2015/130. WIDER Working Paper.

Zhang, D. and G. Smith. "China's foreign aid system: Structure, agencies, and identities". *Third World Quarterly*, Vol. 38, 2017a, 1–17.

Zhang, D. and G. Smith. "China's foreign aid system: Structure, agencies, and identities". *Third World Quarterly*, Vol. 38, No. 10, 2017b, pp. 2330–2346.

Zhu Qianwei. "From new public management to holistic governance". *Chinese Public Administration*, Vol. 10, 2008, pp. 52–58.

Part Three

Evaluation of International Development Projects

Chapter 8

Introduction to Evaluation of International Development Projects

Section 1. Introduction

With the deepening and expansion of international development assistance, the debate on the effectiveness of aid has changed from macro dimension to micro dimension. Issues of particular concern include but are not limited to: Are aid funds spent on where they are needed most? Or are they spent on the most urgent projects and areas? What is the efficiency of the use of funds? What is the effect of aid? All these issues have become the urgent concerns of ODA agencies and multilateral development agencies. As an important part of development assistance, the evaluation of aid projects and funds is directly related to improving the accountability system, effectiveness, and transparency of aid. This section will first analyze the background of the evaluation of international development in detail, then discuss the current development stage, and then analyze the advantages and disadvantages of different evaluation models.

1. Definition and Main Objectives of Evaluation of Development Assistance

In December 1991, the OECD-DAC members unanimously endorsed the *Principles for Evaluation of Development Assistance* in Paris. Since then, the evaluation activities of development assistance projects of governments and multilateral institutions have taken this as the basic starting point. Although this document has been revised several times along with the improvement of evaluation tools, there is no big difference in the definition of evaluation. According to the definition by the OECD-DAC, "[a]n evaluation is an assessment, as systematic and objective as possible, of an on-going or completed project, program or policy, its design, implementation and results. The aim is to determine the relevance and fulfillment of objectives, developmental efficiency, effectiveness, impact and sustainability. And evaluation should provide information that is credible and useful, enabling the incorporation of lessons learned into the decision-making process of both recipients and donors" (OECD, 1991).

Based on its definition, the OECD-DAC further analyzes the purposes of evaluation, which mainly includes two parts.

First, evaluation of development assistance is helpful to improve future aid policies and projects through timely feedback of lessons learned. Although development assistance funding has been increasing, funds for development purposes are scarce compared to the needs. Therefore, improving the effectiveness of aid is crucial, and development evaluation can help to improve it. In particular, if the evaluation can identify effective areas and projects, it will provide a reference for the investment direction of funds. If it identifies invalid areas or links, further waste of funds can be avoided.

Second, evaluation of development assistance provides a basis for government's accountability, including the provision of effective information to the public. Although all countries are increasing development assistance funds, most of them come from public finance. With the increasing accountability pressure faced by governments and organizations around the world, they have to display their performance and more effective development to internal and external stakeholders. A simple record of the consumption amount and direction of funds can no longer meet the expectations of the public. Hence, a systematic development evaluation can help improve long-term sustainability of aid funding. In addition, the provision of the development evaluation results to the public will also help enable the people and the governments of the recipient countries to give more support to the aid projects, promote the dialogue and cooperation between the participants in the development process, and improve the effectiveness of the aid projects.

2. Principles for Evaluation of Development Assistance

Due to the differences in national conditions and aid modes of different countries, there was a divergence of views about how to carry out the evaluation of aid projects. Therefore, the OECD-DAC also drew up guiding principles for evaluation, which are used to manage the framework and system design of evaluation, provide general guidance for evaluation, and ensure the unified standardization of the direction and process of evaluation (OECD, 1991). The specific principles are as follows.

First, evaluation agencies should have an evaluation policy with clearly established guidelines and methods and with a clear definition of its role and responsibilities and its place in institutional aid structure.

Second, the evaluation process should be impartial and independent from the process concerned with policymaking, and the delivery and management of development assistance funds.

Third, the evaluation process must be as open as possible with the results made widely available.

Fourth, for evaluations to be useful, they must be used. Feedback to both policy makers and operational staff is essential.

Fifth, partnership with recipients and donor cooperation in aid evaluation are both essential; they are an important aspect of recipient institution-building and of aid coordination and may reduce administrative burdens on recipients.

Sixth, aid evaluation and its requirements must be an integral part of aid planning from the start. Clear identification of the objectives, which is an aid activity to achieve, is an essential prerequisite for objective evaluation.

3. Process of Development Evaluation

Although the evaluation tools and development are constantly improving, the basic evaluation process is basically similar. The evaluation design process is shown in Figure 8.1.

Generally speaking, the whole evaluation process can be divided into four parts: preparation of evaluation, implementation of evaluation, use of evaluation results, and feedback. In the preparation, the evaluation team needs to identify the purpose of the evaluation, plan and design the evaluation, and determine the methods to be used during the evaluation.

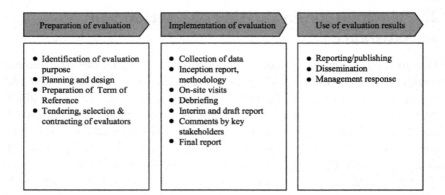

Figure 8.1:   Current process of the evaluation of international development assistance.
Source: Ministry for Foreign Affairs of Finland, 2007.

In addition, the term of reference needs to be prepared and key stakeholders identified. The implementation of evaluation is the core of the whole evaluation of development assistance, including collection of data, preparation of inception report and evaluation tools, organizing on-site visits to understand the actual situation of the project, debriefing the opinions of relevant parties on the aid project, starting to write interim and draft report and sending the report to the stakeholders, revising and improving the report on the basis of their comments, and finalizing it. In the process of the use of the evaluation results, the project team needs to report or publish the evaluation results to the public. Moreover, it is also necessary to use appropriate channels to spread the results and to respond to the feedback at the management level. In the final feedback part, the evaluation team needs to provide the final feedback for the follow-up actions so as to provide reference for future similar projects.

4. Organizational Structure of Development Evaluation

With the increasing role of the evaluation of development assistance in development, the importance of traditional donor countries and multilateral development agencies in the organizational structure of evaluation system has become increasingly prominent. According to the OECD's summary, the current assistance structure is divided into the following two categories.

The first is a comprehensive independent evaluation agency, with Germany, Britain, Sweden, and France being the most representative at present. In 2012, in response to an external evaluation proposal on the German aid evaluation system, Germany established an independent agency-German Evaluation Institute for Development Cooperation (DEval). The evaluation report found that Germany's internal aid evaluation system was too scattered and inconsistent, and proposed to redefine the division of labor and responsibilities of various evaluation agencies and strengthen the number of strategic evaluations so as to enhance the control of the whole evaluation system. In view of this, the newly established DEval is completely independent and is used to evaluate the effectiveness and transparency of the German development cooperation system and to report the evaluation results to the German government. The UK went further. In 2011, the Independent Commission for Aid Impact (ICAI) was set up to evaluate the UK's foreign aid projects and to report the evaluation results directly to the British Parliament, representing the taxpayers' request for the accountability of the British government and relevant donors. The establishment of the commission not only helps to increase the sense of responsibility of the relevant parties to the project but also helps to improve the quality of project operation. The Swedish government put assistance evaluation in a more important position. In 2013, the Expert Group for Aid Studies (EBA) was founded to continuously evaluate and analyze Swedish development cooperation so as to construct a long-term and high-quality knowledge reserve. In terms of independence, the independence of the EBA is even higher than the UK's ICAI and can be independent of the government to freely choose the issues and entities to be evaluated. France is relatively backward in the construction of an independent evaluation agency, but its government has conceived to establish a completely independent evaluation body. However, since the evaluation system of France relies on three different ministries and commissions, which means it has little power, only an observatory entity presided over by Parliament was established to provide suggestions for development cooperation evaluation. The entity provides communication channels for development cooperation stakeholders and the society. Therefore, compared with the UK, Germany, and Sweden, the French evaluation agency, despite being independent, plays a more advisory role.

The second is an evaluation body embedded in existing development institutions. Compared with establishing an independent development evaluation agency, another option is to incorporate the evaluation body into existing development assistance agencies, such as the cases of New Zealand, Australia, and Canada. Generally speaking, the three countries have gradually integrated aid agencies into transactional ministerial agencies. For example, New Zealand incorporated the New Zealand Aid, a semi-independent aid agency, into its Ministry of Foreign Affairs and Trade; Australia also incorporated the Australian Aid Agency into its Ministry of Foreign Affairs and Trade; and Canada similarly merged the Canadian International Development Agency into its Department of Foreign Affairs, Trade and Development. This trend means that these countries combine their development with their diplomacy and trade. With the change in institutional settings, although aid evaluation still focuses on aid projects, the evaluation and research team have begun to expand the scope of evaluation to the whole ministry, possessing a broader scope of responsibility. For instance, the evaluation team of the Ministry of Foreign Affairs and Trade of New Zealand is responsible for the management and formulation of strategic evaluations, including the evaluations of departments, subjects, projects, policies, and practices. This team is an independent body within the Ministry and is directly managed by the Deputy Minister responsible for the international development. Similarly, the Office of Development Effectiveness in Australia, formerly affiliated to the Australian Aid Agency, remains independent within the Ministry of Foreign Affairs and Trade to evaluate the effectiveness of projects, but it must be supervised by the Independent Evaluation Committee to ensure the credibility and independence of the evaluations. Similar settings include Canada. Since the Canadian International Development Agency was merged into the Global Affairs Canada, the original aid evaluation department has been retained to provide evaluation and consultation at the ministerial level and promote mutual learning among organizations.

On the whole, more and more international development institutions have recognized the role of the evaluation of development assistance in improving the effectiveness of development assistance. It is an important part of the international development management system to analyze the cost-benefit of aid interventions through scientific and rigorous evaluation methods. The evaluation of development assistance not only helps to improve the effect of aid resources of the recipient countries, but also helps the donor countries to use public resources more scientifically to allocate aid funds. Therefore, it has been paid more and more attention by international development aid agencies and developing countries.

Section 2. Basic Categories of Evaluation of International Development

With the increasing attention paid to evaluation of international development, the evaluation methods are also evolving. Generally speaking, the main evaluation methods are Monitor & Evaluation (M&E) and Impact Evaluation (IE) which is booming in recent years.

1. Monitor & Evaluation

The traditional Monitor & Evaluation (M&E) is a widely used evaluation method at present. Whether it is the evaluation of national governments or of international development projects, it mainly includes tracking the income and expenditure of the project, the number and level of personnel, the dynamics of the project, the number of the participants, and the generated goods and services. It can be further divided into two stages: monitoring and evaluation.

According to the definition by the OECD-DAC, monitoring refers to the collection of specified data on the progress and dynamics of the project based on continuous and systematic methods, which will enable the management and stakeholders to learn the main indicators of each stage of the project, so as to achieve the final goal of the project and realize the effective allocation and use of funds. The monitoring mainly includes the following aspects:

(a) What is the progress of the intervention?
(b) How are the funds used in the implementation process?
(c) Does the intervention environment change with the progress of the project?

From the perspective of project management, monitoring runs through the whole stage of project management and generates corresponding reports in each subphase to record the progress and implementation of the project. However, in some cases, monitoring is relatively informal, such as discussion and communication. Monitoring-related reports mainly provide basic or core information during the process of project intervention and implementation. In addition, in order to make further analysis, the more systematic and comprehensive the reports of the monitoring stages, the better. Monitoring also plays an important role in identifying existing or potential successful or failed interventions and can make necessary corrections or suggestions for the corresponding situations and implementation. Therefore, in general, effective monitoring is mainly affected by several aspects: good baseline information, clear benchmarks, and clearly defined indicators.

Evaluation refers to the systematic and objective evaluation of ongoing or completed projects, plans or policies, designs, implementation, and results. It aims to determine the relevance and achievement of goals, development efficiency and effectiveness, and impact and sustainability. Evaluation should provide credible and useful information to enable recipient and donor countries to make effective use of the lessons learned from the evaluation in the decision-making process. Evaluation also refers to the determination of the value or importance of an activity, policy, or project, so it needs to assess as systematically and objectively as possible the planned, ongoing or completed development interventions. Compared with monitoring which runs throughout the whole process of the project,

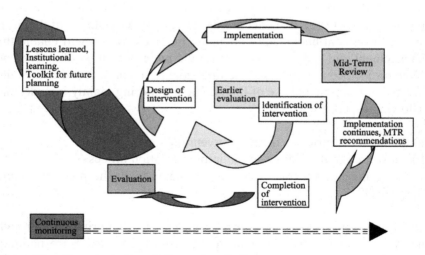

Figure 8.2:   Flow chart of monitoring and evaluation.
Source: Ministry for Foreign Affairs of Finland, 2007.

evaluation is regular and phased. Evaluation usually includes the following:

(a) a mid-term review;
(b) the final evaluation immediately after the completion of the project;
(c) and the evaluation within a few years after the completion of the project in the latest IE.

In general, monitoring and evaluation constitute a complete evaluation process. Monitoring is continuous throughout the whole evaluation process, while evaluation is carried out in sequence and stages. The relationship between the two is shown in Figure 8.2.

2. Types of Evaluation

Generally speaking, the traditional evaluation of international development is divided into four types.

2.1.1 *Country evaluation*

As the name suggests, country evaluation of international development covers a whole set of development interventions of a donor country in a particular recipient country. For most developed countries, country evaluation of international development is mainly organized and implemented by the Ministry of Foreign Affairs, which is in charge of most of the international development assistance work, and the main focus is to evaluate whether the international development cooperation priorities of these countries have been effectively implemented. Generally speaking, country evaluation of international development mainly includes the following aspects:

(a) Implementation of policies at the national level. It mainly makes a comprehensive evaluation of the relevance and effectiveness of policies and the efficiency and sustainability of bilateral development cooperation activities or multilateral cooperation between donors and recipients at the macro level. In the long run, the long-term IE of development cooperation should also be assessed.
(b) Policy recommendations. Country evaluation should also consider the goals, strategies, and plans for future cooperation between donors and recipients.

2.1.2 *Cluster evaluation*

Cluster evaluation refers to the simultaneous evaluation of multiple development items operating or jointly operating in the same field. This type of evaluation refers to the evaluation of multiple subjects rather than collaborative evaluation, which refers to joint evaluation conducted by multiple partners. However, there may be overlap between the two concepts when more than one agency cooperates to evaluate a single or a series of interventions.

2.1.3 *Ex-ante evaluation*

Ex-ante evaluation refers to the evaluation of the potential impact of a new plan or an intervention project. By collecting information, it carries out analysis that helps to determine objectives and ensures that they can be achieved. In *ex-ante* evaluation, the most commonly used tool is cost-benefit analysis. Especially when multilateral development agencies develop projects, they need to do *ex-ante* cost-benefit analysis to ensure the feasibility of the projects. In addition, since there is no *ex-post* project information when doing *ex-ante* evaluation, the parameters and variables of analysis mainly use other similar projects for reference.

2.1.4 *Ex-post evaluation*

Ex-post evaluation is the evaluation of the role of a development project after its completion. It not only evaluates the short-term effects of development projects, but also determines their long-term intervention effects and sustainability. It evaluates the results of the projects' own intention as well as the possible unintended impacts. *Ex-post* evaluation is particularly important for multilateral development banks, because their evaluation agencies, which are usually independent of projects and can hardly run through the whole stage of project implementation, can only conduct *ex-post* evaluation. Nonetheless, although most of the evaluations of multilateral development banks are *ex-post* evaluation, more and more studies believe that evaluation should run through the whole development project process. This is why more and more multilateral development banks begin to introduce IE.

Although the above evaluation methods have been relatively mature and widely used in the field of international development, whether it is a comprehensive and systematic method of M&E, a commonly used country evaluation, or a simple *ex-ante/ex-post* evaluation, it is more of just an input–output evaluation and fails to really assess the improvement of the welfare of the recipient countries and the beneficiaries of projects. Therefore, the demand of academic and policy circles for its improvement has played a great role in promoting the development of the method of IE.

Section 3. Impact Evaluation and Its Importance

1. Definition and Advantages of Impact Evaluation

Impact Evaluation (IE) is an evaluation method that has attracted the most attention in the development field in recent years. It refers to the use of scientific and rigorous methods to quantify the causal effects of interventions on outcomes of interest. Its most obvious feature is the use of causal analysis. For example, the IE of the construction of a hospital can assess whether the investment in the project has significantly improved the health status of nearby residents. In recent years, as international development organizations and donor countries want more solid evidence for the effectiveness of their development projects, there has been growing interest in IE. For instance, the World Bank has specially set up the Development Impact Evaluation (DIME) group to carry out strict IE analysis on its projects so as to better allocate and design them.[1] In 2017, the ADB specially published Impact Evaluation Guidelines to promote the role of IE in it (White and Raitzer, 2017). USAID has also conducted IE on some of its long-term funded projects (USAID, 2015). Although the method of IE was initially used in labor economics and mainly concerned the US, a large number of policy-related IEs have taken place in the field of international development in recent years.

Theoretically speaking, IE measures treatment effects, for which treatment means being exposed to an intervention, such as a new project, and effects are the difference that exposure makes to outcomes, such as income, productivity, poverty, health, and many other aspects. The difference is completely caused by the development project, which means the causal relationship between the two. As shown in Figure 8.3, when a project or an intervention occurs in time *t*, the level of the outcome of

---

[1] World Bank. DIME. URL: http://www.worldbank.org/en/research/dime/overview.

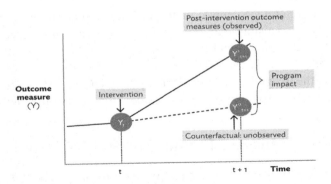

Figure 8.3:   Illustration of an IE.
Source: White and Raitzer, 2017.

interest is Y_t. After the intervention, the outcome of interest becomes Y^1_{t+1}, while it would have been only Y^0_{t+1} without the intervention. The latter is the counterfactual value of Y. Therefore, the difference between the fact and the counterfactual is the impact of the project or intervention.

However, the biggest challenge for IE is to isolate the impact of such project interventions, because to do this, it is necessary to construct the credible "counterfactual" with appropriate control groups, which is almost impossible in reality. For instance, if we want to see whether the distribution of a certain drug in development assistance improves the health status of the recipients, ideally speaking, we should compare the recipients' health conditions before and after taking the drug simultaneously. However, in reality, one person cannot have the two conditions at the same time. Therefore, in practical research, researchers carefully design the "counterfactual" through strict experimental or non-experimental methods so as to obtain a reliable IE of the effects of project interventions. We find that IE is more micro, systematic and scientific than M&E analyzed in the second section. Therefore, IE in multilateral development institutions is usually carried out by the research or project execution departments rather than by independent evaluation departments. For example, the DIME group of the World Bank is led by the Research Bureau rather than the Impact Evaluation Group (IEG).

Compared with traditional M&E, IE has many advantages. The indicators and information obtained by traditional M&E are essentially the conditions of input and output. Therefore, the evaluation results refer to the direct results of the projects, such as the number of the people trained by an employment training project, the electricity-generating capacity of an aid dam, the distance improved by a highway aid project, and so on. By contrast, IE focuses on the effects of the projects and the improvement of the welfare for the related parties, that is, the output. The examples include whether the individuals who participate in the employment training project get jobs or higher incomes, how much the aid dam improves the living standards and industries of the local people, the impact of highway construction on the local income and economic development, and so on. Therefore, we can see that IE is closer to the fundamental purpose of international development than traditional M&E. It is not only more scientific but also more advanced. M&E only evaluates whether the development project is implemented according to the prior provisions and produces the expected output, which is a compliant evaluation and a correlation analysis, whereas IE is to quantify the causal relationship between development projects and development objectives by using effective methods. In recent years, international development agencies and donors have come to realize the advantages of IE. Through the IE of development assistance projects, they can identify the effectiveness and the degree of the impact of the projects and learn the efficiency of the use of development funds so as to improve the allocation and use of funds.

2. A Case of Impact Evaluation: Microcredit

According to the definition by Microcredit Summit Campaign, microcredit is a way to provide low-income and poor people with financial services such as micro loans, so that they can be self-employed and make money to support themselves and their families. As a means of poverty alleviation, microcredit has developed rapidly in recent decades. In particular, Muhammad Yunus from Bangladesh with Grameen Bank he founded won the Nobel Peace Prize in 2006 for promoting micro loans and economic and social development in developing countries. However, the solid evidence that microcredit has a positive impact on the lives of the poor is still limited.

Based on some observational evidence by comparing borrowers and non-borrowers instead of using randomized experimental methods, some researchers claim that microcredit projects are useful for reducing poverty and increasing the income of the borrowers. However, the observational evidence about microcredit projects faces the typical problem of selection bias. Since the borrowers and non-borrowers of micro loans are deliberately selected, there are many invisible differences between them: the borrowers are willing to take risks and exert entrepreneurial ability to improve their lives by launching new business activities, which means that if they do not get microcredit, they are also in a better position than the non-borrowers. Therefore, the conclusion drawn by comparing borrowers and non-borrowers through observation data will overestimate the role of microcredit.

In recent years, the evaluation of the actual impact of microcredit through randomized experimental methods has been rapidly promoted, and the academic and practice in the field of development have begun to use it to test and revise the traditional understanding. These experimental results have a significant policy impact on the international development of microcredit.

Traditional studies using observational data found that microcredit reduces poverty, which has been challenged. Banerjee *et al.* conduct a randomized field experiment in the urban slums of India through a fast-growing Indian microfinance institution (MFI) called Spandana. A total of 52 communities were randomly selected from 104 communities to be granted loans and the baseline data were collected. More than 15 months later, questionnaire data were collected from nearly 7,000 families in the intervention area and the control area. By comparing the surveyed households in all the intervention areas with those in the control areas, the study found that microcredit had no significant impact on average household expenditure, women's status in household expenditure decision-making, children's diseases, school enrollment rate and education expenditure (Banerjee *et al.*, 2015). A randomized field experiment conducted in the Philippines by Karlan and Zinman (2014) also yielded similar results. The prior research believed that, expanding the scope of credit can promote the development of small and micro enterprises and improve their life due to their being discriminated against in the formal financial market. Karlan and Zinman randomly selected 1,600 loan applicants in Manila with credit status slightly higher than the loan standard and granted them personal loans. They found that, compared with the control group, small and micro business owners who received loans reduced the size and scope of their business and even invested money in education rather than business. The results also show that microcredit does not seem to have a direct impact on business expansion. Therefore, together with other studies that have had similar views, the fundamental purpose of microcredit is questioned (Dupas and Robinson, 2009; Burgess and Pande, 2005).

3. Impact Evaluation Cycle

An IE study generally includes evaluation scheme design, data collection, economic model construction, and econometric analysis, as shown in Figure 8.4.

3.1 *Impact evaluation preparation*

IE preparation is very important for the effective evaluation of a project. In particular, two issues need to be determined: the evaluation questions and the identification strategy of the evaluation. Generally speaking, given that IE runs through the whole process of the project, it consumes a long time and a large number of resources, so the problems and

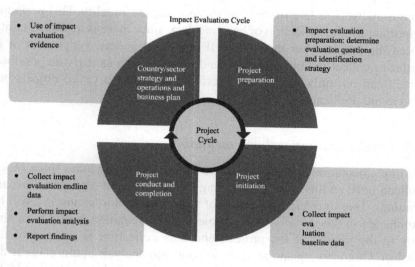

Figure 8.4:   Impact evaluation and the project cycle.

Source: White and Raitzer, 2017.

dimensions of the evaluation should be as extensive and sufficient as possible. For instance, if we want to make an IE of an aided highway project, we can consider not only macro indicators such as economic growth and employment but also micro indicators such as health and education improvement, because traffic improvement can improve local people's access to medical care and education. The identification strategy of the evaluation is also important. Since there are many methods of IE, including non-experimental ones and experimental ones, effective identification tools play an important role in the smooth conduction of the evaluation and the effectiveness of the results. Additionally, since some project staff may be unfamiliar with the design and implementation of IE and staff may change in different stages of the project, how to train relevant staff to carry out IE effectively is also important.

3.2 *Impact evaluation initiation*

IE initiation usually occurs in the early stages of project implementation. The main task of this stage is to collect the baseline data, that is Y_t, which affects the evaluation. Generally speaking, after project approval, there is usually a substantial lag period as procurement contracts are awarded and the groundwork is laid for making project outputs a reality. This period is important for the collection of baseline data, since there is less uncertainty about the project after that. If the IE includes random assignment, it is better to collect the questionnaire and baseline data as early as possible, which can not only reduce the interference of the surveyed objects but also avoid duplicative surveys.

3.3 *Impact evaluation implementation*

IE implementation is the core stage, which mainly includes three tasks: collecting IE endline data, performing IE analysis, and reporting the main findings. Due to the long duration of the project, pilot testing IEs will be conducted in the initial years of project implementation, a mid-term survey in the middle of the project, and data collection at the end of the project. Of course, quantitative estimation and analysis at this stage is the core of the whole analysis, so external experienced experts should be involved. If defects are found in the previous model and evaluation method, they need to be adjusted in time.

3.4 *Use of impact evaluation evidence*

Since the IE results of the development project have been published in the above stage, it is also important to use them. Generally speaking, the role of IE is to identify the effectiveness of the project and the degree of its impact so as to improve the allocation and use of funds. Therefore, the IE results should be integrated into the future strategies, operations, and plans of the countries or sectors so as to make better use of the limited aid funds. For example, if it is found in the third stage that microcredit cannot effectively alleviate poverty or increase income, it should be deleted immediately in future strategies and plans.

References

Banerjee, A., E. Duflo, R. Glennerster and C. Kinnan. "The miracle of microfinance? Evidence from a randomized evaluation". *American Economic Journal: Applied Economics*, Vol. 7, No. 1, 2015, pp. 22–53.

Burgess, R. and R. Pande, "Do Rural Banks Matter? Evidence from the Indian social banking experiment". *The American Economic Review*, Vol. 95, No. 3, 2005, 780–795.

Dupas, P. and J. Robinson, "Savings constraints and microenterprise development: Evidence from a field experiment in Kenya". NBER Working Paper No. 14693, *National Bureau of Economic Research*, 2009.

Giné, Xavier and Dean S. Karlan. "Group versus individual liability: Short and long-term evidence from Philippine microcredit lending groups". *Journal of Development Economics*, Vol. 107, 2014, pp. 65–83.

Ministry for Foreign Affairs of Finland. Evaluation Guidelines between Past and Future, Helsinki, 2007. URL: https://www.oecd.org/derec/finland/47384551.pdf.

OECD. DAC Principles for Evaluation of Development Assistance, OECD, Paris, 1991. URL: http://www.oecd.org/development/evaluation/2755284.pdf.

USAID, 2015. URL: https://www.usaid.gov/node/131331.

White, Howard and David Raitzer. *Impact Evaluation of Development Interventions: A Practical Guide*. Manila: ADB, December 2017.

Chapter 9

Methods of Impact Evaluation for International Development

Impact Evaluation (IE) can be divided into non-experimental methods and experimental methods. Non-experimental evaluation methods mainly include before–after comparison, with–without comparison, instrument variables, difference-in-differences, synthetic controls, and regression discontinuity design. The experimental evaluation methods mainly include the method of randomized controlled trials which is booming in recent years.

Section 1. Non-Experimental Methods of Impact Evaluation

1. Before–After Comparison

As the name suggests, the method of before–after comparison is to compare the situations of specified observed objects before and after participating in a project, and then calculate the impact of the project. Compared with other methods, this method is the simplest in the design of evaluation scheme, and its cost of data collection is also the lowest. If we want to estimate the average effect of the project on the observed objects, we only need to subtract the average value before participation from that after participating in the project. If we can collect individual data and add some time-varying variables, we can take individual specific observations as explained variables and take time indicators (post project observation value being 1 while pre-project observation value being 0) and those time-varying observations as explanatory variables for regression analysis. The regression coefficient of time indicators is used to estimate the treatment effect of the project.

Although before–after comparison provides a simple and effective impact evaluation method, it relies on a key assumption, that is, if the project is not implemented, the status of the project participants (such as health or educational performance) will remain unchanged, that is, $Y_t = Y^0_{t+1}$ shown in Figure 9.1. This strong assumption does not hold water in most cases, so it is difficult to obtain an effective impact evaluation of projects under this method. Once there are changes in macro factors as well as interference of other development projects or intervention measures during the implementation of the project, the status of the project participants will also change. When these confounding factors are very significant, the estimate will be biased if simply attributing the changes before and after the project to the project itself. Figure 9.1 further illustrates this method (Jiang, 2011). It supposes that a group of individuals participate in an employment training program in period t. If we only compare their average wages between the period $t - 1$ (before participation) and $t + 1$ (after participation), the evaluator may mistakenly conclude that since the average wages before and after the project are both

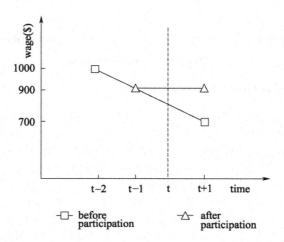

Figure 9.1:   Method of before–after comparison.
Source: Jiang, 2011.

US $900, the training program has no impact on the wage level of the trainees. But in fact, their wages may continue to drop to US $700 without the training program. Therefore, the actual effect of the employment training program is to have increased the wages by an average of US $200. In this case, the method of before–after comparison underestimates the positive effect of the employment training program.

2. With–Without Comparison and Propensity Score Matching

As the name suggests, the method of with–without comparison is to compare the difference in the outcomes of the treatment group and the control group after the completion of the project. Compared with the method of before–after comparison, the method of with–without comparison is not to compare the states of the same group of individuals at different times, but the difference of different groups of individuals at the same time. This method holds that, if other factors are the same or can be completely controlled in the regression model, then the difference in the outcomes of the two groups of individuals can be regarded as the impact of the project. In other words, the effective estimation of this method depends on the most important assumption, that is, whether the unobservable factors which may affect the results of the dependent variables can be controlled.

The method of with–without comparison does not have high requirements for data: cross-sectional data is enough. By observing the cross-sectional data including participants and non-participants, the variable is defined as dummy variable. By estimating a multivariable linear regression model, the coefficient before intervening the dummy variable in regression results is the impact. However, due to the use of cross-sectional data, the estimated coefficients derived from the linear regression model are more sensitive to changes in the model form. Therefore, recently, semi- parametric or non-parametric methods have been introduced to correct the model problems, and the most commonly used method is propensity score matching (PSM).

PSM calculates the impact of a project based on the estimated probability of being in the treatment group given the observable characteristics. The formula is as follows:

$$\text{logit}P(W=1\,|\,X) = \beta X_i + \varepsilon_i.$$

Compared with the linear regression model, PSM calculates $\text{logit} P(W = 1|X)$, that is, the probability of individual i participating in the project, based on a series of observations X_i. Its advantage is that it integrates the information contained in the observable variables into a single variable, which, in terms of the dimensions of variables, is far smaller than the linear regression model requiring that each variable must be processed after matching in regression equation. This is because PSM usually estimates a function of matching variables in a flexible form, which makes the model formal deviation is not as sensitive as in the regression model. What is more, the important assumption of the method of with–without comparison is whether the observers' participation in the project is random, which is too strict because there may be selection bias, whereas PSM can reduce this bias (Rosenbaum, 1987). Although PSM can avoid model bias of the linear model, it also has two disadvantages. First, like the linear model, PSM cannot avoid confoundedness brought about by the correlation between the unobserved variable ε_i and the dependent variable and the independent variable, which leads to the bias of estimate β. Second, when the number of individuals in the observational data is small, compared with regression analysis, PSM as a non-parametric estimation method is less efficient because of its less statistical power.

PSM may be implemented in Stata 13 and 14 using the command "teffects psmatch", followed by the dependent variable, the treatment variable, and a series of other control variables that may determine or differ between treated and untreated groups prior to treatment. An example can be found in Stata 14, where Cattaneo (2010) uses PSM to evaluate the impact of prenatal care in the first trimester of pregnancy on subsequent birth weight in grams, which is the dependent variable (bweight). The treatment variable is dummy variable (prenatal 1), 1 representing taking the hospital examination in the previous 3 months while 0 representing no. Other control variables include whether the mother smoked (mbsmoke), drank alcohol (alcohol), was married (mmarried), age (mage), educational level (medu) and whether it was the first baby (fbaby). If the traditional linear model is used, other control variables and treatment variables are taken as the independent variable. However, many control variables may also affect the treatment variable, for example, the higher the education level, the more likely to go to the hospital for examination, so the impact estimation of the treatment variable is biased. Therefore, PSM can deal with such biases caused by self-selection. For example, Figure 9.2 reports the estimation outcome of the multiple linear regression

. reg bweight prenatal1 mbsmoke mmarried mage fbaby medu alcohol

Source	SS	df	MS			
				Number of obs	=	4,642
Model	90986934	7	12998133.4	F(7, 4634)	=	41.15
Residual	1.4639e+09	4,634	315903.604	Prob > F	=	0.0000
				R-squared	=	0.0585
				Adj R-squared	=	0.0571
Total	1.5549e+09	4,641	335032.156	Root MSE	=	562.05

bweight	coef.	Std. Err.	t	P>|t|	[95% Conf. Interval]	
prenatal1	51.03406	22.4506	2.27	0.023	7.020792	95.04732
mbsmoke	-218.8191	22.29755	-9.81	0.000	-262.5329	-175.1053
mmarried	146.9723	21.43015	6.86	0.000	104.959	188.9856
mage	.1279397	1.834395	0.07	0.944	-3.468348	3.724227
fbaby	-57.18858	17.88803	-3.20	0.001	-92.25763	-22.11953
medu	6.822374	3.780801	1.80	0.071	-.5897958	14.23454
alcohol	-58.06152	47.53652	-1.22	0.222	-151.2557	35.13269
_cons	3195.632	53.95935	59.22	0.000	3089.846	3301.418

Figure 9.2:   Estimation outcome of multiple linear regression equation.

. teffects psmatch (bweight) (prenatal1 mbsmoke mmarried mage fbaby medu alcohol)

Treatment-effects est imation

Estimator	: propensity-score matching		Number of obs	=	4,642
Out comemode	: matching		Matches : requested	=	1
Treatment mode l	: logit		min	=	1
			max	=	68

bweight	Coef.	AI Robust Std. Err.	z	P> |z|	[95% Conf. Interval]	
ATE						
prenatal1						
(Yes vs No)	43.97727	30.37611	1.45	0.148	-15.5588	103.5133

Figure 9.3:   Estimation outcome of PSM.

equation. We find that the coefficient before the variable prenatal 1 is significantly positive, which means that going to the hospital in the first three months can significantly increase the birth weight of infants. However, when we use PSM that can correct the selection bias, we find that the coefficient before the variable prenatal 1 in the regression outcome becomes not significant (as shown in Figure 9.3), that is, the hospital examination does not significantly increase the birth weight of infants. Therefore, PSM can reduce the selective bias and make a better causal evaluation of projects or policies.

3. Instrumental Variables

As mentioned earlier, when the decision-making or qualification of individual participation in a project is affected by observable factors, we can solve this problem by controlling such variables. However, when the influence of unobservable factors (U in Figure 9.4) affects individual participation, and these factors correlate with the outcome of project evaluation (dependent variable Y), selection bias will be caused, which can further cause the estimate of the impact coefficient of the multiple linear equation of regression to be biased, thus misestimating the actual impact of the project. Instrumental variable estimation can be a technique to remove the bias. Instrumental variables are used to obtain consistent estimates of projects by using one or more exogenous variables that affect treatment, but not outcomes, as a proxy for the independent variable. Therefore, the effectiveness of instrumental variables depends on two assumptions. First, the instrumental variable Z must be exogenous, that is, it has no correlation with the unobservable factors (U) related to the outcome. Since facts cannot test this hypothesis, researchers usually need convincing evidence or logic to demonstrate the exogeneity of the selected instrumental variable. Of course, this does not necessarily mean that these instrumental variables are exogenous (Deaton, 2009), and the use of incorrect instrumental variables will lead to expanded or reverse estimation bias. Second, one or several instrumental variables may affect whether the observers participate in the project, but it will not affect the project outcome through any other channels.

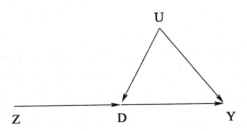

Figure 9.4:   Illustration of instrumental variables.

Due to the strict assumptions of instrumental variables, the method to find instrumental variables is usually through the so-called natural experiments or quasi-experiments (Meyer, 1995), which refer to the exogenous shocks caused by natural and random public policies and legislation, or the exogenous changes in key independent variables caused by some other events. Whether being natural or quasi-experiments, or other exogenous shocks, their occurrence is not controlled by participants or researchers. Hence, we believe that they are a source of the exogenous changes in explanatory variables, which actually play the same role as controlled experiments. For example, Angrist and Krueger (1991) use instrumental variables to estimate the impact of education on income. Personal ability will affect education level and personal income, but is difficult to control, therefore, they can get an unbiased estimate of education income if they can find an instrumental variable which is related to the length of education but has nothing to do with income. They find that under the US Compulsory Education Act, school-age teenagers can only leave school after they have reached the age of 16. As they reach the legal school leaving age earlier, people born in the first half of the year stay at school longer than those born in the second half. At the same time, the labor market does not distinguish the income of workers born in the same year. Therefore, the implementation of the compulsory education law is equivalent to a natural experiment, which enables the people born in the last three quarters to have more educational advantages. Then the birth season is regarded by the authors as an instrumental variable that meets the conditions of both correlative and exogenous, which proves that the education years have a positive effect on income. Instrumental variables are not only used in the domestic policies of the US, but also widely used in the evaluation of international development projects. Duflo and Pande (2007) provide an example of using such instrumental variables. When studying the impact of dam construction on poverty, the authors take the slope of the river as an instrumental variable for dam construction, because the slope of the river where the dam is built has no direct impact on poverty but has indirect impact on poverty due to its impact on irrigation and agricultural production. The downstream area of the river is generally more fertile and less vulnerable to natural disasters. Of course, it remains controversial whether land slope is really a good instrumental variable here (Deaton, 2009).

Of course, the method of instrumental variables also has some defects. First of all, it is a big challenge to find a valid instrument, as many factors that affect treatment also affect outcomes in some way. Second, if the instrumental variable has a weak impact on the project participation, which is commonly known as "weak instrumental variable", it will also lead to biased estimation outcome in the case of limited samples (Bound *et al.*, 1995).

The most popular way to estimate impacts using instrumental variables is to run a two-stage least squares (2SLS) regression. It is represented in the following linear regression models. As the name suggests, 2SLS regressions are conducted in two stages. In the first stage, the evaluator regresses the treatment variable on the instrument Z_i while controlling for the $X_i s$. After running this regression, the evaluator calculates the predicted value of W_i. In the second stage, the evaluator runs a regression

```
. use http: / / fmwww.bc. edu / ec-p / data / hayashi / griliches76 . dta
(Wages of Very Young Men, Zvi Griliches, J . Pol . Ec . 1976)

. ivreg2 lws expr tenure rns smsa i . year (iq=med kww age mrt)

IV (2SLS) estimation
```

Estimates efficient for homoskedasticity only
Statistics consistent for homoskedasticity only

		Number of obs	=	758
		F(12, 745)	=	45.91
		Prob > F	=	0.0000
Total (centered) SS	= 139.2861498	Centered R2	=	0.4225
Total (uncentered) SS	= 24652.24662	Uncentered R2	=	0.9968
Residual SS	= 80.0182337	Root MSE	=	.3249

bweight	coef.	Std . Err .	t	P>|t|	[95% Conf . Interval]
iq	.0001747	.0039035	0.04	0.964	-.007476 .0078253
s	.0691759	.0129366	5.35	0.000	.0438206 .0945312
expr	.029866	.0066393	4.50	0.000	.0168533 .0428788
tenure	.0432738	.0076271	5.67	0.000	.0283249 .0582226
rns	-.1035897	.029481	-3.51	0.000	-.1613715 -.0458079
smsa	.1351148	.0266573	5.07	0.000	.0828674 .1873623
year					
67	-.052598	.0476924	-1.10	0.270	-.1460734 .0408774
68	.0794686	.0447194	1.78	0.076	-.0081797 .1671169
69	.2108962	.0439336	4.80	0.000	.1247878 .2970045
70	.2386338	.0509733	4.68	0.000	.1387281 .3385396
71	.2284609	.0437436	5.22	0.000	.1427251 .3141967
73	.3258944	.0407181	8.00	0.000	.2460884 .4057004
_cons	4.39955	.2685443	16.38	0.000	3.873213 4.925887

Figure 9.5:   Case study of instrumental variables regression.

of the outcome variable Y_i on W_i, while still controlling for the $X_i s$. The coefficient associated with W_i from this second stage regression is the instrumental variables estimate of the impact of the treatment W_i on Y_i.

$$\widehat{W_i} = \beta_0 + \beta_1 Z_i + \beta_2 X_i + \eta_i$$

$$Y_i = \alpha_0 + \beta_3 \widehat{W_i} + \gamma X_i + \varepsilon_i.$$

Although Stata 14 provides the command "ivregress" for the method of instrumental variables, the academic circles and policies generally tend to use "ivregress 2" provided by external users. It provides an example. A study tries to find out the impact of IQ on income. Because of the strong endogeneity of IQ, a simple estimation of the return on education may be biased. Therefore, this study uses a series of instrumental variables such as parents' education level to estimate the young men's education level, and the results are shown in Figure 9.5. The regression outcome shows that the influence of IQ on income is not significant.

4. Difference-in-Differences

The method of difference-in-differences (DiD) was first used by Ashenfelter (1978) to evaluate the impact of training projects on income. Since then, this method has been widely used in empirical economics research and may be one of the most commonly used methods in impact evaluation. As shown in Figure 9.6, the method of DiD requires researchers to collect the data of the treated group and the control group before and after the implementation of the project and then to estimate the average intervention effect by doing two differences. The first step is to calculate the difference between the mean values of the outcome variables of the treatment group and the control group before and after the implementation of the project, that is, the difference between Y_E^1 and Y_B^1, and Y_B^0 and Y_B^0, respectively. The second step is to calculate the difference between the above two differences. Therefore, the explanation of DiD from the perspective of economics is as follows. Before the project intervention, the actual difference between individuals 1 and 0 is Y_B^1 and Y_B^0 If there is no project intervention, because the individuals are randomly selected, the differences between individuals will not change, that is, the development trend should be parallel. Therefore, after the project intervention, the slope of the intervened individual 1 changes significantly, and the gap

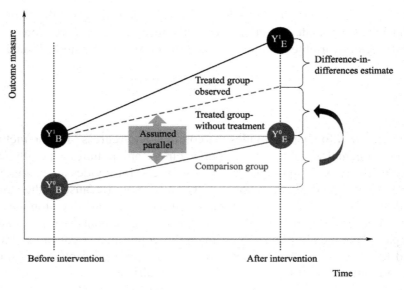

Figure 9.6:   Illustration of DiD.

Source: White and Raitzer, 2017.

between individual 1 and 0 continues to expand. Then the difference between the actual result of individual 1 and the "counterfactual result" is the impact of the project intervention. DiD can also be expressed as follows:

$$\text{DiD} = (Y_E^1 - Y_B^1) - (Y_E^0 - Y_B^0).$$

Compared with the method of before–after comparison and the method of with–without comparison, the hypothesis of DiD is relatively less strict. For the former two methods, if there are unobservable factors, the estimation may be biased, so it is difficult to handle. But DiD is a clever method to deal with this problem. It allows the treated group and the control group to be different in the observable and unobservable factors in the first place, but it also assumes that if the project does not occur, that is, in the counterfactual situation, the results of the treated group and the control group will show the same change trend, that is, their slope change trend is the same. The change in time of the control group is mainly due to the influence of external factors other than the project, which is the same for the treated group. Therefore, although there is an unobservable effect, the fixed difference can be removed by the difference of DiD. In other words, DiD can obtain an unbiased and consistent estimation of the project impact. Therefore, DiD is less dependent on hypothesis than the before–after comparison method and the with–without comparison method.

Although DiD has many advantages, it also needs to be cautiously used. If the key hypothesis is not tenable, that is, if the change path of the treated group and the control group is not consistent, the DiD estimate will be biased. A well-known case is the Ashenfelter's dip (Heckman and Smith, 1999), that is, the observers participating in a government employment training program has generally experienced a dip in income before they receive the training, because they were basically unemployed. If this phenomenon is only temporary, their income will gradually rise even if they do not receive the training. On the contrary, the individuals whose income has not declined are less likely to choose to participate in the training, so their income growth trend may not be as good as that of the trainees at the same time. Then the effect of the training program could be overestimated by the method of DiD taking the non-trainees as the control group. Therefore, it is necessary to ensure the comparability between the treated group and the control group when using the method of DiD. Especially when the outcome variables to be evaluated are dynamic and inconsistent, the DiD estimation of the impact may be biased.

In the regression equation, the use of DiD is easier. In fact, its regression equation is as follows:

$$Y_{it} = \alpha + \beta_1 W_{it} + \beta_2 T_t * + \beta_3 W_{it} * T_t + \gamma X_{it} + \varepsilon_{it}.$$

Y_{it} is the outcome variable of individual i. W_{it} is the binary variable of the treated group and the control group, T_t is the binary variable before and after the intervention, and their interaction term is $W_{it} * T_t$. Coefficient β_3 before $W_{it} * T_t$ is the impact of the intervention and X_{it} is another control variable. From the above regression equation, we can find that DiD is also relatively simple in Stata operation. It only needs to quantify two dummy variables and do the interaction term, while the estimation method is the conventional ordinary least squares. Figure 9.7 estimates the impact of trade union participation on income by using panel data at the national level in the US, with 1980 as the pre intervention period and 1988 as the post intervention period. The regression outcome shows that the coefficient before the interaction is significantly positive, which means that

. reg ln_wage time##union, robust

Linear regression

				Number Of obs	=	3, 574
				F(3, 3570)	=	73.67
				Prob > F	=	0.0000
				R-5quared	=	0.0534.
				Root MSE	=	.47822

ln_wage	Coef.	Robust Std. Err.	t	P>|t|	[95% Conf. Interval]	
1. time	.1377238	.0187794	7.33	0.000	.1009045	.1745432
1.union	.1404369	.0232693	6.84	0.000	.0948145	.1860593
time#union						
1 1	.0885873	.0348885	2.54	0.011	.0201839	.1569906
_cons	1.698597	.0125059	135.82	0.000	1.674078	1.723117

Figure 9.7:   Case Study of DiD.

participation in trade unions can significantly increase the wages of workers.

5. Synthetic Controls

For the method of DiD, if the trends of the control group and the treatment group before the intervention are not consistent, the estimation of impact will be biased. Synthetic controls can solve this problem well. The differences between synthetic controls and DiD are mainly reflected in the following three aspects. First, synthetic controls can relax the parallel trends assumption and build the control by weighing the control group observations such that trends in covariates and outcomes of the synthetic control match those of the treated units prior to the intervention as closely as possible. Second, another difference is the selection of control group. The selection of control group under the method of DiD is subjective, while that under synthetic controls is data-driven, that is, a similar control group is selected as the comparison for the treatment group through data itself. Third, the number of control groups under synthetic controls can be many and their weights will be varied, whereas DiD generally only selects one control group.

Although the method of synthetic controls is widely used and has many advantages, it also has some limitations. First of all, if the treatment group is an extreme sample, it is difficult to find a suitable control group to simulate the trend before the intervention, which will affect the calculation of the outcome difference between the treatment group and the synthetic control group after the intervention. Secondly, this method has a higher requirement for the panel data. The need to simulate the trend before the intervention often requires several years or even decades of panel data, whereas DiD only needs 2 years of panel data. In addition, the variables under synthetic controls cannot be variables with strong volatility, because this will not only affect the simulation effect but also affect the outcomes of the synthetic control.

Synthetic controls can be widely used in the evaluation of public policies and projects. For example, Fan and Liu (2013) use this method to estimate the impact of Chongqing real-estate tax on its housing prices. They first select the control group from 40 large and medium-sized cities from June 2010 to January 2011 and assign them with weighting respectively. Since the purpose of the assignment is to ensure that the weighted house price should be as consistent as possible with the trend of Chongqing's house price before taxing real estate, it is necessary to give higher weight to the cities closest to Chongqing's house price trend, otherwise it will be smaller. As shown in Figure 9.8, through simulation, before the implementation of real-estate tax, Chongqing's actual house price and the synthetic control house price are basically the same. After the implementation of real-estate tax in February 2011, they use the same weight for the control group cities to estimate the counterfactual house price of Chongqing, as shown in the dotted line after February 2011 in Figure 9.8. In other words, the dotted line indicates that if there is no real-estate tax, the dotted line reflecting the change trend of the control group cities will also affect Chongqing. Since Chongqing has implemented the real-estate tax, the actual results are shown in the solid line. Therefore, the difference between the solid line and the dotted line is the impact of the real-estate tax, which shows that the real-estate tax significantly reduces the house price.

Synthesis controls can be realized by Stata. The two commands currently used are not official Stata, so they need to be installed. One command is synth_runner written by Brian Quistorff and Sebastian

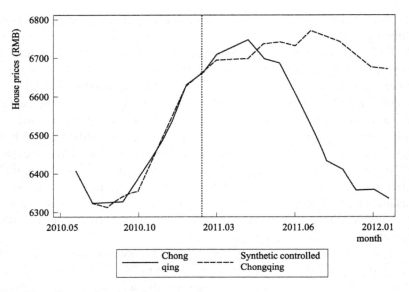

Figure 9.8:   Case study of synthetic controls.

Source: Fan and Liu, 2013.

Galiani (2017), and the other is synth written by A. Abadie, A. Diamond, and J. Hainmueller (2010). There is no significant difference between the two commands except that the former is more concise than the latter.

6. Regression Discontinuity Design

Regression discontinuity design (RDD) is a popular project evaluation method in recent years, which is widely used not only in domestic policies but also in international development field, mainly because it is visual, handy, and highly applicable. The assumption of RDD is that units in proximity to either side of the boundary are sufficiently similar for those excluded from the program to be a valid comparison group. The difference in outcomes between those near either side of the boundary, as measured by the discontinuity in the regression line at that point, is attributable to the program, and whether the treated units participate is determined by the exogenous policy. In other words, RDD is especially suitable for "one-size-fits-all" policies, and the cutoff point is the threshold of "one-size-fits-all" policies. Therefore, the untreated individuals just below the threshold, namely the control group, can constitute the

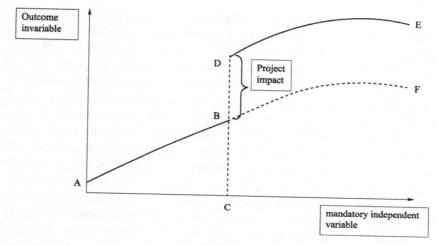

Figure 9.9:   Illustration of RDD.

counterfactual of the treated individuals above the threshold determined by the exogenous policy. The difference in the outcomes between these two groups can be regarded as the impact of project intervention. Figure 9.9 shows this theory. Before the implementation of policy (left of C), it is assumed that there is no relationship between the outcome and the mandatory variable (as shown by the solid line on the left of C). After the implementation of the mandatory policy, the affected individuals are impacted by exogenous shocks and the outcome will move to the solid line. The jump of outcome variable near the threshold should reflect the impact of the project correctly. In addition, since the trend of dependent variables is nonlinear in most cases, RDD should adopt a flexible function about mandatory variables.

The more influential case of RDD is the evaluation of Chile's education policy. In 1990, in order to improve the educational standards of 900 underperforming public schools, the Chilean government introduced a public policy, abbreviated as P-900. The program required schools whose average score of fourth grade examination in the 1988 was below the threshold to participate in the program. The intervention measures included improving infrastructure and carrying out teacher training. Those schools with average score above the threshold did not participate (Chay *et al.*, 2005). Since the average score is set by the exogenous policy, RDD can overcome the potential bias of project impact evaluation.

Of course, according to the degree of the treatment, RDD is subdivided into two types. First, if there is a well-implemented sharp eligibility criterion for the program, that is, individuals just above the cutoff point are similar to individuals just below the cutoff point, except for the fact that individuals just above the cutoff point receive the treatment while those below the cutoff point do not, this situation is known as "sharp RDD". We can see that the probability of receiving the treatment changes discontinuously from 0 (no chance of receiving the treatment) to 1 (100% chance of receiving the treatment) at the cutoff point. Another situation is that, due to various objective reasons, the treatment does not get strictly implemented near the cutoff point. For example, in Chile's P-900 program, government officials reviewed schools that were sorted out on the basis of the average score of examinations, and then disqualified some schools from the program. This type is called "fuzzy RDD" because the threshold is imperfectly applied. What we see is that the jump of an individual's receiving the treatment at the cutoff point depends on the probability. The estimation methods used in these two types are not the same, the interpretations of their evaluation results are not the same, and the requirements of robustness test are also different, but the basic principles of the two are consistent, that is, they both estimate treatment effects by comparing the outcomes of individuals just above and below the cutoff.

Although RDD has many advantages, two problems should be paid attention to when it is used. First of all, the policy of intervention must be thorough. Take the Chile project as an example. Schools that fail to meet the set score line and qualification cannot be allowed to enter the project. Otherwise, it is easy to confound the impact of the project, resulting in biased estimates. Secondly, the observed individuals cannot change their state of intervention. Assuming that the selection of schools for the P-900 program is based on the examination results in 1990 rather than in 1988, if the relevant departments disclose or the schools know the cutoff score in advance, some schools may report their scores lower so that they can be qualified to participate in the program to obtain more policy support. Of course, we can analyze the possibility of such a situation through formal statistical tests, or check and evaluate whether RDD is credible by means of graphs (Imbens and Lemieux, 2008). Finally, other factors that influence policy outcomes cannot also show discontinuities at the cutoff point, because we cannot determine whether the difference in outcome variables is affected by the project itself or by these unobservable factors.

For example, if there were other important policies in the P-900 program in 1998 that would also affect the future performance of schools, then this would not be a "clean" discontinuity, because it is hard for us to determine whether the impact is attributable to the P-900 program or the other policies. These observations should be removed even if the interference policies occur only in certain provinces.

RDD is also easy to use in Stata. Since its command is developed by researchers, it is necessary to make sure that the command for the installation package in Stata is "rdrobust" (Calonico *et al.*, 2014). For example, in the article by Calonico *et al.*, the treatment is whether a member of the Democratic Party wins a US election for a Senate seat representing a State, and the outcome is the margin in the following election. The results of the study are shown in Figure 9.10, which show that the current Democratic Party has a significant jump feature compared with other competitors. This feature is further confirmed by the coefficient of the regression result in Figure 9.11, which indicates that incumbency has a significant positive effect on the margins by which subsequent elections are won.

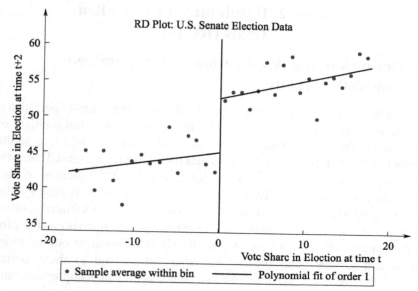

Figure 9.10:   Illustration of RDD.

Source: Calonico *et al.*, 2014.

Order est . (p)	1	1
Order bias (q)	2	2
BW est. (h)	17.708	17.708
BW bias (b)	27.984	27.984
rho (h/b)	0.633	0.633

Outcome : vote. Running variable: margin.

Method	Coef.	Std. Err.	z	P>|z|	[95% Conf. Interval]	
Conventional	7.416	1.4604	5.0782	0.000	4.55378	10.2783
Bias-corrected	7.5099	1.4604	5.1425	0.000	4.64768	10.3722
Robust	7.5099	1.7426	4.3095	0.000	4.09441	10.9255

```
. do "/var/folders/5p/8t5z_ 4qx4msb2y7blbyyzhsm0000gn/T//SD21737.000000"

. qui rdrobust vote margin

. rdplot vote margin if -e(h _1)<= margin & margin <= e(h_r), ///
>   binselect(esmv) kernel(triangular) h('e(h._l}'' e(h_r)') p(1) ///
>   graph_ options(title("RD Plot: U.S. Senate Election Data") ///
```

Figure 9.11:   Case study of the regression result of RDD.

Source: Calonico *et al.*, 2014.

Section 2. Randomized Controlled Trials (RCTs)[1]

1. Definition and Application of Randomized Controlled Trials

Although we introduced several practical and handy non-experimental evaluation methods in the first section, the common potential problem of them is that the observational data are not random or even selective, so the impact evaluation based on such data and methods may be biased. In view this, social scientists in recent years have introduced the method of randomized controlled trials (RCTs) in natural sciences such as biology and medicine to make project evaluation by conducting randomized control experiments in real life situations. The basic operation involves the random assignment of members of the eligible population to one or more "treatment groups" that receive the intervention, and to the "control group" that receives no intervention. With sufficient sample size, the

---

[1] This part is mainly based on the writings of Jiang Yi (2011) and White and Raitzer (2017).

average characteristics of the treatment and control groups are on average the same at baseline, the only difference between them being whether they participate in the project or accept the intervention, hence impact can be calculated as the difference in outcomes between treatment and control at endline. Because randomized experiments are conducted in real life, participants do not know that they are in the experiments, and their behavior will not be affected by the experiments, they are also considered as randomized field experiments. For these reasons, RCTs are also considered the "gold standard" in impact evaluation (Athey and Imbens, 2017).

There are several reasons that RCTs have become the mainstream method in the field of development in recent years. First of all, due to the lack of solid evidence in previous studies to prove the effectiveness of development projects in poverty reduction and economic growth, impact evaluation based on randomized experiments is regarded as the most convincing method to prove the effectiveness of international development projects (Banerjee and Esther, 2008). Secondly, RCTs can not only make a reliable estimate of the effectiveness or impact of a development project, but also be used to study the effect of a specific intervention. Although observational data can also be used to assess a development project with multiple interventions, the impact of a single intervention cannot be estimated. Finally, RCTs can also be used to test some important innovative theories that can only be tested by RCTs (Ashraf and Yi, 2006), as well as to study new measurement or data acquisition methods (Olken, 2007).

The biggest value of randomized evaluation is that it can be used to conduct small-scale evaluation before the large-scale promotion of major projects or policies. The impact evaluation of a pilot project enables the project staff to judge whether the project has achieved the expected results or benefits, thus providing valuable reference for the large-scale implementation of the project. For example, in 1998, Mexico launched a pilot project covering only 1% of 50,000 target communities for education, health and nutrition (PROGRESA). The small-scale RCT proved that it had a positive effect and had won extensive political support, and the project has been running smoothly since then. As of 2000, the project has invested US $800 million (0.2% of GDP), benefiting 2.6 million households (10% of the households).

In addition, RCTs can also be used to evaluate the allocation of resources. When the demand for the project exceeds the capacity of the project, the project participants can be randomly selected by lottery, which is probably the best way to ensure the fairness and transparency of the screening process and also helps to evaluate the impact of the project. For example, in Colombia, vouchers that can be used for private school tuition are allocated by lottery. Angris *et al.* evaluate the project and find a certain degree of effectiveness. In addition, when the target scale of a project is large, it will be implemented in stages. If a part of the beneficiaries are randomly selected in each stage to participate in the project, then we can use RCTs and the unselected individuals will be regarded as the control group (Jiang, 2011).

2. Types of RCTs

There are many different RCT designs. White and Raiter (2017) propose three types and hold that their differences relate to (i) the level of assignment, (ii) different approaches to random assignment, and (iii) the type of treatment combinations assessed.

First, the type based on the level of assignment includes simple RCTs and cluster RCTs. The unit of assignment in an RCT is the unit used for selecting who gets treated. In a simple RCT, the unit of assignment is the same as the unit of treatment and measurement. An example could be a business development program for small and medium-sized enterprises in which eligible enterprises are randomly assigned to treatment and control groups. The outcomes could include firm-level sales, profitability, and employment. However, the treatment group in a cluster RCT are communities or cluster units. For both practical and ethical reasons, a cluster RCT design is often used, in which the unit of assignment contains multiple treatment units. In practical terms, it is more feasible to randomly assign a service with shared community infrastructure, such as electrification or water supply at community or block level, rather than at a household level. For example, rural electrification and roads treat communities, although benefits may be measured at firm or household level. Logistical and ethical questions from creation of visible inequity may arise if assignment is at the household or individual level, such as to some members of a school class but not to others. Cluster RCT designs also help to contain spillover effects and contamination. Knowledge of treatment often spreads within a community. If assignment is at the household or individual level, this knowledge creates a spillover effect that may alter the behavior of the untreated, which biases the experiment if the control group is drawn from untreated neighbors. Cluster RCTs can help to create large and distinct enough units of assignment so that these spillovers are minimized. However, the statistical power of the design is largely determined by the number of clusters in the study rather than the number of treated units. This means that the example program will have to cover a reasonably large number of treatment towns to obtain a sufficiently powered study.

Second, the selection of different approaches to random assignment is very important for the successful implementation of RCTs. There are five approaches. The first approach is random selection. When there is excess demand (oversubscription) for a program or the eligible population exceeds that which can be served with available resources, then random selection, such as a lottery, can be used to determine which of the eligible applicants are included and which are in the control group. Since the program will not be made available to all of those who are eligible, random selection into the program can be the fairest and most transparent means of deciding who gets in. A random number generator can be used, but increasingly public randomization ceremonies are held to increase transparency. The second approach realizes random assignment by slightly altering the eligibility threshold. By relaxing the threshold, it is possible to identify a larger eligible population than can be treated, within which treatment is assigned randomly. For example, a program planning to work in 50 communities can first identify 100 communities and then randomly select 50 communities from this total to enter the program. In this way, not only can there be treatment groups and control groups but also can increase the effectiveness of statistical inference. The third approach is Pipeline or step-wedged designs, which randomize the order of treatment rather than the treatment itself. Implementing agencies often roll out a program in stages, making it possible to randomly select the order in which the participants receive the program. One example of this approach is the Pantawid Pamilya conditional cash transfer program in the Philippines. In its initial phase, the program was a pilot for 140 communities, half of which received the program first and half of which acted as a control group for 2 years (Grover, 2013). Hence, the communities were randomly allocated into the two groups to receive the program in either year 1 or year 3. The fourth approach is encouragement designs, which can be used for programs and policies that are universally available but not universally adopted. The treatment group is provided with an encouragement to take up the intervention, but this encouragement should not be something that affects the outcomes of interest. An example of a suitable encouragement is an information campaign for an ongoing program. The villages where the campaigns will be conducted are selected at random from among all of the villages where the program has been implemented (which may be all villages in the country for a national program). In this case, villages are exposed to the information campaign. The impact of the program on outcomes of interest is measured by comparing the outcome between the control and treatment villages. The fifth approach is stratification or prior matching, which can be used to ensure balance with a smaller sample size. Matched pair randomization matches units (e.g. communities) into pairs based on observed characteristics, randomly assigning one community of each pair into the treatment group and the other to control. This ensures that even if the sample is small, the matching efficiency is high.

The third type is multiple treatments. The ideal of RCTs is to find out the counterfactual of no intervention and compare the results of intervention with doing nothing so as to obtain the impact of intervention. However, in reality, policymakers are often more interested in knowing how doing A compares with doing B. A/B designs, which are extensively used in the medical field, compare two treatment arms, treatment A and treatment B. Normally, treatment B is often called "existing standard of care". That is, the counterfactual is the current policy, and so the evaluation question is "how does this intervention compare with what is currently done?" In this case, A is called an "active control". Alternatively, A and B may be two different approaches to implementing a project. A/B designs are appropriate for adaptive learning to improve project design. More treatment arms may be added (e.g. A/B/C designs), but each arm drives up the sample size requirements. The drawback of this approach is that it is not possible to calculate absolute effectiveness, because what it compares is the relative difference. For instance, the two interventions being tested may produce the same outcome, but both of them are effective and work equally well. If the existing treatment has been shown to work by previous rigorous studies, that problem does not occur. Yet, often it is still useful to have an absolute effectiveness estimate for the purposes of cost-effectiveness or cost-benefit analysis.

3. Steps in Implementing an RCT

An RCT needs to be planned before wide field implementation of an intervention, and its designing usually involves the following steps (White and Raitzer, 2017).

The first step is to identify questions of interest. The overall evaluation design involves selecting evaluation questions derived from the theory of change. Staff of the implementing agency, from top management to field staff, has to buy into the randomized design in order for randomization to be feasible in the first place and to preserve the integrity of the design in practice.

The second step is to isolate treatment(s) of interest. The determination of treatments of interest follows the identification of questions of interest. Clearly defining treatments of interest is important for interventions in a unified way. Additionally, for an RCT, it is also important for external validity: what has been evaluated needs to be clear. In general, the intervention should be as unbundled as possible, with intervention combinations only assessed in factorial or crossover designs. Otherwise, it will not be possible to determine which components of interventions lead to identified effects, and external validity will be limited. In addition, the evaluator should determine whether a placebo should be used for any control arm of the experiment. Placebos can eliminate bias imparted by knowledge of treatment and improve rigor. However, placebos often are not feasible for many real world interventions. This means that placebos are rare in practice for impact evaluation of development interventions.

The third step is to consider spillover effect. If the theory of change suggests that there will be spillover effects, that is, the control group will be affected by the treatment group, then the treated and untreated units should be changed as soon as possible. Generally speaking, there will be no or less spillovers between treated and untreated units if the unit of assignment is aggregated enough (such as from individuals to communities). When spillover effects are expected to be substantial, random assignment may apply to three groups: treated, untreated but subject to spillover, and untreated but not subject to spillovers.

The fourth step is to determine levels of assignment, treatment, and analysis. The randomization design depends on clearly identifying the unit of assignment, treatment, and analysis. Random assignment must occur over a universe from which there is a sufficient listing to randomly draw equivalent treatment and control units. Sample power calculations should be conducted at this point to ascertain that enough units can be included to have a high likelihood of detecting effects.

The fifth step is to determine the types of RCT. The choice of the type of RCT depends on the intervention design and the evaluation questions. The nature of development interventions will usually require a cluster

RCT since projects are assigned by geographic unit, and spillovers often occur within communities. One of the first generation questions is whether the intervention works, which is often highly related to the selection of experimental type. The second generation question is which intervention approach is more effective. Generally speaking, A/B designs are more effective, because it requires shorter time frames and smaller samples.

The sixth step is to identify eligible population (the universe for random assignment). In order to ensure the effectiveness of treated sample individuals and statistics, the identification of eligible population is very important for the effective implementation of the RCT. To do so, the eligibility criteria for the units of assignment have to be clearly defined. Criteria may be geographic or characteristic-based. Several criteria may be combined, but it should be ensured that the eligible population is consistent with the population to be evaluated in the RCT.

The seventh step is to draw sample for analysis. From the eligible or targeted population, a representative sample is drawn. In the case of a cluster RCT, the sampling will be a two-stage design, first sampling clusters, such as randomly sampling villages. The second step is to sample the individuals in the cluster samples to calculate the average value of the cluster samples.

The eighth step is to assign to treatment and control. Eligible units need to be assigned to treatment and control before implementing the intervention in treated locations. The maximum possible size of the treatment group is given by the intended coverage of the project. It is not necessarily the case that the whole treatment population will be in the sample for the impact evaluation, which depends on the sample size requirements as given by the power calculation.

The ninth step is to collect baseline data and check for balance. Collecting baseline data helps to ensure balance between treatment and control. If the difference in quantity between the two groups is too large, it may affect the evaluation effect. Baseline data usually need to be collected before the intervention can have any effect at field level so as to avoid any bias. Once the data have been collected and cleaned, and assignment into treatment has been performed, another balance check should be conducted. If balance is not found, field implementation of the randomization protocol may be compromised, and further investigation should be performed on how randomization was implemented.

The last step is to ensure integrity of the design and monitor for contamination and attrition. The study team needs to stay closely involved as implementation progresses to ensure the integrity of the design, with randomization protocols strictly followed so that treatment groups get treated and that control groups do not. Randomization often means more work for field teams to reach more inaccessible communities, deal with less receptive potential beneficiaries, or do things in an inefficient order. Field teams may thus have incentives to short cut randomization if there is not very close control to ensure that the randomization protocol is followed.

4. Potential Problems and Challenges of RCTs

Although RCTs have made great progress in the fields of development economics and international development in recent years, especially the emphasis on causality has played a great role in promoting the evaluation of projects and development policies, there are still some doubts about this method in academic circles (such as Heckman and Smith, 1995; Deaton, 2009; Deaton, 2018; Ravallion, 2009). The main problems of RCTs are as follows.

First of all, the contradiction between the demand for the treatment group and the control group being as similar as possible and the contamination of the randomized experiment makes the implementation become more and more difficult in reality. On the one hand, in the process of research, when an individual learns of the fact that he is in an experiment, his behavior may change, which will result in the deviation of the evaluation results, namely the so-called randomized deviation. For example, if the control group understands that the project will eventually involve them, their behavior may be affected, and therefore, the contamination of the RCT may bias the impact estimate. On the other hand, RCTs need to assume that the control group is the same as the treatment group except that the former is not exposed to the program, which inclines researchers to choose two groups which are grouped geographically in reality, because this can control other invisible variables as much as possible. However, as information and transportation become more and more convenient, it becomes more and more difficult for the treatment group and the control group to be completely isolated, especially if the two groups are geographically close.

Another challenge for RCTs is the external validity of the evaluation results. Compared with non-experimental evaluations, internal validity of randomized evaluations is higher, that is, the estimates of the evaluation impact are more consistent. However, because the estimation is usually carried out in a specific country or region, and usually in a small geographical area with a specific cultural background, to what extent can the estimation results be generalized? Or if the same experiment is carried out in different countries or regions and different environments or cultural backgrounds, can it produce the same impact? At present, the academic world holds that it is necessary to repeat the same experiment in different countries or regions or even in different cultural backgrounds in order to address the above doubts. Although these repeated RCTs may either confirm or refute the existing experimental results, they all help us to further understand the external validity of intervention and the environment in which it works. However, it also means a corresponding increase in cost and efficiency.

In addition, most RCTs only focus on the average treatment effect of a project on the entire eligible population or project participants. However, in reality, policy makers also focus on other dimensions. For example, they may want to know the distribution of the welfare effect of intervention, that is, the proportion of and difference between the largest and the lowest beneficiaries. However, what an RCT provides is the difference between the treatment group and the control group; it cannot give the distribution of the intervention effect. So, the proportion of and difference between the largest beneficiaries and the lowest beneficiaries cannot be obtained without further assumptions. However, Banerjee and Duflo (2008) believe that the advantage of experimental approaches is that they rely on far less assumptions than non-experimental approaches, but their evaluation results are not only highly reliable but also more likely to reflect the most important dimensions of policies (Banerjee and Duflo, 2008). So, in this sense, their view is actually that RCTs are a method that pays more attention to quality than quantity. However, to what extent policy makers can accept RCTs due to their long duration is a big problem.

References

Angrist, J. D., E. Bettinger, E. Bloom, E. King and M. Kremer. "Vouchers for private schooling in Colombia: Evidence from a randomized natural experiment". *American Economic Review*, Vol. 92, No. 5, 2002, pp. 1535–1558.

Ashraf, Nava, Dean Karlan and Wesley Yin. "Tying Odysseus to the mast: Evidence from a commitment savings product in the Philippines". *The Quarterly Journal of Economics*, Vol. 121, No. 2, 2006, pp. 635–672.

Athey, Susan and Guido W. Imbens. "The state of applied econometrics: Causality and policy evaluation". *Journal of Economic Perspectives*, Vol. 31, No. 2, 2017, pp. 03–32.

Banerjee, Abhijit V. and Esther Duflo. "What is middle class about the middle classes around the world?" *Journal of Economic Perspectives*, Vol. 22, No. 2, 2008, pp. 03–28.

Calonico, Sebastian, Matias D. Cattaneo and Rocio Titiunik. "Robust nonparametric confidence intervals for regression-discontinuity designs". *Econometrica*, Vol. 82, No. 6, 2014, pp. 2295–2326.

Calonico, Sebastian, Matias D. Cattaneo and Rocio Titiunik. "Robust data-driven inference in the regression-discontinuity design". *The Stata Journal*, Vol. 14, No. 2, 2014, pp. 909–946.

Deaton, Angus and Nancy Cartwright. "Reflections on RCTs". *Social Science & Medicine*, Vol. 210, 2018, pp. 86–90.

Deaton, Angus S. "Instruments of development: Randomization in the tropics, and the search for the elusive keys to economic development". *National Bureau of Economic Research*, No. w14690, 2009.

Fan, Ziying and Liu Jiayan. "The impact of China's property tax reform". *World Economy*, Vol. 11, 2013, pp. 117–135.

Grover, D. Sampling recommendations for second wave impact evaluation of the Pantawid Pamilya Program applying regression discontinuity design. *Project Document*, 2013.

Heckman, J. and J. Smith. "Assessing the case for social experiments". *Journal of Economic Perspective*, Vol. 9, No. 2, 1995, pp. 85–110.

Jiang, Yi. *Review on the Latest Developments of Impact Evaluation*. Manila: Asian Development Bank, 2011.

Olken, Benjamin A. "Monitoring corruption: Evidence from a field experiment in Indonesia". *Journal of Political Economy*, Vol. 115, No. 2, 2007, pp. 200–249.

Ravallion, Martin. "Should the randomistas rule?" *The Economists' Voice*, Vol. 6, No. 2, 2009.

White, H. "Using the causal chain to make sense of the numbers". *Evidence Matters Blog*. 12 February 2013. URL: http://blogs.3ieimpact.org/using-the-causal-chain-to-make-sense-of-the-numbers/.

White, Howard and David A. Raitzer. *Impact Evaluation of Development Interventions: A Practical Guide*. Manila: Asian Development Bank, 2017.

Index

A

Abe, Shinzo, 75, 80
Academy for International Business Officials, 225
Accra Agenda for Action (AAA), 32, 85
Accra International Conference Center, 32
Acemoglu, Daren, 22
Addis Ababa Action Agenda, 185
Administration of International Cooperation, 201–202
African Conflict Prevention Pool, 200
African Development Bank, 147
African Development Foundation, 194–195
African Development Fund, 202
African Renaissance Fund, 212–213
African Union, 32
Agrawal, Subhash, 93
AidData, 233
aid effectiveness, 13–23, 118–124
aid evolution, 54–62
aid loans-investment-trade, 51
aid management system, 113–118, 193–203, 205–239

aid ownership, 27–32
Alesina, Alberto, 30
Alliance for Financial Inclusion, 173
America, 37–106
Andreoni, J., 137
Angrist, J. D., 282
An Wenjing, 147
Asian Development Bank (ADB), 74, 144–146, 148, 153, 155–160, 162–171, 225
Asian Development Fund, 202
Asian Infrastructure Investment Bank (AIIB), 33, 100–101, 143–150, 152–153, 155–160, 162–171
Asian-Pacific region, 148–149
Australia, 174–175, 250

B

Bak, Jina, 123
Bandung Conference, 83
Banerjee, Abhijit V., 23, 288
before–after comparison, 263–265
Belt and Road Initiative, 80–81, 146, 149, 224, 232, 235
Big Five Development Intervention, 18
Bill & Melinda Gates Foundation, 6–7

Bolivarian Alliance for the People of
Our America, 85
Boone, Peter, 18
Bräutigam, Deborah, 27
Brazil, 94, 205, 207, 210, 212–214,
216–218
Brazilian Cooperation Agency, 212,
215–217
Brazil's aid management system,
210–212
Bretton Woods system, 28, 144–145
BRICS (Brazil, Russia, India, China,
and South Africa) countries, 8, 24,
94–95, 100, 206–207, 214,
218–219, 227
Brooks, William L., 42
Buenos Aires Plan of Action, 82, 84,
89, 95
Bureau of Complete Sets of
Equipment, 228
Bureau of Technical Cooperation, 228
Burnside, C., 21, 29, 119, 207
Busan Conference, 88
Busan Partnership Agreement, 97, 119

C
Calonico, Sebastian, 279
Canadian International Development
Agency, 250
Cannes DWG, 174
capital flows, 5
Cattaneo, Matias D., 266
Central Committee of the CPC, 226
Central Fund for Economic
Cooperation, 200
Central Fund for Free France, 130,
200
Central Fund for the French Overseas
Territories, 200
China Development Bank, 223, 233,
238

China Export-Import Bank, 225–226,
233
China International Center for
Economic and Technical
Exchanges, 225
China International Development
Cooperation Agency (CIDCA),
221–222, 235–238
China's aid management system,
221–239
China's Department of Foreign
Assistance, 216
China's foreign aid, 223–227
Choi, Jin-Wook, 123
cluster evaluation, 254
cluster RCT, 282
Cold War, 15, 48, 52, 57, 60, 62–63,
83, 86
Collier, Paul, 21–22
Colombo Plan, 38, 40, 195
Colombo Project, 48
Colonial Development and Welfare
Act, 198
Colonial Development Corporation,
198
Commission for Economic Relations
with Foreign Countries, 229
Conservative Government, 198
Consultative Group to Assist the Poor
(CGAP), 177
cost-benefit analysis, 160
country evaluation, 253
Cultural Revolution, 228

D
data and policy research center,
184–185
Deaton, Angus, 6, 19–21, 23
Department for International
Development (DFID), 129, 199
Department of Agriculture, 195

Department of Economy and Cooperation, 208
Department of Foreign Assistance (DFA), 220, 225, 232
Department of Foreign Assistance of the Ministry of Commerce, 117
Department of Foreign Investment and Economic Cooperation, 232
Department of Foreign Trade of the Ministry of Commerce, 230
De Renzo, P., 121
developing countries, 5
development assistance, 245–247
Development Assistance Committee (DAC), 6–8, 38, 127, 130
Development Cooperation Charter, 39, 47, 73, 75, 78
Development Cooperation Forum (DCF), 99
development evaluation, 247–251
development finance, 233–234
Development Impact Evaluation (DIME), 255
development partnership, 92
Development Partnership Administration, 209, 216, 218
Development Working Group (DWG), 171–185
difference-in-differences (DiD), 271–274
Dollar, David, 21, 29, 119, 207
donor countries, 8
Duflo, Esther, 23, 288
Durban Summit, 100

E

Easterly, William, 19
Economic and Commercial Office of the Chinese Embassy, 225
Economic Cooperation Administration (ECA), 49, 193
Economic Cooperation Agreement, 48
economic development, 3, 48–51
Economic Planning Agency (EPA), 197
electronic supervision system, 167
emerging donor countries, 205–239
endogenous variables, 231–233
energy diplomacy, 52, 54, 56
Ethiopia, 233
Europe, 37–106
European Development Fund, 201
evaluation, 251–255
ex-ante evaluation, 254
exogenous variables, 231–233
Expert Group for Aid Studies (EBA), 249
Export-Import Bank of India, 94, 194, 209, 217
Export-Import Bank of Japan, 196
ex-post evaluation, 254–255
Extended Assistance Scheme, 128

F

12th Five-Year Plan for Infrastructure Development, 151
Faure, R., 123–124
financial inclusion, 171–172, 180–185
Financial Inclusion Action Plan, 173
financial services, 183
Financial Stability Board, 178
food aid, 195
Food and Agriculture Organization of the United Nations, 226
forecasts, 161
foreign academic circles, 39
foreign aid, 47–62, 79, 220
foreign aid management, 227–230
foreign aid system, 230–234
Foreign Assistance Act of 1948, 128

Foreign Assistance Act of 1961, 128
foreign direct investment (FDI), 5, 55, 230
four principles, 64, 66, 71, 97
Fourth Middle East War, 51
France, 127, 130–131, 173–174, 202–203, 249
France's aid management system, 200–203
French Development Agency (AFD), 130–131, 202–203
French Global Environment Facility, 202
fund allocation, 217
fuzzy RDD, 278

G
G20 Seoul Summit, 88, 171–172, 182, 185
Gates, Bill, 17
Gates-Melinda Foundation, 132
General Administration for Globalization, 201
General Administration of Economic Relations with Foreign Countries, 228–229
General Administration of Treasury and Economic Policy, 201–202
General Principles for International Remittance Services, 173
Germany, 78, 127–129, 131, 249
Global AIDS Prevention Fund, 201
global governance, 27–32
global market, 84, 89
global partnership, 86, 88
Global Partnership for Financial Inclusion (GPFI), 172–185
Global Remittances Working Group, 173
global SSBs, 185
Going Global strategy, 232, 235

good enough governance, 121, 207
good governance agenda, 119, 121, 207
governance interference, 207
Governance Intervention, 121
governance system, 223–230
Global Partnership for Effective Development Cooperation (GPEDC), 88, 95, 97–99, 119
Great Depression, 171
Great Leap Forward, 228
Great Recession, 171, 221
green concept, 170
Grizzle, C., 137
Grønbjerg, K. A., 136
Group of 77 (G77), 82–83, 90
Growth with Resilience, 173
Guangxi Branch of China Development Bank, 234
Gujarat rural roads, 150
Gulf War, 62
Gulrajani, N., 123–124

H
Hamanaka, Shintaro, 147
Harold–Domar economic growth model, 14, 24
Hattori, Tomohisa, 43
Helleiner, Gerry, 28
High-Level Forum (HLF), 85
High-Level Political Forum, 100
holistic governance, 122, 206, 210
Hook, Steven W., 44
Human Development Indicators (HDIs), 3
Humphrey, Chris, 147

I
Igarashi, Samurai, 42
impact evaluation (IE), 255–259, 263
impact evaluation cycle, 259–261

impact evaluation group (IEG), 256
impact evaluation implementation,
    260
impact evaluation initiation, 260
impact evaluation preparation,
    259–260
increasing returns, 231
independent agency-German
    Evaluation Institute for
    Development Cooperation (DEval),
    249
Independent Commission for Aid
    Impact (ICAI), 249
India, 85, 90, 94, 105, 145, 150, 216
Indian Aid Mission Agency, 208
Indian Cooperative Mission Agency,
    208
Indian Development Partnership
    Administration, 218
Indian Technical and Economic
    Cooperation Programme (ITEC),
    93
India's aid management system,
    208–210
Indonesian Technical Cooperation
    Programs, 95
institutional isomorphism chain,
    135–136
instrumental variables, 268–271
integrated aid agencies, 215–216
integrated aid guiding principles,
    214–215
inter-departmental administrative
    arrangements, 231–233
interdependence chain, 136–138
Inter-ministerial Committee on
    International Development
    Cooperation, 201
internal operation mechanism,
    117, 216–219
International Aid Act, 200
international assistance, 49

international community, 5
International Cooperation
    Administration (ICA), 193
international cooperative governance,
    171–185
international development, 245–255,
    263–288
International Development Act, 114
international development agencies,
    127–131
international development assistance,
    3–11, 13–33
international development
    association, 202
international development coopera-
    tion, 6, 37–106, 113–124, 127–185
international development projects,
    245–261
International Finance Corporation
    (IFC), 177
International Monetary Fund (IMF),
    28, 195
Ishikawa, Shigeru, 45

J
Japan, 37–106, 147
Japan Bank for International
    Cooperation (JBIC), 196
Japanese model, 24–25, 76–78
Japan International Cooperation
    Agency (JICA), 130, 196, 198, 236
Japan–Myanmar Compensation, 48
Japan ODA Model, 50
Japan Overseas Cooperation
    Volunteers (JOCV), 196
Japan's aid management system,
    195–198
Japan's aid model, 24
Japan's foreign aid, 46–77
Japan–US Security Treaty, 48–49, 53
Johnson, John H., 29
Joint Action Plan, 208

K
Katada, Saori N., 45
Kenya, 182
Kim, Eun Mee, 29
Kim, Phi Ho, 29
Korea, 172
Korean War, 48–49
Kosovo War, 70–71
Krugman, Paul, 17
Kubota, Isao, 43
Kyoto Protocol, 66

L
Labor Party, 198
Leaders of the Summit, 177–178
Lend-Lease Act, 193
Lewis, W. Arthur, 14
Lin, Xiaoguang, 41
Lipsky, M., 143
Liqun, Jin, 147
Los Cabos DWG, 174

M
Madhya Pradesh District
  Connectivity Sector Project, 150
Madhya Pradesh Road Development
  Corporation (MPRDC), 155
Marshall Plan, 14–15, 145, 193
Matsui, A., 42
Mawdsley, Emma, 43
Mexican Agency for International
  Development Cooperation
  (AMEXCID), 206
Mexico, 31, 95–96, 174, 177, 206,
  281
Microcredit Summit Campaign,
  257–259
microenterprise, 18
microfinance institution (MFI), 258
Middle East, 52, 57, 67
middle-income trap, 76
Millennium Challenge Act, 194

Millennium Challenge Corporation,
  194–195
Millennium Development Goal, 17
Millennium Villages, 18
ministerial coordination mechanism,
  226
Ministry of Agriculture, 226
Ministry of Commerce, 222,
  224–227, 232, 235–236, 238
Ministry of Economic Relations and
  Trade, 232
Ministry of Economic Relations with
  Foreign Countries, 228–229
Ministry of Economy, Trade and
  Industry (METI), 197
Ministry of External Affairs, 208–209
Ministry of Finance, 197, 209,
  213–214, 217, 220, 224–227
Ministry of Foreign Affairs, 45, 122,
  196–197, 199, 216, 218, 220,
  223–226, 235, 237, 250
Ministry of Foreign Affairs of Japan,
  44
Ministry of Foreign Economic
  Relations and Trade, 230
Ministry of Foreign Trade and
  Economic Cooperation, 228, 230
Ministry of International Trade and
  Industry (MITI), 197
Ministry of International Trade and
  Industry of Japan, 44–45
Ministry of National Defense, 214
Ministry of Overseas Development,
  198
Ministry of Science and Technology,
  226
Ministry of the Interior, 202
Moni, Monir Hossain, 45
Monitor & Evaluation (M&E),
  251–253
Monterey Consensus, 31
M-PESA, 182

multilateral development banks, 100–102, 143–171
multiple linear regression equation, 267
Multi-Year Action Plan on Development, 172, 174
Mutual Security Act, 15
Mutual Security Administration (MSA), 193
Mwase, Nkunde, 27

N
Nairobi Outcome Document, 91
National Coordination Team, 95
National Development and Reform Commission, 236
national interests, 41–42
National Security Strategy, 74–75
natural experiments, 269
neoliberalism, 84–85
Nepal, 208
New African-Asian Partnership, 95
New Development Bank (NDB), 97, 101, 147
New Economic Cooperation Agency, 208
New Economic International Order, 83–84
New South–South Cooperation, 82, 86, 88–89, 104–106
New Zealand, 250
Nishikawa, Yoshimitsu, 43
Non-Aligned Movement, 83–84, 92
non-governmental international development organizations, 131–143
non-military security, 193
non-profit organization (NPO), 132–137, 143
North–South development, 84
Nyerere, Julius, 28

O
ODA Charter, 64–65, 74
ODA/GNI ratio, 128–130
OECD-DAC countries, 4, 15, 24, 33, 40, 85, 94, 124, 245, 247, 251
OECD standard-oriented aid system, 62
Office of Chinese Language Council International, 226
Official Development Assistance (ODA), 4–5, 9–10
Official Development Assistance Accountability Act, 114
Official Development Assistance Charter, 39, 43, 47, 62, 73
oil crisis, 51
One State, One Vote, 15
Organization for Economic Cooperation and Development (OECD), 6–8, 38, 71, 88, 102, 116, 119–120, 123–124, 248
organizational fragmentation, 121–122
Organization of Petroleum Exporting Countries (OPEC), 51
Orr, Robert M., 42
Overseas Development Administration, 198
Overseas Economic Cooperation Fund (OECF), 196
Overseas Food Corporation, 198
Overseas Private Investment Corporation, 195
overseas remittances, 176–182
Overseas Resource Act, 198
Overseas Technical Cooperation Agency (OTCA), 196

P
Paldam, M., 16
Pan American Development Bank Fund, 202

Pan American Development
    Foundation, 194–195
Paris Declaration, 27, 31, 85
Paris Declaration on Aid
    Effectiveness, 119
Paris High Level Forum on Aid
    Effectiveness, 119
path dependence theory, 230–234
Payne, A. A., 137
Peace Corps, 194–195
placebos, 285
Plaza Accord, 54
Point Four Program, 193
political consensus, 92–93
political power, 62–72
P-900 program, 277–279
Prime Minister's Rural Road
    Planning (PMGSY), 152
Prizzon, A., 123–124
Proactive Contributor to Peace, 74
project economic analysis, 154,
    160–169
project expenditure, 134–141
project income analysis, 161–162
project management structure, 155,
    157
project procurement analysis,
    157–159
project procurement policies, 154
project risk analysis, 163–164
project sensitivity analysis, 162–163
Promotion and Participation for
    Economic Cooperation
    (PROPARCO), 202
propensity score matching (PSM),
    265–268

Q
Qinghai Branch of China
    Development Bank, 233–234
Qinghai Central Business District,
    233

Qinghai Province, 233–234
quality of aid, 58
quasi-experiments, 269

R
Raitzer, David A., 282
Rajan, Raghuram, 18
randomized controlled trials (RCTs),
    280–288
randomized deviation, 287
regression discontinuity design
    (RDD), 276–280
regression equation, 273
resource dependence, 135–136
Rich, Sam, 18
risk analysis, 154
Road Construction Department of
    Gujarat, 155
Robinson, James A., 22
Rodan, Paul Rosenstein, 14

S
77-State Declaration, 83
Sachs, Jeffrey, 17–18
safeguards and supervision system,
    154, 164–169
San Francisco Agreement, 48–50
sector allocable ODA, 58–60, 68
Seoul Development Consensus for
    Shared Growth, 172
Seoul Summit, 173
Silva, Michelle Morais de Sá e, 82
Sloan, M. F., 137
small and medium enterprises
    (SMEs), 173–174
SME Finance Forum, 183–184
Smith, S. R., 143
Solow growth model, 24
South African Development Bank,
    213, 217
South African Development
    Partnership Agency, 213, 215

South Africa's aid management
system, 212–214
South America, 56
South Asia, 48
Southeast Asia, 40, 48, 65, 67, 69,
76–77
South–South Cooperation, 8–9, 11,
27, 33, 39, 81–106, 115, 214, 238
Soviet Union, 48, 52, 62–63, 83
Spandana, 258
spillover effect, 285
Standard Setting Bodies (SSBs),
173–174, 177
State Council, 117, 226, 235
State Planning Commission, 228
Stiglitz, Joseph, 17
strategic cooperation, 52, 54
structural adjustment, 66
Subramanian, Arvind, 18
Sustainable Development Goal
(SDG) 2, 183
Sydow, J., 237
synthetic controls, 274–276

T
Tanaka, Kakuei, 52
Tax Working Group model, 181
technical cooperation, 84
Technical Cooperation
Administration (TCA), 193
Tendler, J., 121
Thai International Cooperation
Agency (TICA), 206
The Bottom Billion, 21
Toepler, S., 143
Tokyo Action Plan of 1998, 31
Tokyo International Conference on
African Development (TICAD),
31, 45, 66
Toronto Summit, 172
traditional donor countries, 193–203
traffic flow analysis, 161

Triangular Cooperation, 82
Turkish Cooperation and
Coordination Agency (TİKA), 206
Turkish International Cooperation
Agency, 95
two-stage least squares (2SLS)
regression, 270

U
UN 2030, 180–185
UN agencies, 225
UN Conference on Technical
Cooperation, 83
UN-DCF, 99–100
UN Department of Economic and
Social Affairs (UN DESA), 99
UN Economic and Social Council,
91, 99
UN General Assembly, 64
United Kingdom's aid management
system, 198–200
United Nations (UN), 5, 102
United Nations Conference on Trade
and Development (UNCTAD),
82–83
United Nations Development
Programme (UNDP), 3, 113
United Nations International
Conference, 31
United Nations Millennium
Development Goals, 5, 9
United States Agency for
International Development
(USAID), 18, 128, 134, 138–139,
193–195, 236, 255
United States' aid management
system, 193–295
United States International
Cooperation Administration, 15
UN Security Council, 66, 130
US, 9, 14–16, 18, 20, 39, 48–49, 51,
53–62, 68–69, 127–128, 130, 138,

147, 152, 171, 193–195, 222, 255, 269, 273
US Compulsory Education Act, 269
US President's Emergency Plan for AIDS Relief (PEPFAR), 194
US–Soviet Cold War, 52
US–Soviet Union Cold War, 53
US Trade and Development Agency, 195

W
Wang Xiaotao, 236
Wan, Ming, 147
Washington Consensus, 119
Wasty, Sulaiman S., 29
Watanabe, Matsuo, 45
weak instrumental variable, 270
Weder, Beatrice, 30
Western countries, 8
Western European countries, 58, 77
White, Howard, 282
White, John Alexander, 42
win–win cooperation, 43
with–without comparison, 265–268
Working Group + 1 (international organization) model, 181

World Bank, 6, 28–29, 82, 84, 119, 121, 144, 148, 150, 174, 180, 184, 195, 202, 225, 233, 255
world economic order, 88–89
World Food Program, 226
World War I, 193
World War II, 8, 13–15, 37–38, 41, 47–49, 53, 73, 78, 81, 94, 128, 144, 193, 198, 221
WTO, 227, 230

X
Xi Jinping, 100, 235

Y
Yang, Yongzheng, 27
Yasutomo, Dennis T., 41–42
yonshotaisei, 196
Yunus, Muhammad, 257

Z
Zenawi, Meles, 21
Zhang, Guang, 44
Zhu, Fenglan, 41
Zuo Haicong, 147

Printed in the United States
by Baker & Taylor Publisher Services